CW00920467

Alexander Boddy

Alexander Boddy

Pentecostal Anglical Pioneer

Gavin Wakefield

LONDON ● COLORADO SPRINGS ● HYDERABAD

Copyright © 2007 Gavin Wakefield

13 12 11 10 09 08 07   7 6 5 4 3 2 1

First published 2007 by Authentic Media
9 Holdom Avenue, Bletchley, Milton Keynes, Bucks, MK1 1QR, UK
1820 Jet Stream Drive, Colorado Springs, CO 80921
OM Authentic Media
Medchal Road, Jeedimetla Village, Secunderabad 500 055, A.P., India
www.authenticmedia.co.uk

Authentic Media is a division of IBS-STL UK, a company limited
by guarantee (registered charity no. 270162)

The right of Gavin Wakefield to be identified as the Author of
this Work has been asserted by him in accordance with the Copyright,
Designs and Patents Act 1988.

All rights reserved. No part of this publication may be
reproduced,stored in a retrieval system, or transmitted in any
form or by any means, electronic, mechanical, photocopying,
recording or otherwise, without the prior permission of the publisher
or a licence permitting restricted copying.
In the UK such licences are issued by the
Copyright Licensing Agency.
90 Tottenham Court Road, London, W1P 9HE

British Library Cataloguing in Publication Data

A catalogue record for this book is available from the
British Library

ISBN-13: 978-1-84227-346-3
ISBN-10: 1-84227-346-9

Design by James Kessell for Scratch the Sky Ltd.
(www.scratchthesky.com)
Print Management by Adare Carwin
Printed and bound by J.H. Haynes & Co., Sparkford

Contents

Studies in Pentecostal and Charismatic Issues

Consultant Editors: Max Turner, Andrew Walker
Series Editors: Mark J. Cartledge, Neil Hudson and Keith Warrington

Studies in Charismatic and Pentecostal Issues is a new series of academic monographs, which explore issues of interest to charismatic and Pentecostal scholars, students and leaders. The books will be multi-disciplinary covering:

- **Biblical** studies on the Spirit and spirtual gifts.

- **Historical** studies on Pentecostal-charismatic Christianity.

- Pentecostal-charismatic **theological** studies.

- **Empircal** analysis of contemporary Pentecostal-charismatic Christianity.

Foreword

By the Bishop of Durham, Dr N.T. Wright

I am delighted to commend Gavin Wakefield's thorough and thoughtful biography of Alexander Boddy. There are many reasons why his story deserves to be widely known and pondered.

First, now that the charismatic movement (as we loosely call it) is so well established across denominations and traditions within the worldwide church, it will come as a surprise to many to discover that the whole phenomenon, with 'speaking in tongues' near the heart of it, burst upon a surprised and largely unready western church not much more than a century ago. The dramatic story of those early days of the Pentecostal movement is well worth telling not least because of the clear way it reveals the possibilities, the excitements, and also the puzzles and dangers that new movements of the Spirit bring. It is salutary to see Boddy facing up to the problems with a calm and eirenic spirit, and doing his best to anchor fresh expressions and experiences in the main stream of English church life and prayer. Those who pray for a fresh work of the Spirit in our own day will do well to learn wisdom from such earlier events.

Second, the story of Alexander Boddy and his family is a classic account of self-sacrificial urban ministry. In Wakefield's biography we can hear the pounding and hammering of sheer industrial noise, giving the Boddy family no rest and sometimes taking a fierce toll on their health. Yet for decades they lived, celebrated, proclaimed and applied the good news of Jesus Christ, especially among those at the bottom of the social heap, in the middle of the largest shipbuilding port in the world. Sunderland should be proud to have played host to such a minister. Those who work there and in similar cities today can look back at the Boddy family and take courage.

Third, it is good to cast our minds back not so very long in church history to a time when many things we today take for granted were scarcely thought of. The acceptance of women's varied ministries, including preaching and teaching, shines through in this account, and Alexander's wife Mary, with her own experience and ministry of healing, plays a full part. Women's ordination was not, of course, thinkable at this point, but there are many women in this story who are hardly the shrinking domestic violets we sometimes imagine. In addition – speaking as the present Bishop of Durham – I am warmed to see how supportive were the successive Bishops under whom Boddy served: not least Lightfoot, who called him down to his study one memorable Sunday night, spread out the map of Sunderland, and pointed him to Monkwearmouth; and Moule, who in his long ministry was more friendly to Boddy's unconventional ministry than perhaps any other bishop of the time might have been.

This account highlights, fourthly, several aspects of doctrinal and practical questioning which have continued to this day, at least within Pentecostal and charismatic circles, and are still far from resolved. What do we say about the heightened expectation of the Second Coming, and the speculation about the 'end-time' events that would prepare for it? Can we really tabulate a definite sequence of key spiritual experiences (conversion itself, 'justification by faith' as an *experience*, and then 'salvation by faith' as well)? What is the place of water-baptism within this or similar sequences? And, in particular, how do those Christians who find themselves caught up in the ecstasy of fresh experiences of God's Spirit relate those experiences to the social, cultural and political questions of the day (for Boddy, these included the urgent questions of industrial life when the unions were in their infancy, and the first looming and then devastating questions raised by the First World War)? These questions are not answered in this book, nor could they be; but it is salutary to have them raised from within the story itself, so that they can be pondered in the context of real life and work, not simply as abstract puzzles.

Finally, Alexander Boddy's extraordinary life is well worth reading for its own intrinsic interest. His travels to Russia, North America, around Europe and to Palestine, and his vivid descriptions of the varied characters he met, suggest that had his life taken a different turn he might today be hailed as an early Patrick Leigh Fermor or even William Dalrymple. But his work back home is no less fascinating. His massive and constant labour in Sunderland itself; his broad sympathies and tireless efforts towards unity between Christians of many background and nationalities; his concern for the very poor in Sunderland and his insistence that the better-off needed to see themselves as part of the same Christian family; all these bring the man to life as an attractive and sympathetic character. The obvious warmth and satisfaction of his home life, not without its sorrows and problems, comes across warmly and without cloying. Not everyone will agree with Alexander Boddy, or wish to imitate him. But his life constitutes a record of the unexpected and gracious ways of God, and we should be glad both for that gift and for a book which describes it so clearly.

+THOMAS DUNELM:
Epiphany 2007

Preface

Alexander Boddy is widely acknowledged as the key leader of the Pentecostal Movement that began in Britain in 1907, but there has been no full-length biography of him. This book puts that right. My intention has been to allow this fascinating man to speak for himself whenever possible, quoting from his extensive and readable books and papers. In telling his story I have tried to set him in context, in his time, in his geographical location, and in his church, but the focus is on the man. This book is intended to work as a resource for others, through an accurate account of Alexander Boddy's life and through details provided in the Appendices. I also hope that this book will help both the Church of England and the city of Sunderland to appropriate a part of their history, as well as shedding light on Pentecostal origins in Britain.

My own interest in Alexander Boddy began in 2000 when I was researching the history of Christian mission in the northeast of England and my friend and then colleague, Mark Cartledge, said, 'Of course you will be including Alexander Boddy, won't you?' I had not even heard of Boddy then, but several years on, and after several lectures, presentations, meetings and an earlier shorter study, my friends, relations and students have now had to put up with my being a 'Boddy bore'.

I must thank Mark for his initial help and his continued encouragement to sustain this study, and another friend and former colleague, Steven Croft, for his encouragement at a crucial period.

It has been a delight to write in the context of Cranmer Hall in St John's College: my colleagues have provided stimulus and help, and students have raised awkward questions that have sharpened my perspectives. I am indebted to colleagues who have provided specific information: Alan Bartlett (Victorian church history and Anglicanism), Mark Bonnington (Pentecostalism),

Charles Read (Manchester and liturgy) and Roger Walton (Methodism). I am very grateful to the St John's College Council for their generous grant of a sabbatical in autumn 2005 which enabled me to complete the project.

Many other people have helped me with particular enquiries. I must especially thank Sheila Harker, granddaughter of Alexander Boddy, for family information and a friendship neither of us had anticipated. David Goodfellow, a long-standing member of All Saints Church Monkwearmouth, was another key contact. My thanks must also go to (in alphabetical order) Allan Anderson, Desmond Cartwright, David Garrett, Neil Hudson, William Kay, John McManners, David Morgan, Ian Stockton, Ian Thorpe, and the staff of Durham University Library Archives and of the library of St John's College Cambridge.

I must thank my patient readers, Alan Bartlett, David Day and Fran Wakefield, for their comments and help, and also Nicky Grieshaber, a most careful and thoughtful copy-editor who enabled me to say better what I intended at many points. Between them all they saved me from many potential shortcomings and I alone bear the responsibility for any that remain.

Finally, my thanks to my family for their tolerance of my enthusiasm. This book is dedicated to Fran, who has done so much to make possible the work of the Holy Spirit in my own life.

One

Alexander Boddy's Early Life

The Pentecostal Movement in Great Britain was born in September 1907 at Monkwearmouth, Sunderland. The energetic father was the Church of England Vicar of All Saints Church, Monkwearmouth, the birthplace his church hall. Other members of his family were also present at the birth, and a key attendant at the birth was a Methodist minister from Oslo. The circumstances of the birth were controversial, with Christians divided over the true origins of the Movement and the wider public bemused by sensationalist newspaper reports.

Those attending the meetings might experience unusual convulsions, odd noises and the speaking of strange languages. They might also experience a warmth of Christian love and fellowship and worship they had not previously enjoyed. Other Christians looked on and saw confusion and disorder and, even worse, the work of the devil attempting to lead God's people astray. Powerful emotions were aroused by the events in the autumn of 1907 and the new birth caused both division and new alliances.

Despite the difficulties the infant movement began to grow vigorously and spread across the country under the guidance of its father and other guardians. They sought to protect it from harsh criticism and to nurture healthy habits. Suitable reading material was produced, especially by the father, and he arranged meetings for those who wanted to encourage new life in this way.

Growing up can be a hard process and it came to this Movement just seven years after its birth, in the larger traumatic events of the First World War. Quarrels and misunderstandings broke out, as they sometimes do in teenage years, but reconciliations also occurred, and after the war the Movement was more ready to make its own way in the world.

By the 1920s the father of the Movement had become elderly and tired and a new generation was ready to take over, not always appreciative of its inheritance.

Many dramatic and powerful events, prefiguring charismatic renewal, healing services, large-scale teaching conventions and Toronto Blessing phenomena, had taken place in the church hall in Monkwearmouth before the First World War, and the story of the beginnings of the British Pentecostal Movement is usually told from that beginning. The storytellers generally start, as I have, with the father figure of the Movement, but then move on too quickly to the next generation when new denominations were formed. This study attempts to provide a fuller picture of the earliest days of the Movement by shedding more light on its father.

The metaphor of a father has perhaps been a little over-extended above and it would be unhelpful to take it too far. However, the title *father* itself is worth some defence.

Alexander Alfred Boddy is rightly regarded by Pentecostal historians as the founder of British Pentecostalism, and he was also a key player in the European Pentecostal Movement prior to the First World War. I have called him the father of British Pentecostalism because this term has two resonances of which I believe he would approve.

The first resonance is that of organic relationship: Boddy was concerned to build links between Christians across denominations and across countries and continents. He did not confine his dealings to Anglicans or evangelicals, the two constituencies he was most at ease with, but was ready to work with the whole family of Christians, including Catholics and Orthodox believers, in sharing the faith of Jesus Christ. This attitude is sufficient to suggest that it is appropriate to use a familial term to characterise him.

The second resonance, which takes us more directly to the term *father*, is the paternal, and sometimes even paternalistic, approach he took to his ministry. This was evident in his parish work for many years before the Pentecostal Movement began, and it was true in the way he conducted his oversight of the new Movement. His decisions as Chairman of the Sunderland Conventions and editor of the magazine *Confidence* were of the utmost importance and he was prepared to take them himself if necessary. He was, after all, a product of the Victorian period with all its confidence, strengths and weaknesses.

In addition, Boddy put great store on his own family: his wife Mary had a significant ministry in her own right, leading Bible studies and prayer meetings, with a ministry of healing from the early 1890s, and she was also a prolific writer. Her ministry and her support for her husband were very important in the development of the Movement. As we shall see, their children, especially the two daughters, were also important in the early encouragement of the Movement and one finds the role of human father intertwined with that of the metaphorical father of the Movement.

So then, who was this man?

Boddy was no ordinary vicar, but a seasoned traveller and writer who had travelled widely in Europe, North Africa, the Middle East and North America. He was brought up in a vicarage in a rough part of Manchester and lived most of his life amidst urban industry. He was committed to his 'own beloved historic Church of England'[1] and also had a vision of Christians working together for God's glory and to see souls saved. He was concerned to do something about the harsh conditions of the workers in his parish, and took care of poor people he met on his travels. He was a man of prayer who was passionate about helping Christians to live holy lives in the power of God's Spirit. In all these ways he was prepared to be conspicuous if it seemed necessary.

In order for us to understand Boddy more fully this book first examines Boddy's own family, upbringing and early years in the context of his father's parish and of the Church of England and some of the Christian movements within England in the second half of the nineteenth century. His parish ministry and travelling were important and prepared the way for the coming of Pentecost to Sunderland. As well as looking at the events themselves we shall also examine briefly the spiritual history of Sunderland: not only the father is significant, the birthplace is too. Chapters on the developments of the early years and on Boddy's theological convictions come next. We conclude with Boddy's last years and a discussion of his legacy to later generations.

Family Background

Alexander Alfred Boddy was born on 15 November 1854, the third son of the Revd James Boddy, then the Rector of Red Bank, Cheetham, Manchester and Jane Vazeille Stocks.

Alexander's father, James Alfred Boddy, had been born in 1809 at Beaconsfield in Buckinghamshire. In 1834 James went to St John's College, Cambridge, where he studied a variety of subjects, including classical Greek and Roman literature, theological and biblical topics, and mathematics.[2] This was a familiar route for ordination training at the time. By then James was an author, first of a little moralising book, *Euston Hall*, which he described in the Preface as 'A tale to display some of the excellences of the Christian religion – happy in this life, and to prepare for death and immortality.'[3] He graduated from Cambridge in 1838.

In 1838, the year of his graduation and ordination, James published *The Christian Mission*. This book is of greater interest than his first, and set out a comprehensive vision of mission, both at home and abroad. His book appears to be somewhat derivative from William Carey's seminal book *An Enquiry in the obligations of Christians to use means for the conversion of the Heathens*, but nonetheless is a commendable work in its own right, published when James was twenty-eight years old. He set out a clear theological framework intended 'to stir up the religious world to a sense of the important duty devolving upon them to promote Christianity both at home and abroad'.[4] The book provides a rationale and examples which were to be followed in much of his son's ministry. Its thesis is that mission begins with personal piety and that the main object of mission is 'thy kingdom come'[5] (the primary motivation for mission in Carey[6]). This attention to the kingdom of God is once again the key concept in mission nearly two centuries later.

James was very concerned about the lack of church provision for the burgeoning cities of England, quoting an estimate that eleven million people in London were '*entirely* destitute of the churches' (his emphasis). He drew on a CPAS (Church Pastoral Aid Society) report of 1838 on over-large parishes, citing six cases of parishes with 20,000 people and a total of just nine clergy in those parishes.[7] He was also concerned for the heathen of other lands, who were caught 'in the chains of idolatry',[8] and he desired that Christians would be zealous in self-denial and in preaching the Word of God.[9]

After a discussion of the various objections to mission James moved on to the issue of the personal gifts required of an individual with regard to mission, beginning with prayer and the consecration of gifts, and for ordained ministers 'a willingness to labour where these services are most needed'.[10] James was to put this into practice in his own ordained ministry in a very poor part of Manchester, and Alexander later did likewise in Monkwearmouth.

In the light of Alexander's subsequent ministry it is perhaps significant that James begins and ends the book by quoting St John's Gospel, chapter 20, verse 21: 'Jesus said to [the disciples], "Peace be with you. As the Father has sent me, so I send you.'[11] The next verse describes Jesus breathing on the disciples the gift of the Holy Spirit. These verses have become important in the recent discussion of mission, but were not so commonly used at that period. They do not occur in Carey's pioneering book, for example, though in the *Book of Common Prayer* service for the Ordering of Priests there is a reference to receiving the Holy Ghost and the forgiveness of sins.[12] It seems likely that we see here his father's influence worked out later in Alexander's life. It is not known how widely read the book was, but the evidence of a later edition of *Crockford's Clerical Directory* suggests that it was reprinted in 1845 by the publishers Hall & Rowarth of Manchester.[13]

The same year that his book was published (1838), James was ordained deacon by the evangelical Bishop John Bird Sumner in the then diocese of Chester. He went first to be curate of Goodshaw, in the far north of the diocese, and still a rural parish on the edge of Blackburn. After his ordination as priest in 1839 he was appointed as Chaplain to the Manchester Poor House in the Strangeways district north of the centre of Manchester.[14]

In 1843, while in this post, he married Jane Vazeille Stocks, the third daughter of W. Stocks of Huddersfield in Yorkshire. She was then aged nineteen, having been born in 1824 at Huddersfield. James was now thirty-four and established in his calling. Jane was a descendant of Mary (Mollie) Vazeille, whose second husband had been John Wesley. Mollie had first been married to Antony Vazeille, a French Huguenot, and they had three sons and a daughter, Jane, who was an ancestor of Alexander Boddy through his mother.

The line of descent to Alexander's mother went through daughters: his mother was the great-great-granddaughter of Mollie Vazeille.[15] The family link was clearly valued, for the second son of James and Jane was named Herbert Anthony Vazeille, taking up the name of Mollie's first husband. Many years on Alexander was to give the Vazeille name to each of his own children, and it even passed to his granddaughters in the 1920s. No reason was given for doing this, but besides family self-definition, perhaps we should see a conscious link to eighteenth-century Methodist enthusiasm.

The Parish of Red Bank and Religious Changes

James moved from the Manchester Poor House in 1844 to became the Rector of the new church of St Thomas' Red Bank in Cheetham, a neighbouring district east of Strangeways. This area was a complete contrast to his earlier parish of Goodshaw: despite some quarrying for red sandstone, from which it derived its name Red Bank, it had remained essentially a rural area until the early nineteenth century, However, by mid-century it was expanding rapidly, with coal discovered nearby, and industrial activity was increasing. Besides receiving an influx of people from the surrounding countryside, this overcrowded working-class area, at the foot of Cheetham Hill, attracted immigrants from a number of sources, making for a rich, even bewildering assortment of groups of people.

The planting of a new church in this area of expanding population was no accident, nor simply dependent on the personal commitment of James Boddy and his 'willingness to labour where these services are most needed'. The energetic Bishop of Chester, John Bird Sumner, was acutely aware of the challenges facing the Church of England through rapid urban growth. In the first half of the nineteenth century the population of his diocese, the counties of Cheshire and Lancashire, grew from 87,000 to nearly 2.5 million.[16] In his first Charge to the clergy of his diocese in 1829 he noted:

> [There] are many who imagine, that if the people are not in the established churches, they are in the dissenting chapels, and are therefore not destitute of religious instruction. The truth is

not so . . . The mass of the ADULT manufacturing population is, in point of fact, without religious instruction of any kind.[17]

Up to this point in the century, barely fifteen new churches had been consecrated in the diocese of Chester. Sumner proposed a number of radical remedies, including lay visiting, home instruction in the Christian faith, and – most importantly – the building of many new churches and schools – what would now be described as church planting.[18] By 1841 he reported that 'One hundred and seventy additional churches have opened their doors to receive a people.'[19] As a result, churchgoing in the diocese between 1821 and 1851 grew faster than in the Free Churches, and at least kept pace with the population explosion, possibly even outstripping it.[20]

In all this he anticipated well the findings of the 1851 Religious Census, which the Registrar General, Horace Mann, published in 1853, to general surprise.[21] Probably the most shocking finding to the Victorian public mind was the overall result: only 7.26 million of the 17.92 million people of England and Wales had attended worship on the Sunday of the census, a mere 40.5 per cent of the total population. In his report Mann was careful to point out that allowance should be made for those unable to attend church through illness and other incapacities, but even when due allowance had been made it was clear that less than 60 per cent of the population were accounted for, and a large number of people could be assumed to be choosing not to attend church of any kind.[22]

The same census also revealed the growth of Nonconformist churches. Mann reported that 'about 40 per cent of churchgoers in England and over 75 per cent in Wales attended Non-conformist churches, while in Scotland about 60 per cent of Protestant worshippers attended the Free Church of Scotland or Dissenting churches.'[23] A careful longitudinal study by Robin Gill, examining church attendance records over a thirty year period, has indicated that in fact nearly all denominations were showing an increase in attendance in the generation prior to the 1851 census, with a more complex picture in the second half of the nineteenth century.[24] However, this pattern was not clear at the time, and it was often assumed that churchgoing was in decline. The 1851 census report led to pressure both for the disestablishment of the Church of England and for increases in the provision of church buildings in places where it was perceived that the lack of such provision might be a cause of non-attendance.

This, then, was an important aspect of the background to the founding of St Thomas' Church, Red Bank: it was an example of a wider strategy of the then diocesan bishop to plant churches in urban areas and to support the clergy in those places.

By the time of Alexander's birth in 1854 there was a new diocese of Manchester (formed in 1848), and Sumner was Archbishop of Canterbury, the first avowed evangelical in that position. The evangelical party in the Church of England was at the height of its influence in the nineteenth century: the proportion of evangelical clergy had risen from about 5 per cent in 1800 to 25 per cent or more by 1850[25], while later in the century the Oxford Movement began to overtake the Evangelicals in importance.

Though not explicitly stated by him it seems certain that James Boddy saw himself in the Evangelical party: his book *The Christian Mission* is very positive about various evangelistic efforts, not just from within the Church of England. He cites the zeal of the Moravian church in the West Indies,[26] for example, and is supportive of the work of the Church Pastoral Aid Society (CPAS) and the British and Foreign Bible Society (BFBS), both of which identified with the evangelical party of the Church of England.

A leaning towards evangelicalism can be seen, too, in his theology: David Bebbington, the historian of Victorian evangelicalism, has suggested a broad pattern of evangelical theology in this period: 'For Calvinist Evangelicals – as for Methodists . . . – the holy life had four salient characteristics.'[27] These characteristics of conversion, cross, Bible and activism are very evident later in Alexander's life.

Alexander's father, James, has left less evidence about his views, but they fit the pattern described by Bebbington:

First, there is the importance of conversion: Boddy wrote of his 'anguish that they [the heathen] perish' without Christians being concerned about their fate; Christians are guilty of not preaching to the lost.[28]

Second, the place of the cross was discussed in some detail, both for the saving of sinners and in its role in sanctification by the Holy Spirit.[29]

Third, he continually referred to the Bible. This was not unusual in a Victorian theological work, but there was considerable strength in its use as the final arbiter in argumentation. He also wrote of what might be learned from the Crusaders, who erred in resorting to 'slaughter and cruelty'; but, he argued, we should 'strive with the sword of the Spirit, which is the Word of God'.[30]

Fourth, his desire for an active ministry was found in his discussion of what is required of the individual with regard to Christian mission: it was 'personal piety, prayer and a consecration of his substance, talents, leisure, and influence, to the advancement of religion'.[31] In the serious call to promote the Christian faith the believer was not to fritter leisure time in pursuit of vanity.[32]

Though we do not have details of James' ministry in Red Bank, this prior description in his book coheres well with the brief passing comments Alexander makes much later in the magazine *Confidence*, and with his ministry in urban Manchester for over thirty years, from 1839 to 1871.

There can be little doubt that Alexander grew up in the Rectory at Red Bank imbibing the evangelical passion of his father. As we shall see, the son was no less committed to evangelical theology and practice, even though he was to add other dimensions to his faith. Some clues to the origins of those other dimensions can be found as we turn to examine the social make-up of the parish, in particular two groups which were present as a result of immigration.

The Immigrant Communities of Red Bank

The religious life of the parish of Red Bank and the area around it was most unusual for its time in England. There was a large and active Roman Catholic community, energised by a new-found legitimacy, often in the face of hostility. There was also a growing Jewish community which was becoming confident enough to begin building synagogues and develop schooling. Outside parts of London and a few large ports, this was one of the most cosmopolitan areas of England in the 1850s. It is likely that Boddy's later urge to travel and his emotional ease in doing so was nurtured by this childhood experience. His relative tolerance of people of denominations other than his own and his mixing with people of different faiths seems to have its origins in the assortment of peoples gathered in Red Bank at this time.

Roman Catholics

In the new parish of Red Bank there was a substantial Roman Catholic community. In part this was a reflection of the existence of longstanding recusant families in Lancashire, which was one of the main strongholds of Catholicism from the time of the Reformation right through to the mid-nineteenth century. Further, the combination of industrial growth and the potato famine in Ireland in the 1840s led to large-scale emigration from Ireland: probably one million people left between 1846 and 1851. Though a large number went to the USA, many Irish Catholics landed at Liverpool and stayed. In 1851 about 20 per cent of the population of Liverpool consisted of Irish famine emigrants. Others dispersed inland throughout Lancashire, following the opportunities for employment, and Manchester was a particular focus for settlement. Even before the potato famine there had been a gradual increase in the Irish Catholic community, alongside an inwards movement of English Catholics, especially from the Fylde, Lancashire and Yorkshire.[33]

Already by 1847 the Catholic community in Red Bank was such that it necessitated the building of a new Roman Catholic church, St Chad's. The worshipping community was built up by the Passionist mission led by Father Gaudentius Rossi, an Italian priest, and included for a time Elizabeth Prout, the foundress of a new religious Congregation.[34]

This growth was another local manifestation of a wider trend, in this case the re-legitimisation of the Roman Catholic Church in Britain. In 1829 the Roman Catholic Relief Act was passed, the most important of a series of relief or emancipation measures. Almost all restrictions on Catholics taking part in public life were repealed. The legislation was supported in the House of Lords by Bishop Sumner, making his maiden speech, probably because he was aware of the traditional groups of Roman Catholics in Lancashire and the Irish immigrants in Liverpool and Manchester.[35]

In 1851 the gradually growing toleration of the Roman Catholic Church resulted in the appointment of bishops for England and Wales, the restoration of the hierarchy, despite huge controversy in Parliament.

In England as a whole, the number of Roman Catholics was not great, amounting to just 3.8 per cent of all people attending church in 1851,[36] fewer than 300,000 individuals. However, the Roman Catholic Church was visible once again, especially in the cities where there was significant Irish immigration.

The revival of the Roman Catholic Church in Manchester has been described as the most conspicuous in England: 'the Catholic population grew from 287 English Catholic tradesmen, servants and labourers in 1767 to about 80,000 mainly Irish industrial workers in 1852.'[37] The Passionist mission in Red Bank was intent on assimilating the Irish immigrants into the Catholic Church in England, with the longer-term hope of seeing the country as a whole return to the Catholic fold.

In Red Bank itself St Chad's Church was noted for attracting people of different social classes.[38] The 1851 census showed that Catholics made up some 23.3 per cent of church attenders in Manchester, compared with 3.8 per cent nationally, and even then the Catholic clergy were concerned about the large numbers not attending.[39]

The Jews

The Jewish community in Manchester can trace its roots back to the 1780s, when people took advantage of the opportunities for work in the newly industrialising town.[40] This community was not large at that time, but from the 1850s there was considerable immigration. First came Ashkenasi Jews from Eastern Europe, and later Sephardi Jews, mainly from Spain and Portugal, all fleeing persecution of one kind or another.[41] Often intending to go to America from Liverpool, many of these refugees ran out of funds on the way, and in time Manchester hosted the second largest Jewish population in England.

Most of the immigrants settled in the low-lying areas between Lower Broughton on the River Irwell and Red Bank on the River Irk. The bottom of Cheetham Hill Road, then called York Street, was convenient to the railway station, but was characterised by very poor living conditions. The Red Bank Rectory was here, probably the last remnant of what had been for a relatively short period an area of large middle-class houses.[42]

Red Bank was the heart of the Jewish ghetto, a dirty and noisy environment where steam engines powered clothing factories. Nonetheless, the large houses were easily subdivided and cheap to rent, and the new community gradually became established.

The Central Synagogue was the first to form, serving Red Bank and Strangeways. In 1858 the first purpose-built synagogues were erected: the Great Orthodox Synagogue and the Reform Synagogue. A Spanish and Portuguese Synagogue opened around the corner from St Thomas' at 190 Cheetham Hill Road in 1874, just after the Boddys had left Manchester. It is now the Manchester Jewish Museum.

The impact of these groups on the young Alexander Boddy does not seem to have been recorded by him in writing. However, his daughter was to describe the area as being 'in a very Jewish quarter', a description using words which could only have come from her father.[43] It suggests that the impact must have been considerable.

Living Conditions in Red Bank

The poor conditions in which most residents of Red Bank lived during the 1840s and 1850s were a result of the rapid and unplanned expansion of Manchester. Even more than many other industrialising towns of England it suffered from the lack of a central authority that was able to plan and co-ordinate building efforts and ensure that basic services were provided. It had grown from a series of independent townships, and had been developed by independently minded entrepreneurs who took no account of pollution or the effect of their operations on neighbouring workplaces. The result was a combination of rivers becoming open sewers, regular outbreaks of disease (including cholera), and a smoke-filled atmosphere.

Between 1842 and 1844 Friedrich Engels spent twenty months working in Manchester in the offices of Ermen and Engels, a cotton business in which his father was a partner.[44] While there he took the opportunity to investigate the conditions of the working-class inhabitants. His work has been criticised for its lack of historical judgement and lack of evidence for his statements about social conditions in England.[45] However, in Manchester and Salford he was an eye witness and his vivid descriptions are supported by other sources.

At the foot of Cheetham Hill flows the River Irk, bounding the parish of Red Bank. Engels gave a detailed description, worth recalling, as this was of a major section of James Boddy's parish. He depicts the scene from Ducie Bridge over the River Irk:

> At the bottom the Irk flows, or rather, stagnates. It is a narrow, coal-black, stinking river full of filth and rubbish which it deposits on the more low-lying right bank [the Red Bank side] . . . Above Ducie Bridge there are some tall tannery buildings, and further up there are dye-works, bone mills and gasworks. All the filth, both liquid and solid, discharged by these works finds its way into the River Irk, which also receives the contents of the adjacent sewers and privies . . . There is an unplanned and chaotic conglomeration of houses, most of which are more or less uninhabitable. The dirtiness of the interiors of these premises is full in keeping with the filth that surrounds them.[46]

However, just as it would be wrong to gloss over the horrendous conditions endured by many in Manchester, especially by whichever group was the most recent to arrive, so it would be wrong to ignore the great efforts made to improve conditions, particularly after the granting of the municipal borough charter in 1838 and its confirmation in 1842. Although there were still some obstacles, the new administrative authority was able to begin to deal with the necessary supply of clean water and clearance of rubbish. In the early 1850s water was being supplied from new reservoirs in the Longdendale Valley to many, though not all, of the population of the growing city.[47] Red Bank thus spanned a wider social spectrum, from the poorest slums closest to the River Irk, moving up the hill to more respectable housing, where the Rectory was situated, and to the top of Cheetham Hill, which included relatively wealthy factory owners.

If the varied religious life of Red Bank gave the young Alexander the ability to relate to people of many faiths, the social conditions he experienced also assisted his ministry later on. We shall see evidence of this in the way he related well to people of every social class during his travels and to the working-class people of his own parish of Monkwearmouth.

Alexander's Upbringing

Alexander, then, was born into the middle-class family[48] at the Rectory, with two older brothers: Hugh aged six and Herbert aged nearly four. His father had now been Rector of St Thomas' for ten years, and so Alexander grew up seeing the mature ministry of his father, and indeed into the years when the work became too much. Details of his upbringing are somewhat sketchy, but we can put together an outline from his own reminiscences and a few other sources.

According to Alexander's own later account he was a poorly baby and was expected to die:

> [As] a dying (!) babe, my mother (being utterly worn out with nursing) was persuaded to give me a last kiss, and let me be taken away from her by a nurse to pass away quietly. But the Lord raised me up again when death seemed certain.[49]

This is the first in a list of more than a dozen incidents in which he believed he might have lost his life. Some youthful episodes are recalled in dramatic fashion:

> Whilst climbing in the Alps one summer I suddenly lost my footing, and shot down a terrible and precipitous snow slope stretching downwards for thousands of feet, but He caught me, and gradually, inch by inch, helped me to win my way upwards again, and enabled me to climb back into safety. On the sloping roof of the Manchester Royal Exchange as a youth, whilst watching a Sunday School procession, I slipped on soot-covered glass, and rolled to the edge, but His angels prevented me going eighty feet down into the crowd below.

The list continues with further dangers in the dark of the Egyptian catacombs, forest fires in British Columbia, perils at sea, and even while cycling. He clearly interpreted his deliverances as divine providence, beginning the list by stating:

> Yes, I have reason to praise Him, if only for preserving my life almost miraculously again and again, and so giving me the opportunity of learning MORE OF HIS WORD.[50] (His emphasis)

His strong sense of God's providence, mercy and kindness is reminiscent of John Wesley's experience of being saved as a young boy from a burning house in 1709, the famous incident he later described as being like 'a brand plucked from the burning.'

Alexander's upbringing in a religious and God-fearing household is seen in one of his first memories:

> The earliest religious impressions I had were brought to me by a vivid dream or vision when I was a small child of four or five in a Rectory, sleeping in a cot with very high sides. I saw the Lord and some of the Disciples, and I thought He spoke to me or about me. It was very real to me and I never forget it.[51]

His first formal education is not recorded, but we know that at the age of thirteen he joined Manchester Grammar School, entering Form II in January 1868. At that time the school was located next to the Cathedral, where Cheetham's Music School now is.[52] During this period Alexander began helping in Sunday School work, and he was confirmed by the Bishop of Manchester on 29 October 1870, just before his sixteenth birthday.[53] He said almost nothing about his teenage years, only hinting at his religious life when he wrote, 'The Lord was undoubtedly watching over me as a Grammar School boy.'[54]

In 1871 the life of his family was considerably changed: his older brothers were already making their way in adult life: Hugh training as a doctor[55] and Herbert following in their father's footsteps by studying at St John's College, Cambridge, thus preparing for ordination in the Church of England. His father was now sxity years old and he had spent 30 years working in this poor part of Manchester. The then Bishop of Manchester therefore decided to offer him a post in the County Durham countryside, at Elwick Hall, a parish of which he was the patron. At a similar point in his own life half a century later Alexander recalled the excitement that the Bishop of Manchester, Dr Fraser, came personally to make the offer.[56]

The exact sequence of the events is not now known, but around this time Alexander left Manchester Grammar School and was articled to R. Worsley and W. Parker, solicitors in Manchester. This may have been precipitated by his father's move from Manchester to Elwick Hall, where James became Rector on 10 October 1871.

Alexander moved just outside Manchester to Chadkirk, near Stockport.[57] It was close to a railway line into Manchester, this presumably being how he travelled in to the offices. The parish church was named after St Chad, a key figure from the seventh century in Bede's *Ecclesiastical History of the English Nation*, who had himself came from Monkwearmouth. However, it seems that the teenaged Alexander was concerned less with historical reconstructions than with the building up of the church in his own day, and apparently he continued with his Sunday School work there.[58] Right from the outset he helped with mission room services, and at some point he was commissioned by the Bishop of Chester to act as lay reader and preacher. He was a member of the choir and helped with choir training, and was also involved with working for the Church of England Temperance Society.

At the same time as this busy engagement with church life he was also working hard as a clerk in the Solicitors' offices in Manchester.

It appears that he also somehow found time to play hard: he records a canoe voyage along the north-east coast in about 1874, the first time that he saw Sunderland.[59] He told his children how he had built the canoe himself and had paddled from the Tees to the Tyne. He added how he narrowly escaped drowning in a bad storm on the way, and how he was rescued by fishermen at the mouth of the Tyne.[60] Presumably this incident was connected to visiting his parents and his brother Herbert, who was by this time a curate at Wynyard in the Diocese of Durham.

Alexander seems to have had a restless and curious streak from an early age: his daughter recalled that her father began foreign travel as a young clerk, on one occasion saving 6d of his 1/- lunch allowance each day until he had sufficient funds to visit Paris.[61]

In 1876, at twenty-one years of age, he was admitted as an assistant solicitor, and it seemed as though his future course was clear, especially when he was offered a partnership in the firm, a sign of trust in his business and legal ability. However, as he put it, 'I passed through a spiritual crisis which altered my career' and he turned down the offer.

He did spend two years working as an assistant solicitor and late in life his recollection of this time was very positive: 'My seven years in the law brought me face to face with the seamy side of life and made me perhaps most sympathetic with the tempted.'[62]

What is not so clear is the exact nature of the crisis at this point in his life. How it was worked out takes us into the next chapter of his life, though it was far from the last such crisis that he experienced.

Notes

1 *Confidence*, January 1923, 66
2 Venn, *Alumni Cantab*, 307
3 Boddy, *Euston Hall*, Preface, n.p.
4 Boddy, *Mission*, Preface, n.p.
5 Boddy, *Mission*, 4–5
6 In 1926 one commentator on Carey described this as a lofty tone, unlike many of the more recent cases for mission, which relied on 'a lurid picture of souls streaming into everlasting fire'. See Walker, *Carey*, 80
7 Boddy, *Mission*, 14–15
8 Boddy, *Mission*, 22
9 Boddy, *Mission*, 30–31
10 Boddy, *Mission*, 44
11 Boddy, *Mission*, title page and 120
12 I owe this observation to Alan Bartlett
13 *Crockford's* 1860, entry for James Alfred Boddy
14 *Ecclesiastical Gazette* II.70
15 Jane Boddy, *A.A. Boddy*, 1 gives details of the family links. See the Family Tree in Appendix Two
16 Gill, *Myth*, 114
17 Sumner, *Charges*, 1.96 cited in Gill, *Myth*, 115
18 A detailed discussion of this strategy can be found in Scotland, *Sumner*, 48–60
19 Sumner, *Charges*, 5.10–11, cited in Gill, *Myth*, 116
20 Gill, *Myth*, 114
21 *Parliamentary Papers, 1852–3*, 89, 'Religious Worship'
22 The interpretation of the 1851 Religious Census is complex, but the figures given here are generally accepted
23 Machin, *Politics and the Churches*, 257
24 Gill, *Myth*, 93–123
25 Lewis, *Lighten their Darkness*, 5
26 Boddy, *Mission*, 90
27 Bebbington, *Holiness*, 36
28 Boddy, *Mission*, 23

29 Boddy, *Mission*, 33–39

30 Boddy, *Mission*, 25

31 Boddy, *Mission*, 44

32 Boddy, *Mission*, 53

33 Hamer, *Prout*, 53

34 Hamer, *Prout*

35 Scotland, *Sumner*, 67

36 Gill, *Myth of the Empty Church*, 208

37 Hamer, *Prout*, 46

38 Hamer, *Prout*, 47

39 Hamer, *Prout*, 52

40 Manchester University Centre for Jewish Studies has a useful brief history available at http://www.mucjs.org/EXHIBITION/1MJEWRY.HTML. Accessed 15/7/2003

41 Many details in this paragraph are drawn from *The Jewish Community in Manchester*, from The Centre for the Study of Religion and Education in the Inner City

42 The address of the Boddy family is recorded in the archives of Manchester Grammar School as being 178 York Street in 1868

43 Jane Boddy, *A.A. Boddy*, 1

44 Engels *Working Class*, xxxi

45 See the Editors' Introduction to Engels, *Working Class*, especially xiii–xxxiii.

46 Engels, *Working Class*, 60–62

47 Hamer, *Prout*, 48–49 gives more details of this work and references to official reports of the period

48 Hollenweger, *Pentecostalism: Origins*, 344 incorrectly describes Alexander Boddy as an aristocrat

49 *Confidence*, February 1914, 23

50 *Confidence*, February 1914, 23

51 *Confidence*, February 1914, 24

52 Information about the school in e-mail correspondence from Ian Thorpe, Manchester Grammar School on 8/1/2002

53 Ordinations Register, Durham, 1880, entry 204

54 *Confidence*, February 1914, 24

55 Hugh practised as a doctor in Cheetham Hill all his life. Jane Boddy, *A.A. Boddy*, 1

56 *Confidence*, January 1923, 66

57 The Ordinations Register, Durham, incorrectly notes the parish as Chaskirk

58 The Ordinations Register, Durham

59 *Confidence*, January 1923, 64

60 Jane Boddy, *A.A. Boddy*, 1

61 Jane Boddy, *A.A. Boddy*, 1

62 *Confidence*, January 1923, 66

Two

The Making of a Minister

As Alexander Boddy began adult life he made the commitment to Christ which shaped the rest of his life. Indeed, every aspect of his life before his marriage in 1891 contributed to forming the patterns which led to his involvement with the Pentecostal Movement, and his leadership of it. The records from those years provide fascinating glimpses into his developing personality and interests and help to explain why he eventually became the 'Father of British Pentecostalism'. Here we explore the influences on his call and initiation as an ordained minister in the Church of England.

An Adult Conversion

Boddy himself provided only the briefest of mentions of the important changes in his life in 1876. In 1914 he wrote simply that he was 'then converted to God'.[1] It was in his recollection of his life and ministry as he left Monkwearmouth in 1922 that he wrote, 'I was offered a partnership [in the firm of solicitors], but I refused as at that time I passed through a spiritual crisis which altered my career'.[2]

The testimony of his daughter Jane would suggest that this crisis occurred through a visit to the Keswick Holiness Convention.

> He had been a nominal Christian in his youth but a change came when he went to a convention at Keswick. Then he decided to prepare for ordination, but his parents could not afford to send him to Cambridge, as they had done for

Herbert, so my father saved up enough to go to Durham
University for two years and take his L.Th.[3]

This brief testimony prompts a number of reflections. The first is
about Jane's description of her father as a nominal Christian, a
description she must have got from him, since it involves a
period long before she had been born. Clearly he experienced
something very profound about this time if he had to describe
himself as having previously been a nominal Christian and to
say, as he did in 1914, that he was then 'converted to God'. It
does also seem to represent something of a pattern in his life: a
spiritual crisis occurs, it is resolved in a dramatic fashion, and he
then reassesses his former life.

The information that his parents could not afford to send him
to Cambridge prompts a second reflection about the depth of his
change or conversion. His older brother Herbert had gone to St
John's College, Cambridge a few years earlier, in 1870,
graduating in 1873, thus following in his father's footsteps.[4] It is
not clear why Alexander's parents could not afford to send him
in the same way. In the 1868 edition of *Crockford's Clerical
Directory*, James Boddy's gross income as Rector of Red Bank
was given as £300 a year, with many demands, no doubt, from a
poor population of over 8,000 people. His gross annual income
as Rector of Elwick Hall had nearly doubled to £542, and the
parish population was only 217.[5] The typical cost for a student in
Cambridge at that time was about £70, which would appear to
be well within the scope of James's income.[6] It may have been
that Alexander chose to study in Durham in order to be near his
ageing parents. Whatever the reasons were, he demonstrated his
own commitment by saving up to pay for his fees himself and
attending University College, Durham.

A third significant feature of his daughter's testimony is the
reference to the Keswick Convention. It is known from
Confidence that Boddy attended the Keswick Convention in 1907
and 1908 and he gave the impression that he was familiar with
the Convention. His wife Mary had also attended the Convention on at least one occasion before meeting him.[7] However,
apart from this comment by Jane that he attended it, presumably
in 1876, we have no other specific indication of his attendance
there until 1907. Nonetheless, given the importance of his visit
and the independent attendance of his wife, it is worth drawing

out the characteristics of the Keswick Convention, since it had
features which showed up later in Boddy's ministry.

The Keswick Holiness Convention

The tradition represented by the Keswick Convention stemmed
mainly from the early 1870s, though it had roots in earlier
movements.[8] Its main concern was to give guidance on living a
holy life as a Christian. According to Bebbington, 'The message
was often summarised as sanctification by faith.' It drew on both
the Calvinist tradition and the Wesleyan tradition, synthesising
the two previously contrasting perspectives. The precursor to
Keswick was a series of conferences at Barnet (from 1856) and
then Mildmay Park (from 1864), organised annually by William
Pennefather, the incumbent of the parishes. He was particularly
concerned to emphasise three themes: foreign and home
missions, the second advent of Christ, and holiness. He believed
that Christians were neglecting the work of the Holy Spirit, and
wrote a hymn still sung, 'Jesus stand among us', with the line,
'Breathe the Holy Spirit into every heart'. These conferences
helped to form a constituency keen to hear addresses on holiness
and gave Methodist speakers the opportunity to spread the
message of sanctification by faith.

Pennefather died in 1873 before the first Keswick Convention,
which was organised by the vicar of St John's Keswick and drew
on American as well as British sources. The American root was
associated with the holiness movement begun in the 1830s in the
work of Charles Finney. Finney's argument had essentially been
that human beings could become perfect in a personal crisis in
which they put their faith in God. He had been able to speak
personally in England in 1849–51 and thus exert considerable
influence in this country.[9] The message was picked up by Robert
Pearsall Smith and his wife Hannah Whitall Smith and brought
to England in the period 1873–75. They brought help and
blessing to William Haslam and Evan Hopkins, who became key
leaders of the Keswick Convention when it began in the summer
of 1875.

Bebbington is clear that the movement fits into his definition
of evangelicalism, via the 'quadrilateral' of features discussed in
chapter one: conversion, the cross, the Bible and activism. It was

notable for its encouragement of missionary work as a result of which recruitment to the Church Missionary Society (CMS) went up significantly in the 1880s. However, within evangelicalism it did have a distinctive ethos, in several respects, several of which, as we will see, were relevant to Boddy's spiritual development and life and are echoed in his writings.

Bebbington identified some eight distinctive features of the Keswick tradition, which I summarise here for the sake of convenience:

- Its poetic inclination: Frances Ridley Havergal's hymn 'Take my life and let it be consecrated, Lord, to Thee' is a monument to Keswick spirituality.
- The location in the Lake District, which 'symbolised the appeal of nature for the movement'.
- Crisis as a key element in achieving consecration, though further development was expected after the point of crisis. In the phrase of Handley Moule, later Bishop of Durham, it was about 'Crisis with a view to process.'
- Holiness coming by faith in Christ, trust being very important.
- Its nurture of 'an internal sense of peace and relaxation'. Early on, the sense of peace was somewhat exaggerated and all human initiative given up. Throughout it fostered a calm atmosphere; the music was described as 'soft and low'.
- Repression of sin. Sin was kept under control by the Holy Spirit within the believer, though not eradicated; the result was victory. This was a dynamic concept, derived from a Romantic frame of mind.
- Premillennialist: It was believed and taught that Christ would come before the millennium, so his coming was expected soon. This was related to a Romantic notion of a heroic deliverer about to set the world right.
- A general dislike of dogma, displaying more latitude in doctrine than many other evangelical movements.[10]

Although the Keswick movement had drawn on Calvinist and Wesleyan roots, it was criticised from both perspectives as it developed. From Calvinists it was sharply criticised as being too Arminian in its teaching on perfectionism and its claim that faith alone was necessary for holiness. From the Wesleyan perspective it was seen as deficient in teaching that sin was repressed rather than eradicated. In 1895 Reader Harris of the Pentecostal League, who enters our story again in 1907, challenged anyone to prove from Scripture that sin must remain in a believer. Bebbington sees the origin of the clash with the Wesleyans in a cultural difference between the more 'mechanical' language of the Enlightenment and the more organic language of Romanticism.[11] Ironically, the philosophical roots of the clash with the Calvinists were similar, for they emphasised gradualism and steady progress in faith rather than rapidity and crisis.

Echoes of Keswick in Alexander Boddy's Life

We have already noted the element of crisis in Boddy's experience in the 1870s, a theme which was to continue in his life. He would also place considerable emphasis on faith in the believer's life and, like all evangelicals, locate that faith in Christ. The atmosphere of the Keswick meetings was peaceful, and to a surprising extent this peacefulness was also true of the Sunderland Conferences chaired by Boddy. The sense of sin being controlled by the Holy Spirit within the believer was important to him. He had a strong sense of the imminent return of Christ, and his general dislike of dogma was shown in his readiness to work with people of different denominations.

Boddy was not alone in being a young man attracted to this newer, more Romantically inclined movement, though the ability to attend for a week and to travel to Keswick was limited to the better off, including a large number of university undergraduates. This also meant it tended to be a predominantly Anglican affair. The denominational bias and the prosperity of most of the visitors were in contrast to the way the Pentecostal Movement was to develop early in the next century.

Whatever the details of Boddy's involvement with the early Keswick Conventions, it clearly played a significant part in his adult commitment to faith and in his desire to follow his father James and his brother Herbert in seeking ordination in the Church of England. His attendance in 1907 was to show his continuing debt to this tradition, even as he sought to share his newest spiritual experiences and desires.

Studying and Learning in Ordained Ministry

By the time Alexander was ready to study for ordination in 1878 his main family links were firmly in County Durham, with his parents living in the country parish of Elwick Hall, and his unmarried brother Herbert the Curate of Grindon and Domestic Chaplain to the Marquis of Londonderry. It was thus natural for him to enter University College of the University of Durham to study for the Licentiate in Theology. He was given references by an appropriate set of referees: his employer, the solicitor William Parker; the Curate of Chadkirk, Peter H. Moore, with whom he had worked in the church there; and Charles A. Bullock, Priest-in-Charge of West Hartlepool, next to his father's parish.[12]

The influence of Bishop Lightfoot on ordination training was already being felt and Alexander undertook The Durham Course for the Licentiate in Theology (L.Th.), a specific course of training for ordained ministry and much more focussed than his father's training had been.

His financial situation was eased somewhat by a university award of £30 for his first year, when he did well in an examination and was made a Theological Exhibitioner.[13] Although this was not the highest award – scholarships were also awarded – it demonstrates that Alexander was a good, even if not outstanding, student. The Ordination Register still kept in Durham records both the subjects he was required to study and the examiners' comments on his progress by the summer of 1880. Thus we know that he was assessed as 'very fair' in the Old Testament, Creed and Articles (the Thirty-Nine Articles of Religion being foundational to the Church of England's self-understanding), whilst in the New Testament he did 'fair work', and was 'somewhat better' on Bede. His history was 'weak', his knowledge of the Prayer Book was 'good' and his Old Testament work was 'immature', which may well indicate that he did not follow the latest critical scholarship on the Bible. The result of an examination specifically on the books of Joshua and Judges in December 1880 was that he was 'sufficient but disappointing', and his work on the mediaeval scholar St Anselm was 'moderate'. His last exam in May 1881 on St John's Gospel was 'very fair', though it seemed he had not read the recent commentary by B.F. Westcott and this was to be remedied.

His studies were deemed satisfactory by Bishop J.B. Lightfoot of Durham in September 1880 for him to be made deacon. He first went to be Curate to his sick father at Elwick Hall, in what looks like a sympathetic appointment by Lightfoot. He was also appointed 'to undertake Embleton in Sedgefield', that is to work in the neighbouring parish.[14] Boddy referred to this period briefly in 1914 in his typically flowery language: 'Riding on my horse from farmstead to farmstead, preaching in a lonely mission or in the quaint village church, those were happy days.'[15]

Sadly, these happy days were not to last long, for six months later his father died, on 26 March 1881. 'My beloved father, after a long ministry, was called home, and we buried him beside the grey little stone church at Elwick.'[16] As a result he and his mother Jane had to leave the vicarage quickly, for a new Vicar was in post by the end of June. His mother joined her unmarried son, Herbert, who was soon to be the Vicar at Grindon. She would live with him until her death in 1903, when she was buried with her husband at St Peter's Elwick.[17]

Considering that his father had just recently died, Alexander did well to pass his exams in May 1881 and to be ready for a new post and ordination to the priesthood.

It is not certain how or where he spent the summer of 1881, but it is possible that he visited Sweden during this period.[18] If so it would be an early example of his later desire, and even need, to travel to deal with the emotional demands he experienced.

In October he was moved to be Curate at St Helen's, Low Fell, Gateshead, working with the incumbent William Henry Simons.[19] He was subsequently ordained priest on 18 December 1881.

Boddy does not refer to this period in his life in his later reflections, but it was his main period of preparation and practical training as an ordained minister before his life's work at Monkwearmouth. Some insight into the work there can be found in the Diocesan Visitation returns for 1882. According to these returns the population of the parish was about 2,000 and rapidly growing, as the town of Gateshead expanded. It was perceived by the incumbent to be morally a relatively good area, for he described the moral condition of the parish as 'rather above the average'. The church was reasonably well attended, with average numbers at Matins of 200, and at Evensong of 300; Holy Communion was held twice a month and typically attracted forty-five communicants. The Vicar was an evangelical, encouraging the parish to support the CMS and holding regular Bible classes. The Vicar took those for the women, while Boddy, as an unmarried curate, was given the men's class.

Alongside this training on the job, Boddy was also extending his travelling life in an exciting series of adventures, as we shall see more fully in the next chapter. In 1882 he visited southern Russia, including the Crimea; Turkey, where he saw the Plains of Troy,[20] and, it seems, Milan in northern Italy.[21] This trip was not written up in any published form, but in May and June of the following year, 1883, he embarked on an even more audacious trip to Muslim North Africa. Other trips to northern Russia, the USA and Canada were to follow.

Boddy stayed in Gateshead for three years and he was then briefly Curate at St Peter's, Bishop Auckland in 1884.[22] Moving to Auckland brought him into closer contact with Bishop Lightfoot, who was well known for taking a personal interest in the development of his curates: he himself paid for the training of nearly seventy ordinands,[23] who became known as 'Lightfoot's Lambs' – a sign of the real affection of the Bishop for these young men.

Nearly forty years later, as he was leaving the parish of Monkwearmouth, Boddy looked back fondly to the occasion he was asked by the Bishop to go there. It is worth letting Boddy tell his own story, for it demonstrates the affection felt by him for the Bishop, even if we may feel the picture to be a little ornate.

Bishop Lightfoot, one Sunday evening in November, 1884, was standing with his back to the fire in the quiet drawing-room of Auckland Castle. Supper was ended. Compline had been sung and said in the beautiful chapel, and the 'Sons of the House' were gathered around the good Bishop they each loved – gathered for a short spell of harmless talk, often ending mirthfully.

The writer, then a Curate at St Peter's, Auckland, was there also, and his Bishop, with rather a merry look, was keenly gazing through his eye-glass as he said, 'Wherever is Boddy? Is he so small that I cannot see him?' The young clergyman (then four years in Holy Orders) was firmly pushed forward by the other young men, and he heard the words addressed to him. 'Just come downstairs to my study, I want to have a little talk with you.'

So down those back stairs and along the passage behind the sturdy, saintly Bishop, the young clergyman's heart was beating a little more quickly in the expectation that something important was going to happen to him.

Dr Lightfoot, on arriving in his sanctum, began to look around for some rolled-up maps. He found that of Sunderland and unrolled it. He laid it on the study table. There was silence. 'Ah!' he said at last, 'here is the place. It is a parish in Monkwearmouth. I am thinking of putting you in charge there. Perhaps you would like to go with your brother, the chaplain at Wynyard, and have a look round first.' Then he told me some things that were very sad indeed.[24]

Despite, or perhaps even because of, the 'very sad things' in the parish Boddy soon agreed to the appointed, to be told by the Bishop, 'I'm putting you in the front of the battle.' Before Boddy left for Monkwearmouth the Bishop held a service of blessing for him in the chapel at Auckland Castle, so that, as Boddy put it, 'members of St Peter's congregation, where I had been curate, might by their presence and prayers, hearten me in my new work'.[25]

The fellowship provided at Auckland Castle was important to many ordinands preparing for Church of England ministry – the 'Sons of the House', as Boddy mentioned in his recollections. His was not the only testimony to Lightfoot's generosity and openness, for many were collected after his death, telling of his influence. He himself wrote to Archbishop Benson of its importance when he was being considered for a move to be Bishop of London:

> The wrench of leaving Durham would be even worse than the wrench that brought me here, for an ideal is gradually forming itself of which I can only say that I wish I had the grace and power in any degree to realise it. But it has its centre in the work and men gathered about me at Auckland Castle, and this would hardly be possible elsewhere.[26]

It seems that the warmth of feeling from ordinands and clergy had its origins in Lightfoot's own character and commitment, and that we should not, after all, dismiss Boddy's testimony as overblown.

Vicar of All Saints, Monkwearmouth

The parish of All Saints, Monkwearmouth had been in a bad way almost since its formation in 1844, according to its own *Centenary Booklet*! The parish had been formed out of that of St Peter's, Monkwearmouth, the church of the Venerable Bede, for the undivided parish had a population of 11,000 and virtually no free seats in the church at that time. The population of All Saints parish was about 3,500 in 1851; it provided 550 seats, of which 350 were free.[27] The first Vicar was the Revd Benjamin Centum Kennicott, a son of the perpetual Curate (effectively the Vicar) of Monkwearmouth. This proved to be a most unfortunate appointment. He was unable to cope with the work required in an urbanising parish, where both population and industry were rapidly increasing. As early in his ministry as 1851 he apparently failed to return the Religious Census form.[28] In 1874 he failed to reply to the letter from the Bishop of Durham to all clergy requesting that he fill in the Diocesan Visitation form – a serious failure on his part, and an indication of his lack of engagement with his bishop and his parish.

Some pastoral work does seem to have been done by a series of curates, with four in post at various times between 1858 and 1879.[29] In 1879, soon after arriving as bishop, Lightfoot had put in motion an investigation into Kennicott's behaviour and ministry – or lack of it. Initial charges included 'omitting to perform Divine Service on several Sundays and on a charge of neglecting to publish Banns of Marriage after he had been requested and had been paid the fee to do so', and then several charges of drunkenness. A trial in May 1880 resulted in his suspension for four years and the parish being put into sequestration, a legal arrangement which effectively put the income of the benefice into the hands of the bishop.[30]

By January 1880 the Revd Robert Simpson had been appointed as Curate-in-Charge, and an assistant curate, the Revd James Ousey, was appointed in May 1881. It was Simpson who returned the Diocesan Visitation from the new bishop, Lightfoot, in September 1882. He mentioned a link to the YMCA, and reported that midweek services were held in a mission church. There was also a remark about the incumbent, but unfortunately the key word is now illegible![31]

The situation with Kennicott was clearly highly unsatisfactory and the *Centenary Booklet* summarised his appointment in this way:

> For over thirty years the parish had been under a cloud. The church was forlorn, the vicarage dilapidated, and the income consisted only of the remnants of the stipend after paying the costs of repeated lawsuits . . . The communicants all told hardly exceeded a dozen and the congregation was just a little more numerous.[32]

Despite being prohibited from preaching since 1880, Kennicott refused to resign, so Boddy was appointed initially as Curate-in-Charge after Simpson had left. He was invited to lodge with Canon C.G. Hopkinson in the nearby Monkwearmouth Vicarage (for the parish of St Peter's), opposite what was then the railway station, now a museum.[33] They held in common a commitment to the Band of Hope, an evangelical temperance organisation, and Boddy spoke at a New Year rally in 1885, organised by Hopkinson. Boddy was a lifelong teetotaller and very active in the Band of Hope and the Church of England Temperance Society (CETS), which no doubt made Kennicott's stubbornness and drinking all the harder to bear.

However, it seems that Boddy, with the help of his new Assistant Curate, the Revd Arthur Worsley Smyth, was able to hold services in All Saints and begin his long ministry in Monkwearmouth. Smyth was ordained in 1884 and had joined Boddy by Christmas 1884, a sign of the confidence Lightfoot had in Boddy's ability to cope with the parish and with guiding a newly ordained man. Support was also provided by Lightfoot himself, and a particular highlight in the life of the church in that period was the dedication of a new organ at the end of January 1886, with the Bishop himself preaching at the opening service.[34]

After nearly two years of this arrangement Kennicott died on 15 August 1886. Boddy was soon able to move into the vicarage and was later formally instituted as Vicar of the parish.

It happens that Bishop Lightfoot called for his second set of Visitation Returns on 31 August 1886, and so we have quite a detailed snapshot of the parish just as Boddy was about to become its Vicar. He returned the form on 23 September and was awaiting his institution.[35] Beginning with the practical matters on the Return, he described himself as already living in the small vicarage and 'doing the duties'. The *Centenary Booklet* as quoted above described the vicarage as 'dilapidated', but in this Return Boddy said it was in good repair. Perhaps he had arranged for repair work very quickly, or perhaps by the time of the 1949 Booklet 'the dilapidated vicarage' had become part of the parish mythology. His stipend of £140 was mostly provided by the Ecclesiastical Commissioners (£120), with the further £20 raised in neighbourhood. The gross stipend of £300 was shared with other workers, including the curate. The church building was said to be in good repair and the church wardens were doing their duty. There was also an iron Parish Room between the church and vicarage, which was used for the Sunday School work and weekday meetings.

At this stage Boddy took services according to the familiar Church of England pattern of his day, and even after his Pentecostal experiences he tended to add services and events to the existing pattern, rather than change the provision. This meant that on Sunday the pattern was not dissimilar to that still followed in many larger Anglican churches, with the exception of the afternoon Children's Service:

8.30 Holy Communion (Every Sunday)
10.30 Morning Service (Holy Communion also first Sunday in month)
3.00 Children's Service (Every Sunday)
6.30 Evening Service.

The content would be less familiar to most contemporary Anglicans: apart from the Children's Service these would all be straightforward services from the 1662 *Book of Common Prayer* (BCP), usually accompanied by singing, for Boddy was a fine singer himself and did much to encourage choirs in his churches. The surpliced choir sang from *Hymns Ancient & Modern*, and he reported, 'Men only admitted when Regular Communicants'. The Children's Service Boddy described as 'A very shortened form of Evensong' and it included the catechism of children: 'Every person in the church says the catechism aloud, and illustrations are given.' This is a teaching method not much in use today. Sermons were given at both morning and evening services, and also at the midweek Wednesday evening service. It may surprise evangelicals in the Church of England today to learn that Boddy would take two services on Saints' Days, at 10.30 a.m. and 7 p.m., and during Lent and Advent there were daily services at those times.

There were other opportunities for Christian teaching, including a Communicant Class for Women every Sunday afternoon in the Vicarage, just after the Children's Service.

There were also Bible Classes: one for men on Sunday afternoons held by Smyth, and one for women on Wednesday evenings held by Boddy.

The clergy were also asked about open-air preaching, and Boddy gave the following less than enthusiastic answer: 'A tent has been occasionally placed on the village green at Fulwell during the summer months and services held by the clergy of the parish, but it chiefly attracted those who attended the other services at the church. No effects have been observed.' Later in his ministry he would be much more positive about the value of outdoor preaching and worship in reaching new people.

Bearing mind that he had been in post less than two years, what were the results of this ministry amongst a population of about 5,500 people, who were 'working people and small shopkeepers'? From a base of perhaps 15–20 people there were now about 200 adults at Sunday morning services and 350 at evening services. Weekday services were said to attract about eighty people. He now had sixty-two regular communicants, and about another fifty occasional communicants, well up on the dozen in 1884. These were not unusually high rates of attendance: the neighbouring parishes of St Peter's had 500 attending on Sundays, and that of the Venerable Bede had 930 in three centres of worship. Even if one is inclined to be slightly sceptical about attendance figures provided by clergy there is no doubt at all that Boddy was correct in stating, 'The congregations have increased for the last year and half.'

Further objective evidence comes from the most recent Confirmations held at the church: on 7 June 1885 there were three male candidates and five female. Ten months later, on 7 and 8 April 1886, there were sixteen males and twenty-six females, an overall increase of more than five-fold.

Other topics touched on fill out the picture of Boddy's ministry and understanding: in their visiting they were endeavouring to visit all families in the parish, and as a result were not aware of many people who were unbaptised. At this stage there was just one Society in the church, and that was a branch of the Church of England Temperance Society. He also noted the presence of three Methodist bodies, which had a 'stronghold on middle and working classes'.

At this early stage in Alexander Boddy's ministry in Monkwearmouth we already have a picture of a busy and effective ministry, based largely on widely accepted evangelical and Church of England principles of his day. There was little to mark Boddy out as very different from his contemporaries in Sunderland, except for his regular trips abroad. These demonstrate a very different aspect of his life and work and deserve a full discussion. So before returning in chapter four to Boddy's work at home and his marriage, we go back a year or two and travel with him to North Africa, northern Russia, and North America.

Notes

1 *Confidence*, February 1914, 24
2 *Confidence*, January 1923, 66
3 Jane Boddy, *A.A. Boddy*, 1
4 Venn, *Alumni Cantab*, 307
5 *Crockford's Clerical Directory for 1868; for 1876*
6 *Cambridge University Calendar for the Year 1870* (Cambridge: Deighton, Bell and Co., 1870), 60
7 Jane Boddy, *A.A. Boddy*, 2
8 This section draws on Bebbington, *Holiness*, chapter 4, an excellent summary of the Keswick Tradition
9 Bebbington *Holiness*, 46
10 Based on Bebbington, *Holiness*, 79–85
11 Bebbington, *Holiness*, 87
12 Ordinations Register, Durham, entry 204
13 University of Durham Calendar 1881, 42
14 Ordinations Register, Durham, entry 204
15 *Confidence*, February 1914, 24
16 *Confidence*, February 1914, 24
17 The inscriptions are still obvious on the tombstone
18 Lavin makes this suggestion, *Boddy*, 10
19 Durham Diocesan Visitation Returns, St Helen's Gateshead, 1882. This is the source of the detailed information in the following paragraph
20 Boddy, *Kairwan*, 255

21 Boddy, *Kairwan*, 264
22 His entry in successive *Crockford's Clerical Directories* does not mention the Bishop Auckland post, but it can be found in *The Clergy List* of the time and in diocesan records
23 Robinson, *Lightfoot*, 14
24 *Confidence*, January 1923, 64
25 *Confidence*, January 1923, 64–5
26 Eden, *Lightfoot*, 49
27 Details in Joyce, *Centenary Booklet*, 6–7
28 Milburn, *Religion In Sunderland*, 41
29 Joyce, *Centenary Booklet*, 23
30 Correspondence relating to the sequestration and suspension held in University of Durham archive, All Saints, Monkwearmouth file
31 Durham Diocesan Visitation Returns, All Saints, Monkwearmouth, 1882
32 Joyce, *Centenary Booklet*, 17
33 *Confidence*, January 1923, 65
34 *Sunderland Herald*, 31 January 1886, quoted in Joyce, *Centenary Booklet*, 13
35 Details in this and the following paragraphs are from Durham Diocesan Visitation Returns, All Saints, Monkwearmouth, 1886

Three

An Enquiring Spirit and Restless Feet

During the last twenty years of the nineteenth century Boddy's travels took him further afield. He began by touring western Europe in 1876, and later went to Sweden, Russia, North Africa, Canada and the USA, and on two visits to the Middle East and the Holy Land. He wrote five travel books and a devotional book on the Holy Land, receiving a number of honours for his travel writing. These books provide glimpses of the character of the man and hints about his theological understanding. In this chapter we explore his trips to North Africa, northern Russia and North America, using his travel books to inform us.

Trip to North Africa 1883 – *To Kairwan the Holy*

In his first book, *To Kairwan the Holy*, Boddy provided one of the first accounts of a Westerner visiting one of the holiest Muslim sites in Africa, Kairwan, a city which had been closed to (Muslim) unbelievers for many centuries. The city had been founded in 670, when the first mosque in North Africa was built there, the Great Mosque of Oqba Ben Nafi, commander of the Umayed dynasty in Damascus. According to Boddy's account only half a dozen English people had ever visited the city, the first in 1830.[1] However, in November 1881 a French army had marched in and this had opened up the possibility for more people to visit it. Boddy certainly believed himself to be the first minister of the gospel to visit when he went there in the early summer of 1883.[2]

His book was published in 1885, so the writing most likely took place during his curacy in Gateshead in the latter part of

1883 and the early part of 1884; he had given an informal presentation about his visit at the British Association meeting in Southport in 1884.[3] This presentation was at the encouragement of Dr William Tristram, a Canon of Durham Cathedral and a traveller and naturalist, who had seen Kairwan from outside the walls in 1857.[4] Boddy's account led to him being elected a Fellow of the Royal Geographical Society in 1885.

Well before Boddy described his entry into Kairwan, he wrote about the journey itself in considerable detail, a feature which would continue to characterise his travel writings, both those in his books and those in the pages of *Confidence*, twenty-five years later. He took great delight in sailing and in his relationships with the sailors:

> Nothing could be more inspiring than to stand on the flying bridge and view one of the grandest sights in creation, as the wave mountains of the Atlantic ever rolled past, or to sit on the upper topsail yard as it swung from port to starboard, looking down on the vast tract of heaving waters, bounded only by the distant horizon circle, where the green-blue sea met the grey-blue sky dappled with fluffy cloudlets all torn and wind-driven . . .
>
> 'Beg pardon, sir,' says the boatswain; 'you'll excuse the liberty, sir, but I think they spoilt a good sailor when they made you a parson.' This remark was made one day upon descending from my seat on the upper topsail yard by one of the stays. He had found out that I knew the starboard-vang from the fore trysail, and a buntline from a tripping line. We soon became strong friends, and I did not find the sailors less appreciative when he had our services because I sometimes gave a hand at hauling the braces, or kept above deck in dirty weather clad in oilskins and sou'-wester.[5]

On arrival at the port of Valetta in Malta he was very positive about the variety of people to be encountered there: 'One could never grow weary of gazing at that moving crowd; was there ever such a cosmopolitan gathering? – Arabs, Turks, Capuchins, red-coated English soldiers, Algerians, Maltese lazzaroni . . .'[6] His willingness to mix with and to appreciate the diversity of humanity is as evident in this his first travel book as it is in the travel writings that were to follow over the next thirty-five years. He was at it again whilst exploring Valetta: 'I determined to make friends with the first person who sat down by me,' he said, and described his success. Nonetheless he also took realistic precautions for the journey ahead, buying a six-barrelled revolver and a thick, serviceable stick.[7]

His account of his arrival at Tripoli also demonstrated his appreciation of different peoples and their cultures, as he wrote about meeting people from a variety of black tribes, as well as Arabs and Europeans. He was at ease with religious diversity, observing Muslims and Jews going about their daily business. This passage provides one of the few references to his childhood amongst the Jewish community in cosmopolitan Manchester:

> The Jews, however, are quite different to the Hebrews we met at home. To Europeans these African Jews appear identical with their Arab countrymen. In physiognomy the men often seem very little different. In their dress, however, to one who lives among them there is sufficient distinction. The Jew always wears something blue around his fez, or something blue in it. But the Jews here have superstitious customs which would not be tolerated among their brethren in England.[8]

He does not satisfy our curiosity about the 'superstitious customs', but perhaps says enough to indicate his real knowledge of Jewish practice in England at the time. Later in his description of Tripoli he does briefly allude to the unfounded belief that some Jews were involved in murdering Christian children in order to use their blood in Passover rites. He reported that this had caused a stir in the Levant at that time; he did not openly support the claim, but nor did he obviously refute it.[9]

His visit to the chief mosque of Tripoli allowed him to impart his knowledge about Muslim architecture and practice, and to use and explain Arabic terms. He sought to be fair-minded in acknowledging what he saw as good in Islam, commenting on prayer in the direction of the black stone of Mecca: '(T)his is the only tendency to idolatry I know of in a faith which prohibits the likeness of anything which is in heaven above or the earth beneath.'[10] Nor was he afraid to quote from the Qu'ran, including the call to prayer, Allahu akbar,[11] and he was happy to commend enlightened individual Muslims.[12] Adopting local vocabulary when he arrived in Kairwan he wrote in breathless fashion:

Returning to my room, I push everything against the lockless, boltless door, lie at last on my pallet, very tired, and am soon in dreamland. Yes I am back in the Middle Ages now? Verily it is the year of the Hedjra 1300, and I lie beneath the shadow of the walls of Kairwan! Oh Shade of Okhbah the Mighty, and Spirit of Lord Muhammed's Companion, be hospitable to a Wanderer from the Isles of the North![13]

But for all this he did not regard Islam as a religious equivalent to Christianity in any way. His own attitude to Islam can be found in this reflective passage:

The Muhammedan religion owes all its higher morality to the pure Gospel of Him whom Muhammed certainly recognized, but as a prophet only. Part of its creed is avowed hatred of the infidel, that is, of everyone who is not a Muhammedan. Then it is much easier to be a good Muhammedan than a good Christian. With the Moslem outward observance is sufficient to win for him a sensuous heaven . . .

This surely is less difficult than the strait gate and narrow way of the pure religion of the Nazarene. It is infinitely harder to be forgiving on all occasions, to love our fellow-men as much as ourselves, to be perfectly honest, perfectly pure, perfectly truthful, to seek not self but the welfare of others, and when all is done humbly to feel that we are unprofitable servants, and must trust in an all-powerful Mediator.

The secret of success in the aggressive propaganda of Islamism lies, I think, in the fact that a mere tacit consent is required of the converts, without any thorough knowledge of the doctrines they embrace.[14]

In keeping with his evangelical heritage he desired the conversion of Muslims to the Christian faith, but was realistic about the lack of headway made by missionaries in North Africa.[15] That realism and a desire to explain the lack of evangelistic content in his visit may well be behind the comment he made following his detailed description of the great mosque of Kairwan:

My mission to Kairwan was merely one of personal interest in this African centre of a strange religion. A lifelong training in the midst of this people would be necessary before a missionary could hope to do anything, and then he must be prepared to end a career, possibly of usefulness, and that very suddenly, at the hands of these fanatics.[16]

Reporting another meeting in Tripoli, this time with a Roman Catholic priest, he commented:

With my friend the Emir I went on Sunday afternoon to see the padre prefetto, Father Angelo di Sant' Agata. Religious differences are much diminished in the presence of a common adversary and in a distant country, while a conscientious servant of his Master, like Father Angelo, is deserving of all respect, even from those who look at the Truth from a different standpoint.[17]

Once again, one is conscious of the distinctions Boddy drew between different branches of Christianity all serving a common Master and the Truth, and another religion, even when that other religion was represented by people he regarded as friends. The distinction between a system of ideas and the persons who hold it is not always made, but this allowed Boddy to maintain good relationships during his travels and to retain his personal religious integrity.

A discussion of this trip cannot end without a look at its main object, the city of Kairwan, 'The Holiest Spot in Africa', as chapter XVII is headed. It is a valuable historical description in its own right, and also enlarges our sense of Boddy's ability to learn from very different people and contexts while faithfully holding to his own.

His first impressions were 'unpleasantly mediaeval', with his being woken out of sleep by a call to prayer at two or three in the morning.[18] Once daylight came he obtained permission to enter the city, and he observed the quiet back streets:

We traverse the quiet city by narrow back streets, scarcely seeing any one as we pass along. Women scarcely ever move about in Kairwan; 'it is so very sacred.' That is the reason given, but it is a little uncomplimentary. The Kairwan ladies when they appear out of doors are invariably hidden in black *haics*, which completely envelop them, and their faces are covered with black veils. It is the women of Kairwan who make most of the brilliant carpets which are so much valued, and one of which lies in a northern vicarage.[19]

After passing remains of the Roman period in the form of stones with Latin inscriptions he climbed the Minar, the tower of the Great Mosque, Djama 'l Kebir. The view, both within the city and of the countryside beyond, fascinated him. Tradition told of five hundred mosques; the more accurate figure of sixty mosques plus more than one hundred Marabouts – 'tombs of saintly Muslims' – was impressive enough. Beyond the walls lay dry countryside for many miles, distant mountains and a few tracks across the desert wastes.[20]

In the afternoon came his opportunity to visit the prayer chamber of the mosque. 'Through the great doorway I passed into the darkness of the many-pillared chamber, the Holy of Holies. Vast, weird, and dark as we entered, I felt a sensation of awe which almost chilled me.'[21] However, his critical faculties soon reasserted themselves and he was rather disparaging of the proportions of the building, specifically its lack of height, and somewhat dismissive of the local traditions concerning the many pillars. He went on to give a detailed account of the marble floors and decorations, the huge chandeliers, the elaborately carved pulpit and the Roman origins of most of the stones in the pillars.

He spent a full week in the city, walking the streets, circumnavigating the walls, buying souvenirs and reflecting on its religious history. As it came round to Sunday he was a little homesick, and recorded that it was the second Sunday after Trinity. 'I sit at the open casement reading the lessons for this Sunday, the histories of Deborah, Barak, and Gideon. Now all seems so natural as they are read in an Oriental light. One's surroundings here in wild Kairwan would furnish living pictures for many a sacred story.'

The end of his visit brought a more positive appreciation of the Islamic devotion to God:

The great door of the prayer-chamber is open, and I stand silent and motionless, gazing on the scene within. It is the hour of prayer, and in the semi-darkness of the interior the stately Moors in their snowy dresses lift up their arms, saluting the Omnipotent, their God and mine, or falling on their knees prostrate themselves in adoration, touching the ground with their foreheads.[22]

Here in Kairwan the Christian may learn a lesson which the Collect for this second Sunday after Trinity emphasizes, "Make us to have a perpetual fear and love of Thy Name." The Name of God is indeed had in reverence by the followers of the Prophet, and they could pray the words of that collect of Gelasius most heartily to-day, though, alas! they could not, as we can, hopefully and trustfully offer the petition in the Name which is above every name, "through Jesus Christ our Lord."[23]

Here was a man steadfast in his own faith, and thus secure enough to appreciate that of other people, even when he was convinced that their beliefs fell short of God's revelation in Christ. That attitude, honed through many more years to come of pastoral ministry, enabled him both to remain committed to the Church of England and at the same time to seek its renewal from others outside its fold.

Trip to Northern Europe 1886 – *With Russian Pilgrims*

The next dateable foreign adventure that Boddy went on was his trip to Lapland and northern Russia three years later, in 1886.[24] No doubt he would have had to save up for this kind of costly trip from his adequate but not substantial stipend. Subsequent trips to North America, which cannot be definitely dated, may have been partly financed by income from his first book.[25] Some idea of the detailed planning required is given by his description of examining a land route to his main destination, Solovétsk, through Finland. He discovered that he would encounter problems over finance, the lack of regular travellers through the region, and a lack of dealings between Finns and Russians.[26]

When he set off on this journey in May 1886 he was eighteen months into his ministry in Monkwearmouth, but still not the Vicar – that came in August of that year. The book was not published until 1892, probably reflecting his increased workload as the Vicar and his preparation for marriage in 1891.

The intention of the journey was twofold: to retrace the old trade route of the sixteenth century,[27] and to gain a glimpse of the

Russian church, particularly through a pilgrimage to the monastery at Solovétsk. While his trip to North Africa showed that he was a fluent French speaker and able to pick up the rudiments of a language, he did not speak much Russian. However, he relied on his own ingenuity and a simple letter of commendation from Bishop Lightfoot:

To the Very Reverend the Archimandrite of Solovétsk.

Grace and peace in Christ Jesus,–

The bearer of this letter, the Rev. A.A. Boddy, is a respected priest in my diocese of Durham, for whom I have a great esteem. He is desirous of visiting your great monastery, and I shall be greatly obliged for any kindness that may be shown to him.
Your very faithful brother in Christ,
J.B. DUNELM[28]

The journey began from Sunderland harbour and took him well north of the Arctic Circle into the Arctic Ocean. He spent the time reading the history of earlier explorers and traders, and passed some of that information on to his readers. Never one to miss an escapade he ventured onto an ice floe and wrote a short letter to his mother, with the address line: 'On a Floeberg off Cape Svyatoi Nos'. This was despatched via one of the many passing vessels in that region. A different opportunity presented itself after a conversation with the Captain of the English steamer *Sunlight*, of West Hartlepool: 'Here I left about ten back numbers of our cheery paper, the *Church Evangelist.'*[29]

Boddy's willingness to engage with other Christian traditions is first indicated in this account when he visited a Russian mail steamer which, like his own vessel, was waiting for the ice finally to break apart. In the cabin were icons, one of which 'was almost identical with an icon I bought among the Kozaks of the Don' (on his earlier visit, to southern Russia in 1882).[30] He augmented his collection once in Archangel: 'In the Gostinnyi Dvor (the market) I purchased some Sviatye Obraza (holy pictures or icons), such as the poor people have in their log-houses.'[31]

His stay in Archangel gave Boddy the chance to meet the governor, Prince Golitsin, and obtain a letter of assistance. This was made easier by the fact that the Prince spoke English, having visited England himself.[32] At the other social extreme Boddy also arranged to visit the fearsome prison buildings. 'A prison-like smell hung about – such a smell as assails your senses in some of the cells below our English police courts.'[33] Again, there is an authentic note about the observation, the merest hint of his ministry in Sunderland. After meeting a few prisoners he asked to be shown the worst dungeons, and once there asked further to be shut up in the darkness for a few minutes in order to understand the experience. His sense of proportion may be appreciated from his wry comment, '. . . very soon I was released from my imprisonment, and qualified to compete with M. Stepnyak and Mr. Kennan in writing, say, "Five Minutes in a Russian Dungeon."'[34]

Many instances of Boddy's knowledge and appreciation of Orthodoxy could be given from his book, especially in his descriptions of the monastery at Solovétsk. 'I had been to a great number of services in Russia,' he wrote, 'and am fairly familiar with the Sclavonic use of the liturgy of St. John the golden-mouthed, but never more impressed than at Solovétsk. There was such an earnestness and simple devoutness in these pilgrim faces.'[35] And again, 'I was honoured by being taken within the holy screen at the time of the Consecration.'[36] This is followed by a careful description of the liturgy of St. Chrysostom, the order of services and the most sacred site there, the shrine of two thirteenth-century monks.

Wandering alone through a cemetery on one of the Solovestsk islands prompted a humble comparison between the monks buried there and his own people in England: 'We sometimes think we are more enlightened than these simple children of the North, and that we have a deeper knowledge of the truth, but the God who searcheth all hearts knoweth best, and some of the last, to our astonishment, will be first on the great day.'[37] This monastery was closed soon after the 1917 Revolution and turned into a prison which Solzhenitsyn saw as a paradigm of the gulag system. It was restored as a monastery after 1989.[38]

In the book Boddy also affirms the Russian use of the cross as a symbol of baptism:

> Every orthodox Russian is a cross-bearer. M. Sharvin gave me an old silver krest, in beauty only second to one I once obtained in the Crimean district.

> Except to those familiar with the Russian life it is hard to realise how the baptismal cross is prized. Crosses are kept in the family for many generations. Often they are beautifully wrought. Such a cross I hung round my little daughter's neck when I baptized her.[39]

Clearly he had obtained the cross in 1886 and, valuing the tradition, gave it to his eldest daughter Mary at her baptism in 1892.

His journey home from Archangel was southwards to Moscow by river steamer and then overland. From there it was westwards to St Petersburg, where he was able to catch a boat to Hull. His eye for detail was even more valuable on the homeward leg of the trip, for he was able to engage with a wide range of Russians and to learn their ways. 'Nowhere does one see more of the Russian life and character than during the long journeys on these mighty rivers. From the White Sea to Moscow, travelling by the river Dvina and its southern tributary, the Suchona or Sukhona, is a journey of more than 1000 miles.'[40]

Describing the people he met gave an opportunity for his sense of fun and modesty to be expressed. So, for example, he wrote of his pleasant cabin companion, Nikolai Pavlovitch, and his friendship, but added, 'He only had one grudge against me, and that was that I did not join him at vodka. Total abstinence is not at all popular in Russia.'[41]

Arriving at the town of Ustyug he had to change ships as the river became smaller. His passport was demanded by suspicious officials. 'I was shadowed for a while by a member of the third section (the secret police), and one day, owing to a squeaking door, I had a little joke at his expense.' This had involved careful observation of the policeman's habits, giving a decoy and thus being able to spend the afternoon exploring the town alone.[42]

On one occasion his conversation with peasant women strayed on to more personal matters. 'I spend the day practising Russian with my fellow-travellers and take turns with the passengers of the first-class, second-class, and third-class. Sitting amongst the báby (peasant women) of the latter I rapidly acquired Russian country expressions, and put them down phonetically.' This led to a discussion about a wife, and one girl was suggested. 'Feeling that we were beginning to tread on delicate ground, I hurriedly changed the subject.'[43]

On another occasion it was a group of three clergymen's wives and his companion Nikolai who pressed him about a wife. But Boddy wanted to wait for the right wife, and by 1892 could write, 'I have since done what I could to oblige, and her name is Mar'ya Yakovlevna.'[44] A typical touch, to give his wife's name in the form of the people amongst whom he was travelling, that is, Mary daughter of James.

As on his voyage to North Africa, he enjoyed helping out with the practicalities. On the river steamers the third-class passengers offset their fare by gathering wood for fuel whenever the steamer needed it. Boddy, of course, was in the first-class accommodation, but nonetheless '[w]e had great fun in getting in the wood from the forest this evening. I worked hard at throwing the blocks down the bank, to the astonishment of the correct first class passengers; it was glorious liver-stirring exercise.'[45]

Besides the more light-hearted remarks he also continued to comment on the religious aspects of what he saw. Soon after the start of this long river journey it was Whit Sunday and the steamer was decorated with leafy branches. This feast day gave him the opportunity to remember his friends and to reflect on an impressive painting he had seen in the monastery at Solovétsk:

> Being the only Englishman now within some hundreds of miles, I could not hold any service save by myself, but at half-past ten I knelt in company with those who at the same moment (that is to say, 8.30A.M. in England) were kneeling in All Saints Church in distant Monkwearmouth. We are ten hours before my friends with whom I worshipped on the Pacific Coast. At Tacoma, in Washington Territory, late folk are only going to bed.

> In the dome of the great cathedral and the monastery at Solovétsk is a striking representation of the first Christians gathered on the first Whit Sunday, looking up with glorified faces as the flaming baptism of the Holy Ghost falls upon the infant church. In the centre of the foreground is the mother of our Lord also receiving the gift. Our traditional idea of the power from on high only falling on the twelve apostles does not seem to agree with Acts i.14,15, and ii.6.[46]

It is not clear if this reassessment of the Acts of the Apostles occurred to him while he was in Russia or came subsequently during the writing of the book. Either way it predates a significant spiritual experience he had in September 1892 (which we will come to in the next chapter) and shows how even at this stage in his life there is a clear association of important themes he later developed further: a sense of fellowship with people from other countries and churches, a willingness to learn from people who are different from him, and an emphasis on God's power expressed through the Holy Spirit.

His readiness to learn from other ways of worshipping is illustrated by his comment on the time of worship:

> The Saturday evening service in Russia is one of the best attended in the week . . . One of the chaplains of our church in Russia has in his flock some Russians who have married into English families and worship in the English church. He has the first Sunday service always on Saturday evening, and none on Sunday evening. It is well-attended, he told me, by his people, and fits in with local customs.[47]

In Chapter XXI he gives a report of a funeral in Ustyug, giving details of the service itself, the customs and the clergy, and including many of the prayers in full. He was able to follow the service with the help of King's *Rites and Customs of the Greco-Russian Church* and found himself the object of interest. His reason for attending was, 'I was only a brother in the great family of humanity, and interested to see how these Christians in the East laid in mother earth the body of one of their "Orthodox".'[48]

Trinity Sunday on board the steamer heading south from Ustyug gave a further occasion for theological reflection, first on the use of icons:

> On this Trinity Sunday one is reminded of the very material way in which the Orthodox are taught to remember this spiritual doctrine. In nearly every church are pictures of the Three Mysterious Angels conversing with Abraham by his tent. Also above nearly every iconastas is a picture of a very holy patriarchal face with flowing silvery beard and hair. This benign and serenely beautiful head represents the First Person in the Godhead. With outstretched hovering wings beneath is the Dove, which pictures, to the Orthodox, God the Holy

Ghost, while at the Father's right hand is represented as standing He who alone, as some of us think, should be thus materialised in art, for the Son of Mary alone has worn and still wears a human body.[49]

He was not completely averse to icons, for he had bought a number of them in southern Russia and on this trip at Archangel. Indeed his daughter Jane would remember icons being prominently displayed in the front hall of the vicarages at Monkwearmouth and Hallgarth.[50] What stands out is his desire to appreciate other Christian traditions without losing what was important to him. A second reflection made on the evening of that Trinity Sunday illustrates this appreciation: 'We make a great mistake if we think that the Bible is not read in Russia. The majority of the people who can read, we are told, take a deep interest in God's Word.'[51] This was a view untypical of that held by his fellow evangelicals.

At the conclusion of his account he provides his own perspective on humanity as he quoted from the Acts of the Apostles:

Those who have gone forth sympathetically to view other lands than their own, will join with me, I am sure, in realising that the words spoken on Mars' Hill are true as to our brothers and sisters, though they be Russian brothers ands sisters:-
GOD HATH MADE OF ONE BLOOD ALL NATIONS OF MEN FOR TO DWELL ON THE FACE OF THE EARTH.[52]

Trips to North America c. 1884 – c. 1891 – *By Ocean, Prairie and Peak*

In the 1880s and early 1890s Boddy visited a third continent, North America, and described his four visits there in his book of 1896, *By Ocean, Prairie and Peak*. Unfortunately it is not certain when he went on these trips, but it seems very likely that they were all completed before his marriage in the autumn of 1891, and two of them can be dated to 1889 and 1890. One visit took place after 1890, presumably in 1891, while the earliest cannot be dated; 1884 is the earliest possible date, but it could also be any of 1885, 1887 or 1888, given what is known of his travels.[53]

The exact dates are not ultimately of crucial importance, however; of greater importance is what the book does in helpfully shedding light on Boddy in two respects: First of all, it shows him gaining familiarity with North America, including with something of its religious life, a knowledge which was to prove invaluable twenty years later when he engaged with the Pentecostal Movement; and secondly, we learn something of the motivation for his visits, which goes beyond curiosity or restlessness. The opening sentences of the book act as an apologia for his travelling:

> In a smoke-beaten vicarage, a few hundred yards back from the grey North Sea, emigrants have had farewell talks before starting for new homes in the Far West.
>
> The clatter-clatter of a hundred hammers in the shipyards of the Wear are faintly heard, and the deep thud-thud of a huge steam-hammer mercilessly shakes that home by night and by day. Yet, when all is still with a Sabbath stillness, the 'call' of the tide can at times be heard, and the echoing boom of incoming steamers signalling as they enter the harbour or pass up the Wear.
>
> The incessant strain to body, soul, and spirit of a populous parish, and the constant facing of sorrow and sin, could cause a breakdown if there were not pauses. These pauses – never very long – have from time to time been filled with diverse experiences. Parishioners have protested that they were not true holidays. At all events they were a change of scene and work.[54]

Boddy experienced enormous physical strain through being in the heart of one of the most industrialised places in the world, for Sunderland was a leading shipbuilding town throughout this period.

Added to this was his concern for the spiritual and emotional well-being of his parishioners. By the time of the publication of the book on North America in 1896 it seems that he had not been able to travel for some time, being a married man with young children, and in the next chapter we will see some consequences of that limitation on him.

Once again, the voyage itself gave him opportunities for both spiritual ministry and interesting descriptions. He had an

official position on the ship *RMS Vancouver*, as chaplain to and
for the many emigrants to Canada. This enabled him to hold
services and to give out his newspapers and tracts as he visited
the emigrants. He continued his work for Temperance and was
concerned in other ways for the moral health of the passengers:

> I brought my Temperance Pledge-book with me, and was
> enabled to get several signatures, including one from a poor
> stowaway, whose wretched appearance and condition would
> have softened a very stony heart.
>
> I am never satisfied with the accommodation for married
> people in the steerage. Two or three sets of married people are
> put in one section or cabin. This leads to sin, I am sure. Each
> family should be absolutely isolated. There is sad laxity as to
> morals and self-respect in these quarters, where for more than
> a week together men and women have no real privacy. The
> male stewards should be kept out of those cabins where the
> women are.[55]

During his time as chaplain on the voyage he also experienced
another incident in which his life was only just spared, one to
which he only briefly alluded later in *Confidence*:

> Curiously enough a can of tar fell from the mast above me
> while I was speaking, and just grazed my head. The sharp
> edge would have been too much for the chaplain's skull if it
> had struck that, for it fell at least 100 feet from where a sailor
> was tarring the ropes. Every one but the chaplain realised that
> the service was very nearly concluded abruptly, and the
> chaplain's services entirely dispensed with.[56]

Once again he saw this as God's Fatherly protection.[57]

On arrival in Canada Boddy used his full descriptive powers
to provide a picture both of towns, such as Quebec, and of the
countryside on special excursions and along the route of the
Canadian Pacific Railway. One section from Lake St John
reminded him of Sweden, when he travelled from Gothenburg
to Stockholm.[58] Lake Superior prompted this eloquent passage:

> Winter snow lies on the shores, and the bays are occasionally
> frozen over. White osprey wheel about the fir-clothed islets.

Glints of sunshine play on the lake, and rugged bands of cloud are piled along the horizon line, and clouds of steam occasionally narrow down the view as we dart along near the water's edge or climb up to dizzy heights above and wheel round curling wooden trestle-bridges. We dive into short tunnels, pant along up grades, crawl over ravines, race along rocky cuttings, dodge round the backs of promontories, and re-appear at the edge of the sea.[59]

He also spent time on one trip with Jim, a travelling companion suddenly introduced into the narrative and then later explained as being his brother-in-law, James Pollock, although I take it not his brother-in-law at the time of the trip, but rather a fellow clergyman from Sunderland.[60] (This is the first recorded contact with his wife's family, and may even pre-date his first meeting with Mary.)

His religious observations come from a very different context from those in North Africa and northern Russia, but show the same combination of empathy and gentle critique. So he commented positively about the missionary efforts of the Roman Catholics:

A vigorous move was made to open the country around Lake St John in the form of Roman Catholic parishes generally circling round a rude log chapel, which, as the colony became able, was replaced by a more substantial structure. The Church is the rallying-point, the centre of attraction – a truly beautiful idea.[61]

On Whit Sunday near Winnipeg – at Rat Portage – one year (it is not clear which year) he attended a service where

the rector preached from Acts i.8 – 'Ye shall receive power, after that the HOLY GHOST is come upon you.' Mr Fostin distinguished between 'influence' and 'power'. The apostles were not men of *influence* but they were men of *power*. Men have influence, and may use it for or against the cause of CHRIST, but it cannot be compared with power. We cannot all get much *influence*, but we all receive power, after that the

HOLY GHOST comes upon us. A very helpful sermon, and listened to with sustained and rapt attention.[62] [His emphases.]

Even at this stage of life he was clearly open to and moved by reflection on the powerful working of the Holy Spirit in the life of believers, and keen to share that with his readers. As with his experience of Russian Orthodoxy this encounter with a form of Christianity somewhat different from the Church of England would continue to form him over many years to come.

On Vancouver Island he stayed with 'the Revd Arthur J Beanlands, a graduate of Durham University and well known in that city. His grandfather and a grandfather of the writer were cousins.'[63] Introductions given by Beanlands enabled him to visit China-town and he was able to enter a temple, whose gaudiness rather impressed him. As ever, reflection on other faiths and evangelism came readily to him: 'A representation of some deity – a Chinese figure with a beard – sat in a shrine, cross-legged. Before him were offerings of cold tea and fish. I put my finger into the cold tea, and found it rather weak. The idol was easily pleased.'[64]

In pondering the possibilities of evangelism in China he was also concerned to be fair-minded:

> I have only a slight knowledge of Chinese mythology. Yet one realises a little of the difficulties in the way of evangelizing China's millions . . . I do not know whether the Chinese really fall down and worship the graven image which they have set up. I fancy they are too worldly here to be very religious even in an idolatrous fashion. They reverence their ancestors and are very kind, I am told, to their parents even in life.[65]

He remained hopeful that converts would come. That hope was expressed in another way in his story about one of his return voyages: on the cattle boat he was able to meet with the cattle men and he writes of his interest in their well-being. Among them was a young man who had lost his faith but had become desirous of forgiveness. Boddy took the opportunity to assure him of salvation after repentance.[66] Here was the pastor-evangelist in action, in what Boddy would have seen as a fitting end to this sequence of travel books.

Travelling Man: A Character Revealed and Formed

It is often said that travel broadens the mind, and that can certainly be seen in the experiences Boddy related in his travel books. It is also just as true that unusual conditions, such as travelling beyond the regular routes of one's day, bring out aspects of character which may be less obvious in everyday living. Whichever it was, we can identify a number of important strands in Boddy's character through his travelling. Some are helpfully picked out by Martin Robinson in his pioneering study of Boddy;[67] some I have expanded on, others I have added.

Boddy's adventurous spirit stands out. The very extent of his visits is itself evidence of this. Furthermore, he did not always follow the well-trodden paths, preferring to make his own way, often without interpreters and with only a rudimentary knowledge of the languages. His journey to Kairwan was far from straightforward and involved a real risk of attack, but he was happy to take that risk. He decided not to describe his time in St Petersburg, since it was 'so frequently described, and is comparatively so familiar',[68] a telling remark about what he saw himself doing in his writing. In Canada he took an exuberant ride on the footplate of a train and described himself as 'more boyish then than now'![69]

Here was a man at ease with others from a wide spectrum of social backgrounds. Alexander Boddy loved being with people, and gained their trust very readily, even making a game of it in Valetta in Malta. In northern Russia he appeared equally at home gaining assistance from the Governor Prince Golitsin and learning 'Russian country expressions' from peasant women in the third-class accommodation on a river steamer. He astonished other first-class passengers by helping those in the third class load logs for the fuel. He was interested in trying to visit those in prison in order to understand their conditions.

His travels brought him into contact with Christians of many traditions, which he much appreciated. On his journeys he met, amongst others, Copts, Presbyterians, Roman Catholics, the Orthodox, and Anglicans who prayed for the President, not the Queen. On his visit to the Roman Catholic priest Father Angelo di Sant' Agata he showed great respect for the man and his faith, though this was in face of Muslims whom he opposed:

co-operation with other Christians was in order to advance missionary work. His breadth of Christian fellowship is well demonstrated by comments spread through his descriptions of Russia: for an evangelical he was unusually warm about the Christian beliefs and practices of the Russians, though he was still prepared to critique what they did.

He maintained his integrity doctrinally and personally. His sympathetic approach to people of other denominations and other faiths did not prevent him from making criticisms where he thought them justified. He also demonstrated his evangelicalism within the Church of England: while abroad he regularly visited CMS missionaries, he took care to share his faith whenever he could, and he would distribute Christian literature when possible, as he did on his Arctic Ocean journey. As his parish ministry would also show, he was a firm teetotaller and on a number of occasions politely refused alcoholic drinks, apparently without causing great offence.

He allowed his sense of humour to spill out, sometimes making fun of himself, for example in his remarks about being a sailor. He clearly took delight in being thought worth the attention of a secret policeman and then giving the man the slip; on another occasion he saw no harm in recording the teasing he had about the lack of a wife.

While he was not a great scholar he was a careful observer and recorder of what he saw and experienced. His writing earned him two honours: Fellow of the Royal Geographical Society and membership of the Imperial Geographical Society of Russia. He was well organised in reading previous authors' accounts of the places he was visiting, even giving a list of sixteen books he took with him to northern Russia.[70] His use of other people's study and experience was certainly important later in nurturing the Pentecostal Movement, and its roots probably lay in his father's own writing, and even more in his training in Durham, both at the University and with Bishop Lightfoot.

So here was a man of adventurous spirit, at ease with a wide variety of people, secure in his faith, willing to learn, with integrity and humour, and taking seriously the study of ordinary life and faith. What might God do with such a follower?

Notes

1 Boddy, *Kairwan*, 6
2 Boddy, *Kairwan*, 9
3 Boddy, *Kairwan*, 1–2
4 Boddy, *Kairwan*, 6. On Tristram, there is a brief account in Luscombe, *Groundwork of Science and Religion*, 1–2
5 Boddy, *Kairwan*, 11
6 Boddy, *Kairwan*, 22
7 Boddy, *Kairwan*, 25
8 Boddy, *Kairwan*, 34
9 Boddy, *Kairwan*, 88
10 Boddy, *Kairwan*, 42
11 Boddy, *Kairwan*, 44 and on p. 172 given in English translation
12 Boddy, *Kairwan*, 108–11
13 Boddy, *Kairwan*, 165
14 Boddy, *Kairwan*, 119–20
15 Boddy, *Kairwan*, 118–19
16 Boddy, *Kairwan*, 178
17 Boddy, *Kairwan*, 120
18 Boddy, *Kairwan*, 166
19 Boddy, *Kairwan*, 168
20 Boddy, *Kairwan*, 173–74
21 Boddy, *Kairwan*, 175
22 Boddy, *Kairwan*, 218
23 Boddy, *Kairwan*, 219
24 He never explicitly states that it was his next trip, nor does he state the date, but this information can be deduced by piecing together information from his travel writings. In particular he recorded the comment of the Archimandrite that his previous travels had been in the Sahara desert. (Boddy, *With Russian Pilgrims*, 70)
25 The possible dates are discussed below
26 Boddy, *With Russian Pilgrims*, 73–75
27 See the wonderful route map in *With Russian Pilgrims*, between pp. 10 and 11, his comments in the Preface, p.vii, and a history of those early voyages in an Appendix
28 Boddy, *With Russian Pilgrims*, viii
29 Boddy, *With Russian Pilgrims*, 23
30 Boddy, *With Russian Pilgrims*, 24
31 Boddy, *With Russian Pilgrims*, 47
32 Boddy, *With Russian Pilgrims*, 41
33 Boddy, *With Russian Pilgrims*, 51
34 Boddy, *With Russian Pilgrims*, 55
35 Boddy, *With Russian Pilgrims*, 85

36 Boddy, *With Russian Pilgrims*, 86
37 Boddy, *With Russian Pilgrims*, 153
38 See Wilk, *The Journals of a White Sea Wolf*
39 Boddy, *With Russian Pilgrims*, 156
40 Boddy, *With Russian Pilgrims*, 174
41 Boddy, *With Russian Pilgrims*, 216
42 Boddy, *With Russian Pilgrims*, 220
43 Boddy, *With Russian Pilgrims*, 255
44 Boddy, *With Russian Pilgrims*, 208–10
45 Boddy, *With Russian Pilgrims*, 255
46 Boddy, *With Russian Pilgrims*, 181
47 Boddy, *With Russian Pilgrims*, 233
48 Boddy, *With Russian Pilgrims*, 245
49 Boddy, *With Russian Pilgrims*, 250
50 Jane Boddy, *A.A. Boddy*, 2
51 Boddy, *With Russian Pilgrims*, 252
52 Boddy, *With Russian Pilgrims*, 295
53 The trip in 1889 can be dated by his reference to the burning down of Seattle and his brief visit to the devastated site (*By Ocean, Prairie and Peak*, 178) on 6 June 1889 (Warren, *The Day Seattle Burned*). The visit in 1890 is dated by his reference to 8 May as a Thursday (*By Ocean, Prairie and Peak*, 10). This is the ostensible date of the book, though he also indicated that it was something of a compilation of four visits: 'I do not relate the latest voyage across, but one which was more full of interest; weaving into it incidents and information from earlier and later experiences.' (*By Ocean, Prairie and Peak*, 8)
54 Boddy, *By Ocean, Prairie and Peak*, 7
55 Boddy, *By Ocean, Prairie and Peak*, 17
56 Boddy, *By Ocean, Prairie and Peak*, 14
57 See chapter 1, fn 50, of the present book
58 Boddy, *By Ocean, Prairie and Peak*, 54
59 Boddy, *By Ocean, Prairie and Peak*, 77
60 Boddy, *By Ocean, Prairie and Peak*, 61–65
61 Boddy, *By Ocean, Prairie and Peak*, 53
62 Boddy, *By Ocean, Prairie and Peak*, 82
63 Boddy, *By Ocean, Prairie and Peak*, 170
64 Boddy, *By Ocean, Prairie and Peak*, 175
65 Boddy, *By Ocean, Prairie and Peak*, 176
66 Boddy, *By Ocean, Prairie and Peak*, 199–202
67 Robinson, *The Charismatic Anglican*, 21–30
68 Boddy, *With Russian Pilgrims*, 291, n.1
69 Boddy, *By Ocean, Prairie and Peak*, 184
70 Boddy, *With Russian Pilgrims*, 261–62

Four

Vicar and Married Man

We had left Alexander Boddy on the verge of being inducted as Vicar of All Saints, Monkwearmouth when we joined him on his trips abroad. Now we turn back to his life and ministry at home from about 1886 to 1903, with two further foreign excursions included. In order to make sense of this period in his life we will pick out four themes, beginning with a brief look at his marriage and family life, moving onto his parish ministry, then a period of emotional breakdown and recovery and its relationship to his travelling, and finally some important spiritual encounters during this phase of his life.

Marriage and Family Life

Mary Pollock – "My treasure"

By 1890 Alexander was thirty-five years old – already a little older than his father had been when he had married at the age of thirty-three – and aware of the desirability of marriage, as his conversations in Russia indicated. His own evangelistic and pastoral concerns caused him to arrange parish missions, and when a general mission was held in Sunderland in 1890 he was keen to be involved. It was through this mission that he met Mary Pollock, who became his wife a year later, in the autumn of 1891.

The exact connection takes a little unravelling from the brief information given. In his first essay of recollections in 1914 Boddy wrote of his vicarage home, and wrote only: 'To this home I brought my treasure, my God-given beloved wife.'[1] Though brief, it reflects the affection with which he regularly referred to Mary, and the consciousness that it was God who had given him a wife. His later reminiscences in 1923 expand on this comment a little:

> In the autumn of 1890 a general mission was held in Sunderland, and in All Saints' we had Canon Grant from Kent as our missioner, several others assisting. There were several lady workers also, and to one of these I was married a little more than a year later. She brought great happiness into my home and into the parish, and she is loved to-day as much as ever.[2]

There was another connection, through her brother, the Revd James Pollock. Pollock had been curate in the neighbouring parish of the Venerable Bede, Monkwearmouth from 1888 to 1889; in 1890, it seems, he was helping Boddy at All Saints. They also spent time travelling together in Canada, though exactly which year this happened is not known. His address in 1891 was given as All Saints Vicarage in the 1892 *Crockford's Clerical Directory*, but any position was probably unofficial since it did not appear in his later entries in *Crockford's Clerical Directory*. The Boddys' younger daughter Jane certainly believed that her uncle had played a part in bringing them together:

> James Pollock invited his sister, Mary, who was a trained singer, to come and help [with the mission]. Mary had always lived in the country and was aghast at the neighbourhood at first but she soon got used to it, and when my father proposed marriage she accepted and went to live at All Saints' Vicarage.[3]

Mary had also been brought up in a clergy home. Her father was Scottish and was educated at the University of Edinburgh before being awarded a PhD by the University of Geissen (near Frankfurt, Germany) in 1860. Mary was born about this time in Scotland.[4] The family moved to Scorton in North Yorkshire in 1863 when her father was appointed Principal of Clare College, a school for boys and girls. It had been founded as a Catholic school for girls in 1795 by English nuns of the order of St Clare, who had arrived from Normandy.[5] They handed it on in about 1852/54 when they moved to Darlington. Even now this is a small village surrounded by rich farming country. It would seem that Mary spent her childhood here, until 1879, when her father was appointed to a series of small country parishes: Finghall, a small village east of Leyburn in Wharfedale in 1879, the neighbouring parish of Thornton Steward in 1883, and then as Vicar of Cundall, south of Thirsk.⁶ All were tiny agricultural places, a complete contrast to the urban upbringing Alexander had had in Cheetham, and to his parish when they met in 1890.

This difference in their backgrounds was overcome by much that they had in common. They had a shared outlook on life and Christian ministry, both having a clergy father and brother, though they had ministered in very different social settings. According to Jane's memoir both had valued the Keswick Convention and they shared a burning desire to bring others to the Saviour they loved.

Boddy appreciated Mary as a partner in ministry, for they both had musical ability, and Mary had teaching and pastoral skills and gifts of healing. Women were accepted as ministers within the Holiness tradition, and Mary was able at this point, and even more in the future, to minister in her own right. Though Mary suffered from health problems almost from the beginning of the marriage it does seem to have been a close and sustaining relationship, shown not just in Alexander's words but also in the way he would clearly support and encourage her ministry, both the public and the more hidden aspects.

Mary, Jane and James – heirs to love and an adventurous spirit

Children were soon to follow: Mary Vazeille born in 1892, Jane Vazeille in 1893 and James Alexander Vazeille in 1895. Boddy baptised his children adding his own touches: Mary received the Russian cross and was baptised on her eighth day before her mother had recovered enough to be present. Perhaps she complained, for Jane and James were baptised a little later, though Jane was told, 'He immersed me seven times under the water, much to my mother's consternation, who had a fire lit in the vestry and a warm towel ready to wrap me in!'

Jane Boddy remembered 'a very happy Christian home. We had simple morning and evening prayers.' Her father did not help with domestic chores, but gave much love to his children 'and tried to instil his own adventurous spirit into them'. She recalled jumping into his arms from the top of a wardrobe, being pulled in a little cart behind his bicycle, and visiting the shipyards. A particular treat was to be rowed out to sea by her father, and she remembered one occasion when a warship was anchored in a rough sea and they were the only visitors prepared to go out. She remembered being taken out of bed to look through her father's telescope, and being taught the Lord's Prayer in Greek and to count in Arabic. Around the Vicarage were slides taken on his travels and a variety of objects he had brought back: a Muslim prayer carpet, snowshoes from Canada, a Red Indian mask and icons from Russia.

The image of an interesting man who delighted in life is sustained by this picture of family life. Jane began her memoir by describing her father as 'original in thought and behaviour', and his family life would appear to have fitted that description, no less than his travelling life did.

Parish Ministry

Pastoral care

We saw in chapter two the beginnings of Boddy's parish ministry, first in the highly irregular circumstances of having to work round the drunken incumbent, and then in his first year as Vicar. Within this short time he and his curates had already brought Sunday attendance and other activities into line with neighbouring parishes.

Very soon pressure of population growth and successful parish ministry led to the desire to expand the buildings available to the parish. Mention of this can be found in letters which survive from Boddy to successive bishops of Durham.

In the first of these, on 30 September 1887, the main discussion is about a parish hall erected between the vicarage and the church. Boddy was pleased to be able to report to Lightfoot that the hall had been more than doubled in size and that the £100 debt had been paid off. His lawyer's mind also went into details about the legal ownership of the hall, complications which remained from the messiness of the previous incumbency. Having made the point that they were now completely free of debt he also looked ahead, indicating that a Vestry was needed next.[7] He added a rather touching detail: 'Our Russian Village was less successful than we had hoped. Visitors were pleased but they did not leave their money with us as we should have liked.' Clearly he was hoping to make use of his travelling experience of the previous year to raise funds for the church.

He did spend some of his time giving 'lantern lectures', for he later described his hobbies as

> travel, book-writing and lecturing. I was enabled the better to endure cheerfully the smoke pall and the steam hammer, and the rattle of machinery night and day, by getting away for a few weeks, in some years, to distant lands . . . In those years I was much pressed by my clerical friends to give lantern lectures, and gave more than 100 of such lectures, going sometimes long distances, but not more often than once a week at the most.[8]

This rather suggests that this was the late 1880s before he married: 'Ere long I limited my lecturing journeys, and soon refused all invitations, keeping strictly to my own work in the parish.'[9] Perhaps by 1923 he was also keen to dispel any impression that he had always been off travelling and not paying proper attention to his parish work.

In fact, his parish ministry was well received. His concern for his parishioners is well illustrated by his action during a prolonged miners' strike in 1892. The strike was against the intention of the pit owners to reduce the wages, following a fall in the price of coal and coke. It began on 9 March and did not end until 3 June. More than 80,000 men were immediately out of work, and many thousands more in related industries soon affected, for County Durham was one of the most industrialised parts of the world at the time. Within Monkwearmouth many hundreds of ironworkers were 'laid off' because of the strike. Eventually a resolution was reached, significantly through the mediation of Bishop Westcott, who had succeeded Lightfoot as Bishop of Durham in 1890.[10] Before that the hardship was widespread and Boddy took a lead in supporting the men from the neighbouring ironworks, S. Tyzack's, and their families, writing in this affecting way to *The Times* a month into the strike:

Sir, There is a class deserving of more sympathy than the miners. There is work for the latter if they accept a reduced wage, but for thousands of artisans and labourers there is now no work to be got at any wage. Starvation is approaching, and all through the lack of coal. Smokeless chimneys, cold furnaces, our rivers full of ships laid up, and the weary pacing to and fro of men who long for work! The children are suffering; there is nothing for them in the house and no credit at the shops. Some are almost on the verge of desperation, and in this locality what can we do but appeal to the public? We ask those who, perhaps, have not known what it is to be hungry to help as they can. That there is a true Christian generosity among member of our wealthy classes has been shown by the wonderful sum sent to our starving fellow-creatures near the Volga.[11] May the same warm-hearted philanthropists help those who live near the Tyne and Wear, and who, through no action of theirs, are in this pitiable condition!

Send help to any responsible persons whose lives are lived among these people.

If money is entrusted to me it will be used to alleviate cases of genuine distress in this parish, or handed on, if it proves to be more than sufficient, to neighbouring parishes.

Yours, &c Alexander A Boddy All Saints Vicarage, Monkwearmouth, Sunderland April 18th

PS We have established a soup kitchen and hope to feed some hundreds of half-starving people who have nothing to do with the strike and are innocent sufferers.[12]

Boddy's writing ability was put to good use as he drew on his talent for description and added that poignant postscript.

It worked. According to a later report in *The Times* Boddy raised £535 for the workers and their families from newspaper readers and through local efforts.[13] His efforts were much appreciated and after the strike a special gathering was held in a beach café, where the workers presented him with a silver communion set and Mary with an urn. These they continued to treasure many years later.[14] The communion is inscribed: 'Presented to the Rev. A.A. Boddy by the workmen of S. Tyzack

& Co. Sept. 24th 1892' and it is still in use at All Saints for sick communions.[15]

This is the most obvious of many instances in which Boddy can be seen working as an evangelical Anglican slum priest.

Perhaps it is no coincidence that Boddy's first felt and recorded personal encounters with God through the work of the Holy Spirit took place about this time, when emotions were running high. We shall return to this soon.

Pastoral prayer

We learn of Boddy's prayerful work in the parish from the personal account of his daughter Jane and the formal replies to Visitation forms from the Bishop of Durham. Jane Boddy saw her father as doing his best work as a faithful parish priest, who 'loved his people and they loved him'.[16] Her memoir once again provides vivid details, which seem to cohere with other information about her father and his ministry. In a touching passage she explained:

> He loved his people and they loved him, for he never spared himself and was available day and night. There was a lot of drunkenness in our neighbourhood, especially at the week-ends, and on Saturday nights my father used to go round the public houses and take drunken men home. The street just opposite the vicarage was the worst and housed some very poor, low-class people, mostly a family in each room, sometimes more. The children played in the street and were practically always bare-footed and in ragged clothing. There was a beer shop at the end of the block and, as a child, I remember listening to the bell ringing as customers went in many times during the evening until I fell asleep. There was also a big public house called 'The Cambridge' further down the street and father used to hold open-air services outside it, often on a Sunday evening after the service in Church, which usually ended about 8 pm.

She was prepared to be faithful to her own memories: 'My father was not a brilliant preacher, but his sermons were simple and practical.' She also remembered the singing talents of her parents: 'my father, who had a deep bass voice and was very musical, took the choir practices . . . and when there were Oratorios my mother sang the soprano solos. I remember her glorious voice best in *The Messiah*.'

Bishop Westcott sent out his Primary Visitation form in August 1892, and some of Boddy's answers are especially interesting.[17] He was clearly not content with the religious practice of most of his parishioners. Asked about Sunday observance by different classes his response was typical of many clergy of the time: 'The lowest classes rarely observed it. The middle classes to a large extent observe it. The highest classes only to the extent of 50 per cent.'

When asked, 'Is Family Prayer frequent among your people?' he replied that it was 'scarcely known', though he 'frequently urged it both in public and private ministrations'.

On the other hand he was more positive about the use of lay workers, a distinguishing feature of his replies at this stage and even more so in later Visitations: 'A fair number of earnest workers are joined in a Church Guild. Our workers are District Visitors and Sunday School Teachers.'

Finally when asked, 'What will bring the Gospel to bear more effectually upon ordinary life?' he had two parts to his answer, one for all Christians, and one for the clergy:

a. A greater co-operation with all who are in Christ Jesus. A cultivation of the spirit of <u>love</u> [his emphasis] to those who are in Him whenever it is possible to work with them and accept their aid.

b. Meetings of clergy simply to pray for a greater filling by the Holy Ghost for service.

This emphasis on God's love and the greater filling by the Holy Ghost is noteworthy, for the comments were made before any particular Pentecostal experience he had, as far as we can tell; they mostly likely stem from the teaching at the Keswick Convention. This was an aspiration as much as a lived experience at this stage of his life. It also contrasts somewhat with the answers that other local clergy gave: they wrote about activities perfectly good in themselves, including visiting, education, preaching, Bible classes, good example and personal influence – all of which Boddy himself engaged in, but even at this stage he saw the need to go behind them to something more fundamental, in reliance on God's love and the work of the Spirit.

The Sunderland YMCA published a glowing account of the man and his work. Even allowing for some element of uncritical admiration we gain a picture which fits with what we know of him later in life. His passion for unity was noted, for he had a 'catholicity of Spirit and a deep spirituality of mind'. He was seen as combining the best of several traditions, for he 'seeks to combine Church order with evangelistic zeal'. He was said to hold three prayer meetings each week, to support Church Army work in his parish and to be a devoted Bible teacher.[18]

Further detail of his continuing parish work is found in the 1896 Visitation return to the Bishop of Durham. In connection with evangelistic activity Boddy reported: 'I cannot report any increase in zeal for Evangelistic Work. We have open-air preaching in connection with our regular Church Army Services.'

He continued to hold regular Bible Classes on Sunday afternoons and Tuesday evenings after Service in order 'to strengthen spiritual life and to teach Bible Truths'. He also held 'Mission Services' in two hired rooms, one being 'a cottage with the wall between two rooms removed'. Going beyond the Prayer Book, he also mentioned that '[p]rayer meetings and testimony meetings are also held at which opportunities are given for "extempore" prayer and "witness"'. This last sentence was marked by the Bishop, though it is not specified why, and it is not likely that he took any action. The effect of the Mission Services was not great in numbers, but Boddy noted they added 'a few very earnest people'.

In a tradition going back to the eighteenth century, Boddy was also willing to hold Cottage Meetings, rather in the way a century later house groups became popular: 'Cottage Meetings held in succession for some six weeks in the same neighbourhood seem to do good. After that it seems well to stop for a time. These Cottage Meetings seem as helpful to the Workers as to anyone present.'

Comparison with other parish returns in the diocese suggests that this was a minority activity, though some other clergy were also very enthusiastic.

With both the Mission Services and the Cottage Meetings we get a glimpse of a minister willing to try new things in order to bring spiritual life to as many people as possible, and in the prayer meetings and testimony meetings to go beyond many of his fellow Anglicans.[19]

As mentioned above, in the early 1890s the growth of the population and the steady work of Boddy, his curates, Church Army Captains and lay workers led to a desire for further church buildings. This was not easily achieved, and some of the correspondence between Boddy and Bishop Westcott indicates the drawn-out process.[20] In 1893 the Bishop visited a proposed site for a new church building in Roker and then the Ecclesiastical Commissioners gave half an acre of land and promised £500 towards a permanent building, costed at between £1,500 and £2,000. One local man, Mr Tone, promised £100, but a lack of commitment by many other lay people to the project delayed it, and a temporary iron building, dedicated to St Aidan, was eventually erected.

In a later letter of 1901, to the next bishop, Handley Moule, Boddy wrote positively about the daughter churches of St Aidan's Roker and St Mary's Fulwell as answers to prayer. He and the congregation of St Aidan's were apparently content with the building, though Boddy also noted that the £500 from the Ecclesiastical Commissioners was still on offer and he hoped that some devout person would have their heart touched to complete the work.[21] He also drew the bishop's attention to their work towards a new Sunday School building; they had raised £920 in cash and promises towards the £2,100 needed. (This would seem to be the same building as the parish hall on Fulwell Road, opened in 1904, and later the venue of the Sunderland Whitsuntide Conventions.)

Related to the concern for buildings was a longstanding proposal that the parish be split, since it was now over 10,000 people and still growing. Boddy's dislike of the idea reveals something of his methods of working:

> Your Lordship will understand however my own shrinking from this arrangement. Since 1886 I have been the Vicar of Roker and have relied upon the help of its better class residents to help my very poor parishioners in other parts of the parish. Bishop Westcott in thinking it over shook his head and said 'I can never be a party to cutting off the poor from the rich.'

[handwritten margin note: burned down St Aidan's Chapel of ease]

If it is done, perhaps it would only be fair to myself not to do it while I am here – but when a young man full the zeal of freshness in the work could be appointed to All Saints – and from the first be accustomed to work without the help of Roker. The Roker church people in large measure are the personal friends now of my wife and myself. Her Friday Bible Class at this Vicarage has a great influence over many of their lives, and I do not think that they would wish to be separated from us.[22]

Here was a clear admission that the richer folks of Roker were essential to the ministry he had in the poor end of the parish, around All Saints itself – a situation found repeatedly in the Church of England at the time. The appeal to Westcott's words shows that the discussion was not a new one. We also get a glimpse of Mary's influence through her Bible Class, which in fact was to continue until they left the parish in 1923. A mention earlier in the letter of services taken by the Revd F. Smith is a reminder of the work done by Boddy's curates. He usually had at least one curate with him, sometimes two and on one occasion three.[23]

Eventually in 1903 money was found to pay for a new church of St Andrew's in Roker when John Priestman, a local shipbuilder, put forward £6,000 towards the substantial £9,000 cost of the building.[24] The new building was opened in 1907 and the new parish of St Andrew's Roker formed. The new church was built to a very high standard and has frequently been called the 'Cathedral of the Arts and Craft Movement', but it plays no further part in our story.

In the mid 1890s all this successful building work was only a dream and Boddy felt under considerable pressure from the spiritual stress, as he hinted in his book of 1896, *By Ocean, Prairie and Peak*: 'The incessant strain to body, soul, and spirit of a populous parish, and the constant facing of sorrow and sin, could cause a breakdown if there were not pauses.'[25]

The time came shortly after this when he did break down.

Travelling in the Holy Land: Devotion, Breakdown and Recovery

Boddy's son James was born in 1895, but he still made a solo visit to the Holy Land, or Syria as he called it, in the autumn of 1895 in order to write a 'life of our Lord'.[26] Perhaps we should infer that he was in serious need of a break from the parish. His book was published in 1897 as *Christ in His Holy Land* and it went through the life of Christ from the Forerunner and the Annunciation to Ascension and Pentecost, giving word pictures of the places associated with Jesus' life in forty-five pithy chapters. It was a devotional work and he would continue making use of the material to the end of his life, giving lectures and sermon series based on his observations.

In a subsequent book, *Days in Galilee and Scenes in Judaea*, he gave a more familiar travelogue account of his 1895 visit. As on other visits, he was concerned to be in touch with missionaries and local Christians, and he had conversations with CMS missionaries about the realities and difficulties of working amongst Muslims. On other occasions he met Mr Khalil Jamal, a Syrian clergyman of the Church of England mission, and was given the opportunity to preach to a congregation in Nazareth; he also attended a Church of England service in Arabic at Shechem.[27] He was spiritually overjoyed to reach Jerusalem: 'To a reverent mind such a moment is impressive, for whilst looking at the actual one also looks forward to the spiritual. One thinks of the day when one may see the heavenly Jerusalem also for the first time.'[28]

This visit provided an opportunity for various themes in his life to come together: his contacts with Jews and Muslims, and a concern for conversion; ecumenical relations with a variety of Christian churches; links with the Russian Orthodox church and her pilgrims – all were to feature in his time in the Holy City.

The end of his visit gives a further illustration both of his energy and his willingness to be outspoken for fellow Christians. On learning from the Russian consul and others that Christians were in some danger from certain Muslim fanatics he hurried back to England and went direct to the offices of *The Times* newspaper to write a short article requesting that the government of Lord Salisbury send gunboats to patrol the coast and deter the violence.[29]

A second visit to the Holy Land followed in 1897 after his health broke down. Boddy never referred to this publicly, but gave hints of the strain he felt, as indicated above and also in the book he wrote about this second visit, *From the Egyptian Ramleh*:

> The strain of a large parish, and the depression caused by living in a vicarage often overshadowed by a pall of smoke and always shaken by a vindictive steam-hammer has been mitigated during the last fifteen years by occasional glimpses of strange sunny scenes, from which he [the writer] has returned invigorated and strengthened for his welcome work in the homeland.[30]

Years later he gave this account of the industrial setting of his Church:

> All Saints' Church, Monkwearmouth, stands in the midst of industry. On two sides extends a great Rope Manufactory, giving employment to hundreds, both women and men. On the other side are Iron Works, whose furnaces are blazing night and day in ordinary times. A visit at night time takes one among fires almost at white heat; men sweating and toiling, molten slag running from the fires, great steam hammers, with resounding and colossal blows, driving dross out of great masses of soft and glowing metal. Rolling mills turning this into rails. Rivet machines turning out thousands of rivets. Purification and sanctification through much tribulation. Eventual usefulness is the outcome, a great change from the rough ore to the shapely rail. A visit at night is a weird experience, as one steps from darkness into glare and noise, and the ceaseless rush of these iron-workers. But far down below, a mile deep, other men are working or hastening along dark, cavernous passages to their distant cavils.[31]

Right throughout Boddy's ministry Sunderland was at the heart of industrial Britain, and the largest shipbuilding port in the world. This was the demanding location of Boddy's parish, and that was the reason he found he needed time to recuperate, as did the more well-known slum priests of the East End of London. It is only in a private letter to Bishop Moule that he wrote more directly of the fact that he did have a breakdown of some kind, whether physical or more likely emotional.

The letter he wrote to Moule in 1901, mainly about the proposed new church at Roker, also contained two sentences indicating what he had been through: first he wrote, 'I am 47 now. But better in mind and body than I have been for many years.' Then he mentioned that he had been offered a post in a less demanding parish: '. . . the late Bishop offered me Escomb when my health once gave way, but that instead I took eight months in Egypt as Chaplain of Ramleh but that I am most happy in my work here.'[32]

His time in Ramleh, a suburb of Alexandria on the Nile Delta, gave him the opportunity to visit the Holy Land again in October and November 1897. He was licensed by Bishop Blyth in Jerusalem for his work at All Saints, Ramleh and stayed until the summer of 1898. On this occasion it seems that Mary joined him, though she was not able to stay for the whole time, as their three children contracted scarlet fever and she returned home.[33]

Boddy also developed his skills in photography, illustrating his books as a result and being able to give lectures on the Holy Land once he had returned home himself.

Just as his exact illness is a mystery, so we are told nothing of his recovery. However, he appeared to remain fit and well from this point onwards, even as he continued to seek to know God more deeply.

The Missing Link: Power from on High

1892: Forgiveness and power

Boddy's physical travels had their spiritual counterpart, for he constantly sought a deeper spiritual life, whether at home in Monkwearmouth or in other parts of the world where God seemed to be at work. This was seen in his life as early as 1876 when he attended the Keswick Convention for the first time and continued throughout this period of parish ministry, and into his final years.

By the end of 1892 he made two significant steps forward. First he realised that what was missing in his spiritual experience was the personal appropriation of justification by faith.

Though God has, in His great mercy, permitted me now for more than twenty-nine years to be in His ministry, I have to confess that in the earlier part of that time I was not truly and experimentally 'Born from Above'. I believe that in those earlier days I honestly endeavoured to live up to, and preach up to, my light; but I do not wonder at a worthy parishioner once writing a letter of fatherly rebuke to me.

He told me in it that he missed in my ministry the preaching of the glorious doctrine of Justification by faith. No wonder, for I could not honestly say then that I knew that my sins were forgiven, though in a way, I did seek to preach Christ.[34]

He wrote the following about what happened when he met and prayed with a visiting missionary from Ceylon: 'We knelt together, and I arose with full assurance that my sins were forgiven me for His Name's Sake. I now had a real message to give, and had not much need of my old manuscript sermons.'

But this was not enough for him: 'I still yearned for more power with souls, and God showed me that he was willing to fill me with His Holy Spirit because he had commanded me to be filled (Eph. v.18).'

He then went on to describe how God met him in a profound way during a service of Holy Communion on St Matthew's Day:

It was on the 21st September, 1892, at about 8.40 in the morning, in All Saints' Church, Monkwearmouth – my church in Sunderland, that the Holy Spirit in infinite love came upon me, when I was taking part in the Communion Service. I was reading the Epistle for the day (St Matthew's Day), 2 Cor iv. 6, when the Holy Spirit came in power. As I read these words (the sixth verse) He fell, 'For God which commanded the light to shine out of darkness, hath shined in our hearts to give the light of the knowledge of the glory of God in the face of Jesus Christ.' It overwhelmed me; my voice broke, and tears were in my eyes. I knew He had come, and that I was 'fulfilled with His grace and heavenly benediction'. When the service was over I praised Him in the words of the Doxology. The longing of my heart was satisfied: my constant prayer was answered.

The second half of this testimony made four points which he was to reiterate frequently in his teaching in his *Confidence* magazine: the first fruit of love, testing by the devil, not trusting in experience or emotion, and keeping Christ central, not the Holy Spirit.

His longer testimony five years later in February 1914 did not refer to the experience of Justification by faith, but did reprint the central portion of the description of his experience on 21 September 1892, that printed above, along with a short paragraph about the fruit of love.[35] This no doubt reflects the emphasis of his ministry by then on the appropriation of a Pentecostal experience.

What he did not refer to in any of these printed testimonies was that 21 September, the Feast of St Matthew, was when he was accustomed to celebrate the anniversary of his ordination in 1880 (the actual date was 19 September). His daughter's testimony, however, did refer to this anniversary, and made it the final paragraph in a nine-page document.[36] There she wrote: 'My father's ordination was on St Matthew's Day, and each year he celebrated Holy Communion that morning.' She also high-lighted as especially loved the same verses from the Epistle, 2 Corinthians 4:5-6. The implication seems to be that this pivotal experience occurred just after the stress of the Miner's Strike and the subsequent presentation of gifts by grateful workers he had supported, in the context of his annual remembrance of his ordination by Lightfoot, of whom he was in some awe. This commemoration each year of his ordination is a further and hidden confirmation of the centrality of his self-identification as an Anglican clergyman.

The personal experience of being 'Born Again' and then of being overwhelmed by the power of the Holy Spirit changed the direction of his ministry: his evangelical doctrine came alive for him, and he desired to know God more deeply.

Another testimony he wrote in 1909 supports this charac-terisation of a serious change of direction: he wrote of his early motivation for travelling, that it was 'not in order to preach Christ, but to write books of travel and to be somewhat of an authority on the people he thus studies'.[37]

1895: *The Spirit and power*

Some sense of his developing spirituality can be seen in 1895 when he published a short book, *Laying on of Hands*, for young confirmation candidates, putting Confirmation in a very positive light as a basis for Christian living, and including a defence of infant baptism and the Creeds. It contained much that would be familiar to other Anglicans, on renunciation, faith, obedience, prayer, Bible Reading and the Holy Communion.

His emphasis on the supernatural nature of Confirmation may seen as drawing on The Order of Confirmation in the *Book of Common Prayer* which includes this prayer by the bishop for the candidates: 'Strengthen them, we beseech thee, O Lord, with the Holy Ghost the Comforter, and daily increase in them thy manifold gifts of grace.' Boddy wrote: 'there is specially sealed to us supernatural power to enable us to live in union with the Incarnate SON of GOD.' He went on: '(W)e now "take" the HOLY GHOST in His Divine fullness as our strength.'[38] As he was to do later, he incorporated testimonies from people he knew, using anonymous contributions from an ironworker, a hat trimmer and a glassblower. He tended to assume the validity of infant baptism, and in keeping with his background in the Holiness tradition he was mostly concerned to see people live out the implications of their baptism, realising that the Holy Spirit gave them supernatural power to live holy lives.

Also in 1895 he visited the Holy Land for the first time, and his spiritual development was shown in a sermon preached at St George's Church, Jerusalem when he urged unity amongst Christians and mutual respect. He was concerned that: 'Too often each [Christian] is ready to condemn others, and to do it, perhaps, in great ignorance . . . Earnest, Christ-loving men, devoted servants of the Cross, are at times even suspicious of one another.' The solution, interestingly, was to pray for the Holy Spirit to pour out his love:

> Oh, for an outpouring of the Holy Ghost until hearts overflow to one another in love! There is no other solution of these difficulties but the yielding to the full possession of the Spirit's power. The spirit of condemnation and criticism in our Church, at home and abroad, will be flooded out with the spirit of love.

While discussing how peace might be achieved he stressed the importance of individual Christians having peace with God, and quoted Romans 5:1, 'Being justified by faith we have peace with God through our Lord Jesus Christ.'[39] Thus he sought to be true to his evangelical roots, but saw the sadness of Christians divided and believed that the experience he had had of God's love through the Spirit was what was needed to bring unity.

1899: The Holy Spirit and healing

A further experience of the Spirit came in 1899, when Alexander and Mary were profoundly influenced by her healing from asthma.

In her own testimony in 1907 Mary described how her eagerness to work in the parish led to poor health, especially chronic asthma and bronchitis. She began to read the Scriptures on the matter of Divine Healing and became convinced that Christ could bring physical healing. 'After many months of prayer, God *spoke* to me from John v.,39–40, on the 23rd of February, 1899, and as I believed the Word and *received* Jesus to come into me as my physical life, He did so, and I was made whole.'[40]

Mary went on in her testimony to discuss the reality of sin, and to be positive about the possibility of 'sinless perfection' (a Wesleyan doctrine), emphasising the finished work of Christ on the Cross.

As a result of her healing Mary discovered she had a gift of healing and regularly prayed with and laid hands on sick people. Their daughter Jane remembered that the family rarely saw a doctor, for if they were ill her father would anoint them with oil and her mother lay on hands. According to Jane her father did not have the gift of healing but used a service of Anointing the Sick and taught on the subject of healing. She believed that his prayers, faith and compassion helped many. She herself asked him to pray with her when 'in a bad mood as an adolescent' which she found brought her peace.[41]

Boddy's own later reflections were that he began to anoint sick people with oil from 1892, and it was after Mary's healing that they rarely consulted doctors.[42] This length of involvement in a healing ministry was to prove invaluable later, and Mary began an extensive teaching ministry by writing of 'Health and Healing in Jesus' in the second issue of *Confidence* in 1908.[43]

By about 1900 it was clear that the energy Boddy had previously been putting into his foreign travels was now going into developing his understanding of the work of the Spirit. Turning from travel books he wrote a series of twelve 'Roker Tracts' on spiritual renewal, some of which were reprinted later in the magazine *Confidence*. All this indicates that during the 1890s and into the early 1900s while Boddy was working hard as a parish priest he was also extending his theological and spiritual horizons. The major turning point came in 1904 when he heard about the Welsh Revival and he believed that this was what he had been waiting for.

Notes

1 *Confidence*, February 1914, 24
2 *Confidence*, January 1923, 66
3 Jane Boddy, *A.A. Boddy*, 2. This memoir by Jane Boddy is not entirely accurate, especially when she gives details from before her birth or early childhood, but this part of her account is consistent with the rest of the evidence. It is used in the following paragraphs to illustrate their family life
4 1901 Census
5 From information transcribed from *The National Gazetteer of Great Britain and Ireland* 1868 by Colin Hinson ©2003, http://www.genuki.org.uk/big/eng/YKS/NRY/Catterick/Catterick68.html accessed 27 April 2004
6 Pollock's career details from *Crockford's* 1892
7 Letter dated 30 September 1887, University of Durham archive. All Saints Monkwearmouth file
8 *Confidence*, January 1923, 65
9 *Confidence*, January 1923, 66
10 Westcott, *Westcott*, 115–31
11 This is a reference to the Russian Famine Fund set up earlier that year, and to which Boddy himself had been a significant contributor, raising money through his lectures. *The Times*, 12 May 1892, 10
12 *The Times*, 19 April 1892, 10
13 *The Times*, 27 September 1892, 5
14 *Confidence*, January 1923, 66
15 Seen by the author in All Saints Church, Monkwearmouth, 5 March 2002
16 Quotations here from Jane Boddy, *A.A. Boddy*, 3
17 All responses from Durham Diocesan Visitation Returns, All Saints, Monkwearmouth, 1892
18 'Rev Alex. A. Boddy F.R.G.S.' *YMCA Flashes* Vol. 11, No. 8 1895, 86
19 All responses from Durham Diocesan Visitation Returns, All Saints, Monkwearmouth, 1896

20 Details here are drawn from letters held in University of Durham archive. All Saints Monkwearmouth file. Dated 11 May 1894 and 26 June 1894

21 After a fire in 1907 burnt down the first St Aidan's church a new stone church was built on the site and opened in 1910

22 Letter to Bishop Moule, 10 December 1901. University of Durham archive. All Saints Monkwearmouth file

23 The full list in given in Appendix Two

24 *The Times*, 16 November 1903, 8

25 Boddy, *By Ocean, Prairie and Peak*, 7

26 Boddy, *Days in Galilee*, ix

27 *Days in Galilee*, 72, 120

28 *Days in Galilee*, 138

29 *The Times*, 20 November 1895, 7

30 Boddy, *From the Egyptian Ramleh*, 2

31 *Confidence*, April 1912, 67

32 Letter to Bishop Moule, 10 December 1901. University of Durham archive. All Saints Monkwearmouth file

33 Jane Boddy, *A.A. Boddy*, 2

34 These and the immediately following extracts are from 'The Writer's Testimony', *Confidence*, April 1909, 98. The reference to Ceylon is from a report by Pastor Polman in *Confidence*, September 1908, 19

35 *Confidence*, February 1914, 24. He also reprinted the entire testimony in one of the last issues of *Confidence* in October 1922, 52–53, 56

36 Jane Boddy, *A.A. Boddy*, 9

37 *Latter Rain Evangel*, February 1909, quoted in Lavin, *Boddy*, 36

38 *Laying on of Hands*, 7, 8

39 Quotations from *Days in Galilee*, 341, 342

40 Mary Boddy, *'Pentecost' at Sunderland*, 2

41 Jane Boddy, A.A. *Boddy*, 5

42 For the first see *Confidence*, April 1922, 21; for the second see *Confidence*, January 1910, 15

43 See chapter 8 for discussion of his theological understanding of healing

Five

'Pentecost Comes to Sunderland'

The Impact of the Welsh Revival

In 1904 revival broke out in Wales.

Although it appeared to arrive spontaneously and grew rapidly, the revival was not without preparation and warning. There had been previous revivals, notably through Methodism in the eighteenth century and in 1859 a national awakening. At the start of the twentieth century there were groups of people in several places praying for revival. In 1903 in Cardiganshire two Calvinist Methodist ministers, Joshua Jenkins and his nephew John Thickens, came under the influence of the teaching on holiness of the Keswick Convention. They began to hold meetings, at which they encouraged people to confess their sins and to seek the power of the Holy Spirit. This led to conversions and then further evangelism by young people.

Evan Roberts

It was at such a meeting on 29 September 1904 at Blaenannerch that Evan Roberts, then aged twenty-six and wanting to enter the ministry of the Calvinistic Methodists, was convicted of sin and felt called to evangelise.[1]

Evan Roberts quickly became the best-known leader in the revival, though he was not alone, and he went on seven trips to South Wales, Liverpool, North Wales, ending in Anglesey in June 1905. He gave a prominent place in his meetings to women – they sang, gave testimony and occasionally preached. He changed the emphasis of the revival meetings from preaching to public confession of sin and calling on the Holy Spirit. A contemporary account noted the conditions Roberts believed necessary for revival, which in essence were the confession of sin and amendment of life, followed by fervent prayer for the Holy Spirit. At first meetings were quite disorderly, with people calling out their sins or laughing, crying or singing, which Roberts saw as evidence of the presence of the Holy Spirit. However, he later became more critical of the outpouring of emotion and came to emphasise a more cerebral belief in God.

Alexander Boddy's response

Boddy heard of the revival quickly, and he asked Roberts to come to Sunderland. But when Roberts replied he was too busy to come, Boddy decided to travel to Ton-y-Pandy in the Rhondda Valley to see for himself what was happening, in December 1904.[2]

He later described the Welsh revival as an important preparation for the outpouring of the Holy Spirit in Sunderland, writing in an article in 1910 that it 'made hearts more hungry for the living God'.[3] He himself 'was present at some of the most Spiritual of the wonderful gatherings of the Welsh Revival, and was in the pulpit with Evan Roberts'. He took back with him encouragement from Roberts to 'believe the promises' and saw himself as passing on the fire he had experienced. He was welcomed to do so in Methodist Chapels, Mission Halls and other places.

In his 1910 article Boddy provided three extensive extracts from newspaper reports about the meetings he had held, presumably in 1905, and probably into 1906. These meetings themselves were punctuated by cries of 'Amen', 'Praise God' and 'Hallelujah', and included an address by Boddy, citing the prophecy of Joel, itself quoted by the Apostle Peter on the Day of Pentecost according to Acts 2:17. Boddy noted that in Wales sermons were being replaced by praise, prayer and testimony. He would encourage his hearers to believe that God would bless Sunderland in a similar way, and then they would turn to prayer. After each prayer or prayers he apparently led the singing of a gospel chorus. He described these prayer meetings as 'Revival on a small scale'.

On one occasion he organised a United Revival Service which began in All Saints Church with an address from an evangelist from Wales. They formed a procession which included 'Church of England clergymen, Congregational ministers, a Baptist minister, the leaders of the two great Bible Classes in the town, Local preachers and many Church and Nonconformist laymen'. About 15,000 people assembled outside the Roker Park football ground, which was in the parish and was the home ground of Sunderland football club. This was perhaps the most prominent of many open-air services which Boddy held.

In addition, Boddy was inspired to start a prayer meeting for revival: 'A little circle of earnest young men met night after night in prayer in my Vestry for further Revival – for a great Outpouring of the Holy Spirit.'

Bishop Handley Moule

Boddy was fortunate to have had Handley Moule as Bishop of Durham since 1901. At the age of seventeen Moule had experienced in his father's parish in Dorset the effect of the 1859 Revival, an event he regularly referred to until his death.[4] Later he was challenged by the teaching on holiness of the Keswick Movement and in 1884 he made a fresh commitment to Christ at the Convention. He remained a strong supporter of Keswick until his death, regularly attending as a speaker.[5]

Moule was probably the first Bishop in the Church of England to write publicly and positively about the Welsh Revival of 1904. *The Times* published a short article by Moule in which he mentioned a positive report from a friend who was a vicar in the Borders. Moule compared the current revival favourably with the revival of 1859, and he appealed for a welcome for the movement, ending the article with reference to the 'power of the Paraclete' and 'Come Holy Ghost, Creator, come.'[6]

Early in 1905 there were two further references in *The Times* to Moule's comments on the revival. The first quoted from a long letter that had been sent by Moule to the Wearmouth ruridecanal conference.[7] Intriguingly, the second was a report of an address given in Monkwearmouth by Moule, in which he said that 'the Welsh revival was a movement of God'. The report noted that he 'prayed that the revival might spread through England'. Moule was also quoted as stating that a meeting of thirty English bishops had been of one feeling and hope that the blessings received in Wales might also come to England.[8]

It seems reasonable to suppose that both Moule's letter and his attendance in Monkwearmouth arose out of requests by Boddy. Given Boddy's previous use of *The Times* for drawing attention to the plight of ironworkers in his parish and to that of Christians in the Holy Land, one also wonders if he was behind the publishing of these remarks. Whether or not that was the case, the public support for the Welsh revival by Moule would certainly have helped Boddy in his own promotion of revival in Sunderland.

A search in the archives of *The Times* reveals only one other bishop speaking out in this way: Edward Carr Glyn, the Bishop of Peterborough.[9]

Mary Boddy

In this same period Mary Boddy was on her own spiritual journey. Her healing from asthma in 1899, mentioned at the end of chapter 4, had led her to a healing ministry in her own right and a desire to know and experience God more fully.

Some letters she wrote in 1905 have been preserved in a memo written by a Mr A. Blackburn of The Mission House, Hisehope, Waskerley, high in the Pennines above Weardale.[10] There are excerpts from three letters written by Mary in March and April that year. In the first Mary asked for prayer that 'I may very soon receive a real Baptism of Fire and the Holy Ghost.' She went on to explain this came from her experience of healing and her desire to help those who were coming to her:

> God healed me 7 years ago and has lead [sic] me into the Resurrection Life of Jesus for soul and body And has wonderfully blessed and used me in healing and getting many through into Life – but I have a great longing for the conscious presence of God Himself for power in healing the many sick that come, and to the large Bible Class I have.

An interesting comment about God's presence comes in a later sentence, apparently referring to September 1904, before the Welsh revival started:

> Last September the power of God came upon me wonderfully and shook my whole frame, but I think I was a little afraid

then of the <u>full</u> Baptism. Now I want it just for His work and glory. He sends so many to me for help, and I quite think the same signs should follow now as in Apostolic days. M.B.[11]

Mr Blackburn replied to this letter and received a second one from Mary, in which she mentioned the devil tempting her 'after a time of great filling in which God used me to heal 2 people at once and 2 others were visibly anointed with the Holy Ghost – with laying on of hands – The power of God went through and through me'.[12] After a difficult time she had clearly found Blackburn's letter helpful.

This ministry must be seen in the context of the influence of the Welsh revival and Alexander's own attempts to encourage revival in Sunderland. We have no further knowledge of the claimed healings, nor of what was visible about the anointing, though one might suspect shaking, but this went beyond earlier evangelical practice towards something like a Pentecostal practice of ministry.

The third and final letter in this memo struck a positive, even ecstatic note throughout:

Last Monday (Easter Monday) while some of us were in prayer, the Heavens seemed to open and I saw the Light of God come right down to me from the Living personal Christ. And as I thanked Him, He filled my mouth with laughter. Our very house was filled with the presence of God, so that our maid who is in the Spirit felt afraid to be alone.[13]

The reference to laughter here is very unusual, for though emotions were regularly mentioned in reports about the Welsh revival they tend to be about fervour and excitement.[14]

It is clear that Boddy's visit to Wales and the aftermath of Mary's healing had considerable impact on them and their ministries in 1905 and onwards.

International Encouragement

Meanwhile, news of the events in Wales soon spread well beyond Britain, and it stirred people as far apart as India, Scandinavia and North America. The Welsh revival led to the encouragement of prayer for revival by Frank Bartleman in Los Angeles by April 1905. In June Pastor Smale of the First Baptist Church, Los Angeles, returned from Wales and began prayer meetings for an outpouring of the Holy Spirit.[15] These meetings inspired by the Welsh revival helped to prepare the way in Los Angeles.

By the beginning of the twentieth century Los Angeles had been a rapidly growing city for just one generation, and people had flooded in from many parts of North America. Many had come in search of an earthly heaven of sunshine and wealth, but were becoming disillusioned.

In this dynamic, multiracial and restless city there were those who offered a more traditional heavenly vision, based on Holiness teaching and what had become known as 'Latter Rain' ideas.[16] This was a conviction that, as foretold by the Old Testament prophet Joel, God would pour out blessing in great abundance just before the end of history in the second coming of Christ. The Welsh revival and Boddy's own expectations owed something to these concepts.

The influence of Azusa Street

Among the newcomers to Los Angeles in 1906 was William Seymour, recently fired up by the message, though he had not yet had the personal experience of baptism in the Holy Spirit and speaking in tongues. Unable to preach at the little storefront church where he had expected a welcome, he organised prayer meetings in the homes of black sympathisers.

It was on 9 April that the first people spoke in tongues, and Seymour followed three days later. With his friends they took over an abandoned building in Azusa Street, holding their first service on 14 April 1906, within days of their first experience.

Their eschatological message – here is the Latter Rain, evidenced by the Spirit, the harbinger of judgement – was reinforced a few days later, when San Francisco was nearly destroyed by an earthquake on 18 April. In these circumstances the message and the experience spread quickly and its influence spread throughout the USA, at first through individual contact and soon through the Azusa Street magazine *The Apostolic Faith*. People were drawn by the conjunction of familiar teaching about end times and a fuller experience of the Holy Spirit, all in a heady context of blacks and whites, males and females worshipping and leading worship together.

A copy of the first issue of *The Apostolic Faith* in September 1906 was received by a Norwegian Methodist pastor, Thomas Ball Barratt, on a visit to New York. This was to prove of great importance in Boddy's own spiritual journey. At the time Barratt was a minister in the Methodist Episcopal Church of Norway, though his parents were Wesleyan Methodists from Cornwall, England. Following an early call to an evangelistic ministry he was now in his mid-forties and seeking financial support from American Methodists for a City Mission project in Norway which he was wanting to sustain. Failure in these appeals led him to a point of spiritual desperation and he began to read in search of renewal. It was in this context that he read of Azusa Street.

Meeting with other sympathetic people he had a profound religious experience on 7 October 1906, and experienced speaking in tongues on 15 November. This gave him a new framework within which to see his mission and spirituality, and he left New York for Oslo (then called Christiania) on 6 December 1906. When he returned home he held meetings to spread the Pentecostal Outpouring, as it was being called.[17]

Boddy's prayer meetings for revival were sustained through this period, with lasting effects. In one later account he described the participants as 'a prepared people here at Sunderland, eager to receive the very fullness of God, and longing to honour the Lord Jesus',[18] and in another mentioned that 'our beloved people were very much blessed, and they determined to press on for more of God.'[19] Later still he wrote, 'through the winter of 1906–7 a band of young men were praying night after night, sometimes in the church and sometimes in the vestry, laying hold of God, at times in perfect stillness before him for half-an-hour at a time.'[20]

News of the events in Azusa Street in 1906 and then in Oslo in early 1907 reached Boddy and in March 1907 he visited Barratt's meetings in Oslo for four days. In one account he described his motivation as that of having heard 'that they were speaking in Tongues as at the beginning'.[21] In a later account it was more generally put as 'to enquire into the Movement of the Blessed Holy Spirit'.[22] He found the meetings in a Mission Hall at Torvegaden Seven, Oslo, very powerful, being surrounded by Norwegians who were speaking in tongues. He was invited to speak to the meeting, and on 5 March 1907 himself received what he described as a baptism, though he did not speak in tongues.

Boddy's time in Oslo was hugely important, and it was clearly what he had been hoping and praying for.

On his return home he began publishing a series of very brief leaflets, each titled *Leaflet on "Tongues"*, which are undated, but clearly come from this period, since the first one referred to his visit to Norway and the sixth one described the visit in more detail. *Leaflet on "Tongues"* No. 1 was primarily an exhortation as to the scriptural nature of the phenomenon. Later leaflets contained more by way of testimony.

In Leaflet 6, 'Tongues in Norway', he wrote in forceful terms of the impact he had felt:

> I stood with Evan Roberts at the Ton-y-Pandy meetings, but never have I witnessed such events as in Norway . . . Boys and girls around me – from say seven to twelve years of age – were seeing visions and speaking in "tongues" as well as older people.'[23]

He seemed much taken by the participation of children in these meetings, and he also drew attention to the involvement of men and women, and the positive effect on 'inquisitive folk or scoffers'. He commented on the content of the revelations to people: '[t]he near coming of Christ seems to be impressed upon everyone who thus comes under the power of the Spirit. The message of nearly everyone is "Jesus is coming".' This was to prove a continuing theme in later meetings.

A further noteworthy feature of the Leaflet 6 is the short personal testimony he gave of the effect of the prayers on himself:

> I knelt in the mid-day meeting at Torvegaden (No. 7) and six persons speaking in tongues knelt or stood around me . . . Power from on high seemed to thrill from them through me. Tears of joy coursed down my cheeks, and the spirit of holy laughter took possession.[24]

Boddy subsequently described this experience in a number of ways. In 1907 he called it 'a great inflow of his Spirit', in 1908 a 'wonderful anointing of the Holy Spirit', and in 1910 a 'blessed and wonderful "Baptism" of the Holy Ghost'.[25] By 1914 he was to write, 'It was one of about seven occasions in my life when I felt the presence of God and His touch in a very marked way.'[26] In this account of 1914 he continued to describe his experience of 1892 also as 'the Baptism'. The reference to 'holy laughter' is also significant, coming as it did after Mary's experience of laughter in 1905; the implication of Boddy's testimony seems to be that he was experiencing in the Oslo meetings what others around him were too.

Besides the privately published *Leaflet on "Tongues"* series, Boddy also wrote a number of articles for Christian newspapers, including 'Glossalalia in Christiania' for *The Record* and two articles on the Scandinavian revival for *The Layman*. For *The Christian* he wrote a long article in favour of the Pentecostal Blessing, which he claimed in 1910 was 'the first and last favourable article on this subject which ever appeared in that widely-read, helpful paper.'[27] The articles resulted in publicity for what was happening and for Boddy's work, and he received considerable correspondence in consequence.

Much of the correspondence was encouraging of his comments, but this was not universally true. In particular the prolific writer Mrs Jesse Penn-Lewis wrote negative comments in *The Christian* and *The Life of Faith* about Boddy's articles. During the Welsh revival Penn-Lewis had written a weekly column in *The Life of Faith*, partly chronicling the spread of the revival, but also increasingly offering her assessment of its spiritual value. She became very concerned about its origins, believing there to be considerable demonic intrusion. When Evan Roberts began to doubt what was happening in the revival he was invited in 1906 to stay with Penn-Lewis at her home in Leicester. In her later book *The War on the Saints* she indicated that she believed that in this and other revivals, leaders, including Roberts, had been deluded by evil spiritual forces.[28]

Although Boddy did not know Penn-Lewis personally he decided to write to her about her comments, unsure if it would make any difference: 'If I knew you personally I should be better able to judge whether it is of any use my writing to you at the time of on the subject of "tongues" as a sign which shall follow them that believe.'[29] At this early stage Boddy was already very anxious about public comments from fellow Christians. 'As *The Christian* and *The Life of Faith* now resolutely close their columns to any but unfavourable and warning statements it seems almost hopeless to expect that the subject should receive fair treatment at the hands of those connected with the papers.'

He went on in strong terms to say that this blessing was foretold by the Lord and should not be all condemned as from the devil. He referred to the 'physical outworkings' in the days of Wesley and George Whitefield. His more usual conciliatory nature reasserted itself somewhat at the end of the letter, as he pleaded, 'We must not forbid to speak with tongues must we', and expressed this concern: 'at present there seems a mighty effort to keep out of Great Britain this sign which the Lord is giving . . . but let us not merely warn – but let us point the way to the blessing – otherwise He may pass by.'

Not surprisingly, perhaps, this letter did not bring about a reconciliation of their views and further communication and further opposition were to come in the autumn of 1907.[30]

Later in the summer Boddy attended the Keswick Convention (one of only three definite dates we have for his attendance), taking many thousands of copies of his pamphlet *Pentecost for England*. The pamphlet began by claiming that at least 20,000 people across the world were known to have 'spoken in tongues', but only half a dozen in Britain, yet he believed that a time would soon come when many more would have this experience, not least because of the bands of people praying for 'Pentecost with signs following'. He also included the testimony of Mrs Price of Brixton, believed to be the first person in Britain to have had this experience.[31]

It was in this context of increasing publicity and expectation, and growing numbers of participants in prayer meetings that Boddy was urging T.B. Barratt to visit his parish, in the hope that Pentecost might come to Sunderland.

The Visit of Thomas Barratt to Sunderland

Alexander Boddy worked hard to get Barratt to come to Sunderland. In fact, Boddy's lobbying had begun in Oslo in March 1907. Barratt wrote in his diary at the time: 'He did not only come to see the revival, but also to receive a blessing for his own hungry soul. Immediately he started begging me to visit his congregation in Sunderland.'[32] According to Barratt's diary, Boddy continued to be in touch by letter, with prayer requests and repeated invitations during the middle part of 1907.

While he was hoping that Barratt would visit, Boddy continued with the prayer meetings and contacting friends. His publications in newspapers, the Roker Tracts, the *Leaflets on "Tongues"* series, and Mary's healing ministry meant they were known by a wide circle. Through this activity a high level of expectancy had been created, and apparently one young man had already received 'the precious gift of the Holy Spirit' – almost certainly meaning speaking in tongues – at a prayer meeting in the nursery at the All Saints Vicarage.[33]

Barratt himself was concerned that too much was expected of him and he was worried that his grasp of English would be insufficient, but Boddy remained enthusiastic.

After Barratt had finally agreed to come, Boddy wrote to him in July 1907: 'Hungry folk from all parts of the land will flock to Sunderland hoping that God may permit you to be a channel of blessing to them.'[34]

Barratt finally arrived in Monkwearmouth on Saturday 31 August 1907. He arrived earlier than expected and was able to attend an evening prayer meeting in the Vestry which he clearly found very powerful. On the next day (Sunday), afternoon and evening meetings were held. Barratt spoke to the congregation after Evensong and those who wanted went into an 'after meeting' in the Vestry, with the express intention of receiving the Holy Spirit. It was at this meeting that the first 'baptisms in the Holy Spirit' occurred and the meeting lasted until four o'clock in the morning.

On Tuesday, 3 September Barratt wrote ecstatically and in some genuine surprise: 'Honour to God! He has started a great work here in Sunderland . . . I believed it was a possibility for me to go to England, but that the first to invite me should be a state-church-minister was the last thing I could have thought!'[35]

He also wrote, 'an English state church minister allows that a man not ordained in their church to preach in the church just after Evensong'. This was at a time when the Church of England did not allow its own licensed lay readers to preach from the pulpit, and had allowed any preaching only since 1904, and then not at services of Holy Communion.[36]

As we saw when discussing Boddy's travels he was always open to Christians of other traditions, and the significance of that openness was clearly not lost on Barratt at this crucial period.

Boddy was less effusive about the first meetings and gave more details: 'On the evening of Sept. 1st, three who were seeking Him entered right in and went right through into Pentecost with signs following; to encourage others God allowed them to be dealt with tenderly.'[37]

The three were all from one household, though unrelated. The first had been through serious personal difficulties – here was the pastor in Boddy making time for a personal conversation with the woman a few days after this experience – and she was now expressing gratitude for God's help. The other two women may have been lodging with the first, for they had arrived only a month earlier, with the purpose of praying and offering to work in any way they could, a point that Boddy emphasised. They were Margaret Howell and Mabel Scott, who quickly became secretaries to Boddy in handling the enquiries, literature and soon the conferences. Their testimony to God's presence and 'coming' on the night of 1 September was included in the first edition of *Confidence*.[38]

A pattern of two meetings a day continued, with a gradual rather than dramatic build-up of interest and numbers. Initially, nearly all the visitors were believers, though by 19 September Barratt noted that interest amongst outsiders was growing; nonetheless he was not seeing the repetition of large-scale conversions he had seen in Norway.

The meetings may have begun in a gentle way, to encourage others, but before long more extreme and emotional events were occurring, as Barratt recorded in his diary:

> A young man who was preparing to be a school master was also filled that same evening. He began by shouting 'Glory!' continuously. At last he rolled over on the floor, then after some time he arose with a beaming face proclaiming 'Where have I been?'[39]

The following week he wrote after what he called 'excellent meetings':

> In one case the tongues came very slowly as I have noticed it sometimes in Scandinavia. All kinds of strange sounds. A

stranger would have thought it like the quacking of a duck and the barking of a dog twice, but it was only the commencing syllables of a word constantly repeated.

He went on to give an indication of the opposition they were receiving. 'People unacquainted with this have evidenced it as a counterfeit and of the Devil, but she was under the Blood, constantly trusting Jesus and longing for the salvation of souls.'[40]

Such experiences became associated in the 1990s with the 'Toronto Blessing', and the reports of joy and physical sensations are also similar to later descriptions of Pentecostal and charismatic phenomena. A clear example of 'Holy Laughter' was provided by James Techner, a Salvationist leader, in his testimony:

On December 2nd, 1907, in a most wonderful manner I spoke in other tongues, and then I went into uncontrolled Holy Laughter. I learned something of what David meant when He said, 'Then shall thy mouth be filled with laughter'; and I believe for something like half-an-hour my whole being was convulsed in Holy Laughter.[41]

Techner was later given the honour of jointly welcoming people with Boddy at the first Whitsuntide Conference, and he was to become a regular platform speaker.[42]

Pentecost for the Boddy family

Amongst the earliest recipients of the baptism in the Spirit, as evidenced by the gift of speaking in tongues, were the members of Boddy's family. Alexander's wife, Mary, began singing in the Spirit on 11 September, and their daughters Mary and Jane received the gift of tongues on 21 September.

In her testimony Mary recounted some of her earlier spiritual journey, including her healing from asthma in 1899, and her subsequent learning that God had dealt with her sin. She emphasised the centrality of the Cross as the point at which all sin was dealt with, the importance of 'shedding of blood' and the concept that she had died in Christ. She also mentioned the experience of 1905 when she had a vision of Christ from whom a wonderful light emanated, and when she had laughed as never before. At the time she believed this to be 'the Baptism'.

It happened that she was away from home when Barratt arrived, only returning on 10th September. By her own account she was surprised to be uninterested in what was going on in the meetings. Yet she was able to go to the meeting on the evening of 11th September, apparently not joining in but 'resting in God'. When hands were laid on her by Barratt she '*felt* nothing' but emphasised that she believed God the Holy Ghost had come to her:

> What followed I cannot describe, and it is too sacred to do so, but I *knew God* had come. Though never unconscious, I was quite oblivious to everyone around, just worshipping, then my mouth began to quiver, my tongue began to move, and a few simple words were uttered, as I just yielded to the Holy Ghost.

After that she had 'a vision of the Blood'. She went on, 'In one moment, what I had believed in for years was illuminated as a reality.'[43]

It is a moving testimony written just days after this experience, and hence full of extravagant language and emphasis, yet also of a piece with her prior beliefs and, as her writing in *Confidence* was to show, her subsequent beliefs.

The testimony was completed just after 21 September 1907, as it included a reference to the experiences of their daughters Mary and Jane. The teenagers were quickly writing their own testimonies, for *Leaflet on "Tongues"* No. 10, 'Young People at Sunderland', comprised three testimonies: that of a young man who had received the gift of tongues on the same evening as the older Mary, and those of the daughters, apparently written on the next day.

Losing no time, Jane also gave spoken testimony to 600 children in the Parish Hall, since the 22nd was a Sunday. It is instructive that she included the detail that it was 'the Anniversary of when father first got the Holy Ghost, and he had been praying all day'.[44] As mentioned in the previous chapter this was also the anniversary of his ordination, which he marked each year with a service of Holy Communion, according to Jane.

Their brother James was not involved as he was at the boarding school in Monkton Coombe.

Mary's brother, James Pollock, also received baptism in the Spirit about this time. Barratt thought it 'remarkable' and recorded it in his diary for 13 September. He noted that Pollock had been seeking this experience for some months and received prayer with laying on of hands more than once:

> On one occasion he fell to the floor. But the night he received his Pentecost he was filled with a marvellous power, and prophesied and spoke in tongues with a more than usual intensity. He leaped for very joy and praised God with a loud voice.[45]

Sadly for Boddy, this led to a difficult time as Pollock, his friend and brother-in-law, came to see this event as demonic within a few weeks of receiving the gift of tongues.[46]

Alexander himself did not speak in tongues until 2 December, well after Barratt had left Monkwearmouth, at the same meeting at which Techner was convulsed with 'Holy Laughter'. In his 1914 account Boddy wrote of his overwhelming desire to praise God, and how the assembled group joined in singing a doxology. On the following morning he walked on the sands at Roker, singing loudly 'in unrestrained tongues . . . The Lord seemed to make up to me for having to wait so long. Yet the waiting time had been very precious – amongst the best times in my life.'[47]

Even by then numbers were not huge and Boddy estimated he was about the fiftieth person to receive the gift. This is a good indication of his care in recording and reporting facts, in some contrast with those who claim many numbers of converts or healings in their meetings.

It also seems that he took some delight in being the fiftieth person, for on 3 December he also took time to write to Jesse Penn-Lewis, inviting her to rejoice with him, and briefly giving the circumstances of his experience. He ended his short letter saying, 'I am the 50th here to receive the Sign of the Tongues (Pentecost means "Fiftieth"). Seven have been thus blessed this weekend.'[48]

The News – and Opposition – Spreads

The number of people attending the meetings had begun to increase when newspapers started to take an interest; the first seems to have been the *Sunderland Echo* on 30 September.

According their report about 100 people, mostly female, attended the open meeting and about thirty stayed for the 'after meeting'. The London papers (firstly the *Morning Leader*, by 3 October, and the *Daily Chronicle* – by 5 October) picked up the story and press interest rocketed, especially in what were seen as the more spectacular aspects.

Reports also soon appeared in *Lloyd's Weekly* and the Scottish papers *North Mail* and *Evening Dispatch* (the latter being especially scathing).

It appears that Barratt was not very concerned by the implication of notoriety, but Boddy was less sanguine if his later recollections are accurate when he said of the reporters, 'We did not want them, but could not help it, and so prayed the Lord to overrule. The reports, while often grotesque, raised deep interest.'[49] In the same place he went on to write about mischief-makers and the 'pain and anxiety' he felt.

Boddy and Barrett were able to publish some of their own material about the meetings in September and October in *The Christian Herald and Signs of Our Times*.[50] On 24 October 1907 the regular column 'World-Wide Revival' began with positive reports from Sunderland and included sections of a letter from Barrett. The following week the column began with a long account from Boddy which reminded readers of his many travels and then called this the 'best six weeks of my life'. He noted that this mission did not need 'lavish advertising', unlike his previous experience in seeking publicity. Indeed, from around the country 'newspapers without any request sent their representatives' thus providing widespread free publicity. Already by 31 October they were sending material to other parts of the world, and he specifically mentioned South Africa, America, Jamaica and India. They had received 'visitors from all parts of Great Britain', and he mentioned sixteen towns, from Sidmouth to Edinburgh, and Dublin to Windsor. In line with his eye for accurate reporting he was able to state that 'more than fifty long-distance visitors have come'.

Reader Harris

Opposition was found not only in the secular newspapers: serious theological opposition came from an itinerant preacher called Reader Harris who happened to be holding meetings in

Sunderland at the same time as Barratt's visit to All Saints. Harris was the leader of the Pentecostal League, which he had founded in 1891, and Boddy was himself a member of the League and had been for some time. Indeed, he had mentioned it in a letter to Bishop Moule in 1901 when he wrote:

> Then lastly a very personal matter. I am a humble member of the Pentecostal League of Prayer for the Holy Spirit. I do not like all the methods of its leaders, nor the way in which doctrines they teach are often enunciated. But I have been drawn to join it because of their wholeheartedness in loving and honouring God's word, in holding up my crucified and ascended Lord as our life in the power of the Holy Ghost – and their desire never to limit God's power by unbelief in his promises. I rarely put the Pentecostal League forward – but I have a quiet meeting in this Vicarage every week and I take part also in its central meetings.

He also added a somewhat ingratiating postscript: 'Mr Reader Harris K.C. told me that he was brought to Christ by your "Christian Sanctity".'[51] This was a devotional book which had been published by Moule in 1885.[52] This letter incidentally confirms the way in which Boddy had sought spiritual renewal over a long period of time, and also his willingness to work with people that he did not necessarily fully agree with, provided there was important common ground.

The Pentecostal League of Prayer had been started by Harris to promote the concept of entire sanctification or Christian perfection originally associated with John Wesley and the Methodist movement.[53] Harris had been converted in the 1880s, apparently through reading Moule's booklet *Christian Sanctity*, as we've just seen, while associated with an evangelical Anglican church in Clapham, and he remained an Anglican throughout his life. He had strong interdenominational tendencies, and despite his own privileged social standing he sought to work across both ecclesial and social barriers. As Wesley had done, he saw scriptural holiness as comprising both personal and social elements; for example, starting from Speke Hall, Battersea, London in 1887 he ran evangelistic events and provided blankets, coal, clothing and books for people in the slums of the area. In 1890 he called the Hall a 'Pentecostal

Mission', with the League of Prayer beginning a year later. The League was 'dedicated to praying for the filling of the Holy Spirit for all believers, for revival in the churches, and for the spread of Scriptural holiness'. By 1900 there were nearly 150 prayer groups throughout Britain, with 17,000 members. They met in Methodist, Baptist, Congregational and Anglican churches. With these emphases it is not surprising that Boddy should be part of this movement, and he was the secretary of the Monkwearmouth group. More copies of their newspaper were sold in Sunderland than in any other town.[54]

However, Harris's terminology was not the same as that of either Wesley or the emerging Pentecostal Movement. Wesley had not linked entire sanctification with baptism in the Spirit, while Harris equated the two. The Pentecostal Movement tended to link baptism in the Spirit with speaking in tongues, which was a significant part of Harris's objection to what he saw in Monkwearmouth in September 1907. Well after Harris's death the League continued to insist, in its incongruously named magazine *Tongues of Fire*, that it was not connected with the 'Tongues movement'.

In addition to different usages of the term *baptism in the Spirit*, Harris was also disturbed by what he saw as extreme emotion and immoral conduct being generated by the meetings led by Barratt. In a strong attack he described the outpouring as a Satanic counterfeit. In particular, Harris wrote of

> confusion, errors of conduct, and the loosening of the marriage tie . . . Errors of conduct is a mild term to describe the rolling on the floor of women and men from which all true believers and indeed all decent people, should hold aloof.[55]

Barratt was especially forceful in his response, with the argument being aired in the local newspaper at the beginning of October.[56] As the title of Harris's later article 'The Gift of Tongues' indicates, much of the controversy arose from the emphasis that Barratt placed on people receiving the gift of tongues as evidence for the baptism in the Holy Spirit. Harris saw this as unnecessary, and objected to carnality which 'seemed to haunt movements of this kind'. Barratt in turn defended his emphasis on tongues as a gift from the Spirit, and denied that carnality was any greater problem in Pentecostalism than in other churches or movements.⁵⁷ According to his diary, Barratt had decided by 17 September that he had to address the opposition, for 'I have already finished . . . a leaflet on "Pentecost – not of the Devil".'⁵⁸

While Boddy may have believed that there had been too much of an emphasis on tongues – his descriptions of baptism in the Holy Spirit consistently referred to the fruit of love as the evidence – he was steadfast in his support for Barratt. He wrote warm letters to him after Barratt's return to Norway (for example on 29 October 1907) and spoke positively about him in public.

In these circumstances a split between Boddy and Harris was inevitable. In 1910 Boddy reflected sadly on the failure of other Christian leaders to support the Pentecostal Movement and went on: '"This work is of the devil" boldly asserts this or that great leader. But it is not the great enemy who is causing so many to be "Scripturally born again".'⁵⁹

Other opposition

Other significant opposition came from Jesse Penn-Lewis, with whom Boddy had previously been in correspondence.

Boddy had written to Penn-Lewis on 17 June 1907. We have no record of a reply from her until 9 November, after Barratt's visit had ceased, and Boddy had written again on 4 November. She had not been to the meetings in Monkwearmouth but had studied newspaper reports, both secular and Christian, and Boddy's own pamphlets and had heard from people who had attended the meetings. She began by insisting, 'I am in the very deepest sympathy with you in the longing you have for a full and mighty "Revival in England".'⁶⁰ She also repeatedly expressed her concern 'for you, and your dear wife'. She believed, however, that 'there are "other spirits" at work in your midst' and that this would cause 'terrible trouble'. She went on to suggest that Barratt's ministry came not from the Holy Spirit, but was 'a strong force of animal magnetism, making him almost like a galvanic battery'. She expressed her own concern to meet with the Boddys in order to clarify the matters between them, hoping they would come to her. In a postscript which seems not to have been sent she offered out the possibility of a meeting with Evan Roberts, who by this time was convalescing with her, worn out by his work in the Welsh revival. It may be that she thought better of this as an inducement, having read Boddy's desire for Roberts to go to Sunderland.[61] It seems that such a meeting did not take place.

Given Boddy's propensity for letter writing it is possible that he replied to Penn-Lewis, but the next surviving letter from him was the one mentioned above, dated 3 December, the day after he spoke in tongues for the first time. Citing a number of New Testament texts, he hoped that Penn-Lewis would rejoice with him. This did not happen and Penn-Lewis went on to write against the Pentecostal Movement in *The War against the Saints*.

There were other negative statements, public and private, attributing the observed phenomena to hypnotism by Barratt, to the extent that Boddy wrote to the *Christian Herald* to reaffirm his conviction that what was happening was the work of the Holy Ghost.[62]

All this opposition from other evangelical leaders is enough to explain Boddy's 'pain and anxiety' at this time.

Encouragement

Nonetheless, there were also considerable encouragements for the Boddys during the autumn of 1907, as they received a steady stream of visitors from various parts of Britain and Europe.

Smith Wigglesworth

Perhaps the most notable of the British visitors in 1907 was Smith Wigglesworth, a plumber from Bradford who had long worked with the Salvation Army as an evangelist. He had developed a powerful healing ministry and had also been helped by Reader Harris's Pentecostal League. Nevertheless, he had come to desire a deeper experience of God and in November he visited the Boddys in Sunderland.

According to his own testimony in a letter published by Boddy in his *Leaflet on "Tongues"* series, he had been familiar with a ministry of healing for fourteen years but had been desirous of other signs described in the Acts of the Apostles. He had heard of the meetings in Monkwearmouth and so went expectantly. He spent time in 'waiting much on God', worshipping with the Salvation Army in Roker Avenue and then attending the Holy Communion service at All Saints. Two days later, after further attendance at the prayer meetings, he was ready to ask for prayer. Mary Boddy laid hands on him in the vicarage – in the kitchen – and he received a vision of the empty cross, Jesus glorified and then the gift of tongues.[63] This was the beginning of his long ministry across many churches and of a long friendship with the Boddys. Over the next twenty years letters and articles about or by Wigglesworth were to appear in the pages of *Confidence* magazines.

Engagements beyond Sunderland

In addition to receiving visitors the Boddys began to receive invitations to speak in other parts of the country and as 1907 turned to 1908 both Alexander and Mary were to find they had ministries which were to take them well beyond Sunderland.

But before we move on to those ministries it is worth pausing to reflect on the reasons the British Pentecostal Movement really began in Sunderland at this time.

Why Sunderland?

It is clear that a major reason the Pentecostal Movement began in Britain was Boddy's own spiritual quest and leadership. His character and life experiences were very significant in the leadership he gave from 1907 onwards in the movement. But there were also factors in the locality which helped to release the potential of Boddy's leadership.

It may be over-fanciful to point to the legacy of Bede and the seventh-century monastery at Wearmouth, though Boddy was conscious of living next to this ancient site, referring to 'Modern successors to choir-boy Bede' at the end of his first travel book.[64] More plausibly it is important to appreciate the non-conformist tradition in Sunderland, reaching back to the seventeenth century.

The French sociologist of religion Daniele Hervieu-Leger has made an extensive and innovative case for taking seriously the local history of religion. She has argued that a collective chain of memory and tradition is important in helping individuals become part of a religious community. She writes: 'Of its essence fluid and evolutionary, collective memory functions as a regulator of individual memory at any one moment.'[65] The history of Sunderland provides ample evidence of the passing on of religious memory, with repeated episodes of intense religious experience.

Church and chapel

The local church historian of Sunderland, Geoffrey Milburn, has published a number of studies of the churches and chapels of the district, providing a rich description of the developments in the town. As the town grew in population it became clear that the Church of England was not capable of keeping up with the number of people. In 1780 there were three parishes and just four buildings. Two of the parishes, Monkwearmouth and Bishop-wearmouth, had ancient and decrepit buildings (St Peter's and St Michael's) and the clergy were generally slow to respond to the enthusiasm of the non-conformist chapels. There was a particular issue in the case of Bishopwearmouth, for this was a very rich living, worth at least £1,200 around 1800 and about £3,500 by 1850. By the mid-nineteenth century extensions were being built to existing church buildings, and new parishes created, as happened with All Saints, Monkwearmouth in 1844.[66] Nonetheless, this had left considerable scope for non-conformist developments.

Even in the seventeenth century Sunderland was said to have been a strongly puritan town, with Milburn attributing the outspokenness and tolerance of the community to it being a seaport. Perhaps as a result the parish churches of Sunderland and Monkwearmouth had evangelical leanings, and John Wesley was able to worship and preach regularly in both churches.[67]

Charles Wesley was the first to preach a Methodist sermon on Wearside, on 16 June 1743, and wrote in his journal: 'Never have I seen greater attention in any at their first hearing.'

John went on to visit Sunderland more than thirty times between 1743 and 1790, and preached at St Peter's, Monkwearmouth at least fifteen times. He was especially positive about Sunderland folk, noting on one of his earlier visits in 1752, 'I rode to Sunderland, where I found one of the liveliest societies in the north of England.'[68] And on his last visit in 1790: 'Here it is plain, our labour has not been in vain!'[69]

The Primitive Methodists

The work of Methodists in Sunderland was extended by the early arrival of Primitive Methodists in the 1820s. They quickly became established, with the town being a circuit centre by 1823 and a year later one of four District Centres for England.[70] The Primitive Methodists had begun in 1807 as a revivalist movement within Wesleyan Methodism; its leaders were much influenced by an American Methodist revivalist, Lorenzo Dow, thus providing an early example of the important interaction between American and British revivalist movements.[71]

Among the features of the movement were a commitment to open-air evangelism, camp meetings for preaching and prayer – with prayer seen as central to evangelism – and an emphasis on the Love Feast, over against Holy Communion.

The movement had a strong appeal to coal miners, shipyard workers and artisans in many parts of England. It enabled its members to gain responsible positions within the Primitive Methodist organisation, and this was notably true in Sunderland. By 1832 they were writing of a revival in their Circuit and were not only able to pay for a second preacher, but had £20 in hand to fund a missionary to the Channel Islands, where they had contact through converted seamen.[72]

The 1851 Religious Census showed that Methodism as a whole – it was in five groupings – was strong in Sunderland, with just over 40 per cent of all worshippers attending the variety of Methodist chapels, compared with a national average of about 25 per cent. Remarkably the Primitive Methodists in Sunderland had an attendance slightly in excess of the Wesleyan Methodists, who were the direct successors to the society founded by the Wesleys themselves.[73]

Sunderland continued to be a strong centre of Primitive Methodism in the second half of the nineteenth century. The first theological college of the movement was set up in Sunderland in 1868 and had trained about 300 ministers by the time of closure in 1882.[74]

However, all was not well: in 1875 a new chapel was opened at Tatham Street in a more affluent area and this crystallised a growing division between a centralising tendency in the national leadership and resentment at this amongst local people. In a desire to maintain 'its original simplicity and power'[75] over

300 members withdrew from Primitive Methodism to form 'Christian Lay Churches'. The term 'Runaway Ranters' was also applied to them, perhaps hinting at a less than positive reputation.

The episode is an indication of the continuing independence of thinking in Sunderland in a denomination which was becoming more established and respectable. It is not fanciful to suggest that such thinking played its part in helping to create a pool of people ready to respond to Boddy's meetings in September 1907. Much later Boddy certainly recalled long-standing friendly relationships with Methodists and other Non-Conformists 'on the North-side'[76] (that is, the north bank of the Wear), which lends support to such a view.

Further suggestive evidence of spiritual zeal in the town comes from the powerful celebration in May 1907 of the centenary of Mow Cop Camp Meeting. Some 90,000 people gathered for the first meeting, and the celebrations included the themes of renewed evangelism, personal dedication and recovery of the old spirit of the movement.[77] Books were written celebrating the movement and the national newspapers carried warm reports of the centenary events. From the perspective of this study it is worth noting that the Newcastle/Sunderland District raised one of the largest amounts of money for the Centenary fund, indicating the continued strength of the movement in the area.

The impact of visiting preachers

Some visiting preachers contributed to the religious fervour. For example, the town was included on the itineraries of American preachers Walter and Phoebe Palmer in 1859 and of Moody and Sankey in 1873. Milburn records that there was a local revival in the pit villages around Sunderland in the 1860s and 1870s, largely lay led, by both men and women, and in the town William Gelly was employed as an evangelist from 1870.[78]

Around 1879 a young Bramwell Booth, son of William and Catherine Booth, was holding 'All Nights of Prayer' in Sunderland. These events combined a call to holiness of life and prayer meetings, to help anyone seeking deeper spiritual experience', according to Catherine Booth. In a letter to his father, Bramwell gave a vivid picture of the results of one such event:

I preached last night at Sunderland . . . It was a remarkable night . . . Of course, we went straight on in the Holiness line. There were thirteen pipes, with several tobacco pouches, a scarf pin and a lump of twist, two or three cigars, two snuff boxes, then feathers, a string of flowers and a brooch, voluntarily surrendered amidst a scene of sobbing and shouting rarely surpassed.[79]

With this wealth of religious memory in the area and the contemporary pool of religious seekers encouraged by the Pentecostal League of Prayer, the Methodist chapels, the Salvation Army and Boddy's own work it becomes plausible that the new religious experience should take hold in the town.

Despite the opposition he had encountered, Boddy remained convinced of the importance of the prayer meetings and he began to receive some support from other parts of the country. Events in 1908 would show whether this was a short-lived phenomenon or a movement with real spiritual potential. As a previous study of Boddy pointed out, 'Much would now depend on the leadership of Alexander Alfred Boddy.'[80]

Notes

1 This account of the revival is based on Pope, Robert, 'Wales and the great awakening', *Church Times* 26 March 2004

2 *Confidence*, February 1914, 24

3 This and subsequent quotations from Boddy's reminiscences of the beginnings of the Pentecostal Movement in Sunderland. *Confidence*, August 1910, 192–97

4 Harford and MacDonald, *Moule*, 14

5 Harford and MacDonald, *Moule*, 127–31

6 *The Times*, 30 December 1904, 5

7 *The Times*, 28 January 1905, 8

8 *The Times*, 2 February 1905, 5

9 *The Times*, 21 February 1905

10 This memo is preserved in the archive at Mattersey Hall

11 These excerpts are from a letter dated 28 March 1905

12 Letter dated 4 April 1905

13 Easter was on 23 April in 1905, so this letter was probably written in the last week of April

14 For example, William Kay has indicated that he did not know of any reports of laughter in the Welsh revival. Personal communication, 2 September 2004
15 Bartleman's account in *Confidence*, April 1916, 64
16 Cox, *Fire from Heaven*, 45–65 offers a convenient reflection on the Azusa Street outpouring
17 Bundy, *Thomas Ball Barratt* provides these and further details on Barrett's own history to this point, based on Barratt's diaries and letters
18 *Confidence*, August 1910, 194
19 *Confidence*, February 1914, 24
20 *Confidence*, October 1916, 169
21 *Confidence*, August 1910, 194
22 *Confidence*, February 1914, 24
23 Boddy, 'Tongues in Norway', 1
24 Both quotes from Boddy, 'Tongues in Norway', 2
25 *Confidence*, August 1910, 194
26 *Confidence*, February 1914, 25
27 *Confidence*, August 1910, 194
28 See the refutation offered by Boddy and others in *Confidence*, July 1913, 136 and the strong denunciation by a German author, *Confidence*, August 1913, 157
29 This and the following excerpts are from a letter from Boddy to Penn-Lewis, dated 17 June 1907, in a typescript version at Mattersey Hall
30 This and the later opposition are discussed in Hudson, *Early Days*, 55–57
31 Some extracts from the pamphlet are found in *Confidence*, August 1910, 195
32 Barratt, *Diary*, 154, from a translation held in the archive at Mattersey Hall
33 *Confidence*, October 1916, 169
34 Letter to Barratt, 12 July 1907
35 Barratt, *Diary*, 3 September 1907
36 Cranston, *History of the Reader* accessed at {http://www.futurechurch southcoast.com/time_line3.htm} on 24/1/2005 (information from Anna de Lange)
37 'Tongues in Sunderland', 1
38 *Confidence*, April 1908, 5
39 Barratt, *Diary*, 5, 13 September 1907
40 Barratt, *Diary*, 8, 19 September 1907
41 *Confidence* August 1912, 182
42 *Confidence*, June 1908, 6
43 All quotations from Mary Boddy, *"Pentecost" at Sunderland: the Testimony of a Vicar's Wife* – italics as in the original
44 *Leaflet on "Tongues"* No. 10, 2
45 Barratt, *Diary*, 6, 13 September 1907
46 Reported in Robinson, *Charismatic Anglican*, 63. Also see G.H. Land, *The Earlier Years of the Modern Tongues Movement* (Florida: Conley & Schoettle,

1985), 50. Any rift does not seem to have been permanent: there is a record of Boddy visiting Pollock in 1922 (*Confidence*, October–December 1922, 5, though this is one of very few references to Pollock in the pages of *Confidence*)

47 *Confidence*, February 1914, 25
48 As cited in Cartwright, *Wigglesworth*, 29
49 *Confidence*, August 1910, 195
50 Copies of these editions are in the archive at Mattersey Hall.
51 Letter to Bishop Moule, 10 December 1901. University of Durham archive. All Saints Monkwearmouth file
52 Harford and MacDonald, *Moule*, 367
53 The next two paragraphs draw on Randall, *Pentecostal League*. As a web page it is a continuous piece, so it is not possible to give more precise citations
54 Cartwright, *Wigglesworth*, 25
55 Harris, 'The Gift of Tongues', *Tongues of Fire*, November 1907, 1–2
56 'Speaking in Tongues: Rival Pentecostals', *Sunderland Echo*, 2 October 1907
57 See Hudson, 'Earliest Days', 57 for a brief discussion of these points
58 Barratt, *Diary*, 7
59 *Confidence*, August 1910, 196
60 This and the following excerpts are from Penn-Lewis, letter to Boddy, 9 November 1907, in a typescript version at Mattersey Hall
61 This invitation was given in Boddy, letter to Penn-Lewis, 4 November 1907, typescript version at Mattersey Hall
62 'Worldwide Revival', *Christian Herald*, 31 October 1907, 411
63 'An Evangelist's Testimony. His Pentecost with Tongues', *Leaflet on "Tongues"* No. 12. The full text is reproduced in Cartwright, *Wigglesworth*, 33–36. This biography provides a helpful and readable account of Wigglesworth's life and ministry
64 Boddy, *With Russian Pilgrims*, 295
65 Hervieu-Leger, *Religion*, 124
66 Based on Milburn, *Church and Chapel*, 2–12
67 Details in this paragraph from Milburn, *Travelling Preacher*, 51–61
68 Wesley, *Journal*, iv, 24
69 Wesley, *Journal*, viii, 72
70 Milburn, *Primitive Methodism*, 44
71 Milburn, *Primitive Methodism*, 5
72 Letter from the Sunderland Circuit, *Primitive Methodist Magazine*, 1832, 230, reprinted in Milburn, *Primitive Methodism*, 23
73 Milburn, *Religion in Sunderland*, 33
74 Milburn, *Primitive Methodism*, 41
75 Letter to *Sunderland Daily Echo*, 16 February 1877, reprinted Milburn, *Primitive Methodism*, 45
76 *Confidence*, January 1923, 66

77 Milburn, *Primitive Methodism*, 82
78 Milburn, *Primitive Methodism*, 44
79 Cited in Kent, *Holding the Fort*, 332–33
80 Robinson, *The Charismatic Anglican*, 63

Six

Leadership Exercised: *Confidence* and the Sunderland Conferences 1908–14

In 1904–05 the Welsh Revival had raised hopes of an extended renewal and even revival of the churches in Britain. While there were some continuing effects the Revival was soon over and Evan Roberts, one of the key leaders, burnt out. The Pentecostal Revival of 1907 might have had a similarly short lifespan, but instead it led to lasting results before and after the First World War, although it did not achieve any major impact on the historical churches. This persistence was due in no small way to Boddy's leadership of the movement in the years 1908–14. With his long experience of pastoral ministry – he was in his fifties, compared with Roberts, who was in his twenties – he provided stability to the new movement and guidance to a generation of younger leaders.

In Britain his leadership was exercised through his writing ministry and through the numerous conventions in which he became involved, most importantly the annual Whitsuntide Sunderland Conferences and Conventions. Beyond Britain he was influential through the Pentecostal Missionary Union (PMU) and especially through an itinerant ministry. In the next three chapters we explore these four themes and his theological convictions. This is the period of Boddy's life for which we have most material, mainly because of the *Confidence* magazines, which were monthly throughout this time.[1] These chapters therefore seek to provide an accurate overview of these aspects of Boddy's ministry and thought, but they cannot be completely comprehensive. A chronological overview is provided by the timeline of his life in Appendix One.

Alexander's Writing Ministry

As we saw in the previous chapter, Boddy was quick to be involved in writing about the Pentecostal outpouring in Monkwearmouth. However, he soon found that existing Christian magazines and newspapers were not receptive to his perspective. In part he tackled this antagonism by producing free literature: as he had done with the Roker Tracts, so he now produced the *Leaflets on "Tongues"*, with twelve issued before the end of 1907. These were very brief pieces, of about 700–800 words each.[2] Their contents imply that Boddy had several purposes in mind: information about the events in Sunderland and elsewhere (Leaflets 1, 5, 6, 8, 9), testimony and encouragement from those who had received this gift (2, 4, 10, 12), exegesis of appropriate biblical passages (3, 7) and even a prophetic message given by a Norwegian woman and supplied by Barratt (11).

Early in 1908 he wrote a slightly longer essay of about 1,500 words entitled *The "Pentecostal Baptism"*, which was 'Counsel to Leaders and others' on various spiritual gifts, beginning with that of speaking in tongues.[3] In this paper Boddy emphasised 'the Holy Comforter' and following 'the blessed Holy Scriptures'. Besides discussing the gift of speaking in tongues the essay also provides a snapshot of his thinking about prophetic messages, discernment of spirits, physical manifestations of the Spirit, charges of immorality, opposition, and even the use of the word *Pentecostal*. It clearly reflects a situation in which some people were pushing to receive 'the "power"', while Boddy's advice was that God might be teaching more in a time of waiting, and that pushing for a blessing might lead to evil consequences. There was also reference to misunderstandings and crushing circumstances.

The insight of the Boddys into the realities of spiritual life is further shown by a final paragraph written by Mary, headed 'As to darkness, etc.' This discussed the way in which 'the Wilderness of temptation' generally follows 'full Baptism of the Holy Ghost'. She wrote: 'We really only begin to see our own emptiness and powerlessness, so we must not be discouraged, but keep in stillness of soul and let the Blessed Holy Spirit reveal and glorify the victorious Christ in us.'[4]

A third edition of this essay, also undated, is in the Mattersey Hall archive and has an additional paragraph by Boddy, headed

'Calls to Foreign Service'. It addressed the belief of some that their gift of speaking in tongues enabled them to speak a foreign language (xenolalia) sufficiently well to constitute 'a call to the Foreign Mission Field'.

Boddy had probably contributed – if unintentionally – to this belief through the publicity he had given to certain testimonies, in particular that of his daughter Jane, which was widely published and given in detail. Some prominence was given to the claim that she had spoken words of Chinese; it was included in her testimony in *Leaflet on "Tongues"* No. 10, along with Barratt's claim that her sister Mary had spoken words of Norwegian. A report on the events in Monkwearmouth in the newspaper the *Morning Leader* included the prominent headline 'VICAR'S CHILD TALKS CHINESE'[5] and at least during October 1907 Boddy continued to draw attention to this in interviews for other newspapers.

His later comments in the third edition of *The "Pentecostal Baptism"* came after reports of people going abroad believing they had this gift to enable them to engage in missionary activity. Boddy bluntly stated: '(We) have not yet received one letter stating that they have this gift.' He did go on to write: 'I long to receive or see such a letter.' His advice was that this might be a call 'to be an Intercessor for that particular field', and that a further call to go might come later. This short paragraph could be seen as a demonstration of Boddy's naivety, but it is also a powerful combination of spiritual openness and pastoral realism. Such qualities had been created over many years of ministry and life experience and were to be shown again and again in the pages of *Confidence*.

Confidence-building

At the beginning of April 1908 Boddy set up his own magazine, which he called *Confidence*. From comments in the first edition we deduce that there were two main reasons for doing so.

Firstly, according to his own testimony Boddy encountered difficulties in the autumn of 1907 in getting material published in existing Christian newspapers and magazines. At the end of the first edition of *Confidence* he reprinted a letter from Barratt which gave a different account from those in other religious papers of a conference held in Germany and wrote: 'As we cannot obtain any opportunity of reply in the columns of these papers we have been led to issue "Confidence", where the strengthening and affirmative side may appear.'[6]

Secondly, the quantity of written material he was generating and the huge demand he was finding for his concise leaflets seem to be the other factor that led him to set up his own magazine. Commenting on this he wrote: 'Scores of thousands of testimonies and other publications have been sent for, and have travelled to Jamaica, Cuba, Canada, USA, India, South Africa, Switzerland, Holland, Italy, Ireland, Wales, Scotland, and all parts of England.'[7]

He also discussed the title, acknowledging that one suggestion had been *Pentecost with signs*, but stating that he was keen to see the newspaper as a means of grace and encouragement 'to lonely ones and to scattered bands', a reflection of the relative isolation and small numbers involved in the Movement at this stage. He explained his motivation in these words: 'They will find from these columns that they are not alone, as regards even human fellowship, but that there are many who have perfect "Confidence" that this work is of God, and who will be rejoiced to know that His Pentecostal Blessing is spreading all the time.'[8]

Once again his pastoral concern was to the fore.

Confidence *and other magazines*

Confidence – which was subtitled 'A Pentecostal Paper for Great Britain' – quickly established itself as the leading written source for British Pentecostals. Furthermore, it became important throughout the English-speaking world, doubtless building on the demand for '[s]cores of thousands of testimonies and other publications'.

The magazine was published monthly until January 1917, when an increasing gap between income and expenditure, blamed on the war, forced a reduction in the frequency of publication.[9] Six editions were published in 1917; from 1918 to 1924 it became quarterly, and there were only single editions in 1925 and 1926. Throughout this time Boddy was editor and often the chief contributor of articles – a remarkable achievement, spanning 141 editions.

Boddy's achievement is put into perspective when the history of *Confidence* is compared with that of other Pentecostal

magazines. Neil Hudson, a historian of the Pentecostal Movement, has surveyed the various magazines in circulation in this
period, and concluded that '*Confidence* was the premier agency
of news for British Pentecostals.'[10] The circulation built up
rapidly: there were 3,000 copies of the first edition printed in
April 1908, costing a total of just over £15.[11] In less than two years
this became 4,000 copies[12] and by the following year it had
increased to between 5,000 and 6,000. Boddy even printed a
picture of the bundles ready to be dispatched. Of these he states
that 2,000 copies are sent out singly, with the rest in bundles of
varying sizes up to 100.[13]

Hudson also draws attention to other magazines circulating
from 1910, beginning with *Omega*, produced by Pastor Moncur
Niblock based in Paddington, London.[14] Niblock had already
featured in the pages of *Confidence* regularly, including the very
first edition. He had received his own Pentecostal experience at
Sunderland, before the first Whitsun Conventions, and was a
platform speaker.[15] *Omega* included items from writers such as
Pascal and Thomas à Kempis, and Early Church writings such as
the Shepherd of Hermas and Chrysostom, as well as from
contemporary authors.[16] It was one of three monthly publications listed by Boddy, along with four occasional papers. He
both commended these papers to his readers and also pointedly
reminded them:

> We are sure none would like "Confidence" to suffer. For a
> long time it was alone in the field. We hope that the
> multiplication of papers may not bring difficulties to the old
> friend that has stood through stress and storm in the
> endeavour to spread Pentecostal truth in Great Britain.[17]

In fact, these potential competitors did not significantly dent the
pre-eminence of *Confidence*: two – *Abundance of Grace* and *Spirit
of Truth* – were short-lived, while Stanley Frodsham's *Victory*
lasted from 1909 to 1916, but closed in debt. *Fragments of Flame*,
published by Boddy's friend Cecil Polhill,[18] lasted from 1908 to
1925 and survived because of its missionary emphasis. Malcolm
Taylor, who has also examined the history of Pentecostal
publishing, has argued that this was the only other magazine
that was not a 'publishing fiasco'.[19]

One other magazine in Boddy's list of 1910, *Showers of Blessing*, lasted from 1910 to 1926, mainly because it was a denominational paper from the Apostolic Faith Movement.

In all, despite Boddy's concerns, it was his magazine which was the most durable, financially viable and influential of this period. This was achieved through his enterprise, his hard work and his familiarity with the publishing process, gained in his younger days. He was already a published author with a wide-ranging list of publications, which gave him a positive public profile and trust.

It was Boddy's faith in God that gave him a willingness to take the considerable risks involved in launching a magazine without a subscription base or any paid advertising. As Taylor has shown, even *Confidence* struggled financially, with most issues in deficit. In 1911 Boddy's faith faltered and he introduced a cover price (3d), but this resulted in a loss of circulation, and the price was reduced to 1d and then dropped altogether.

Crucial to the endurance of the magazine was the support of Cecil Polhill. According to Taylor's research Polhill regularly gave large sums of money to cover the deficit, including £20 (very roughly equivalent to £1,000 in 2006) in February 1911 and another £24 in September 1913. In the declining years of the magazine he gave no fewer than fourteen contributions totalling £169 10s between January 1921 and November 1924 – there can be no doubt about Polhill's faith in Boddy's editorial work.[20]

Components in Confidence

The contents of the magazine have already been indicated to some extent by the use made of them in this book so far. A typical issue contained a great variety of items, often jumbled together. It demonstrated its voluntary and independent nature by printing a list of subscriptions and costs on the inside front cover. The first substantial item was usually a long piece by Boddy, sometimes describing his travels and encounters with Christians elsewhere. Sometimes it was a reflective or devotional piece. In many issues Mary wrote a devotional and theological article. Teaching from other people was included, especially sermons and talks given at the annual Conventions. There was news of events in the Pentecostal Movement, comments about books, and some reflection on wider issues, notably including the First World War from its outbreak. Several pages were devoted to the work of the PMU, and Boddy was generally keen to encourage missionary work. Through it all, one is aware that the Editor was in charge as a benevolent autocrat, and his gentle firmness still comes across.

A significant feature of all the issues was the number of letters, both from around Britain and from many other parts of the world. They indicate the major international network built up by the Pentecostal experience and sustained by magazines such as *Confidence*. The longevity of Boddy's relationships is shown in these letters: for example, Barratt was quoted from his own letters until at least November 1916, and as late as April 1922 was quoted in a letter from a Danish correspondent: 'Pastor Barratt sends his love to the dear friends in England.'[21] In the penultimate issue of May 1925 there was a letter from Smith Wigglesworth, who was returning home after a long tour of New Zealand and the USA.[22]

It was not just the people Boddy had met who were recorded in *Confidence*: right from the start there were letters and news from many places. In the first edition there was news and correspondence from: Sunderland (no surprise!); Lytham, Lancashire; Bradford (Wigglesworth); Brixton, London; Cudworth, near Barnsley; Carlisle, Southsea; Bracknell, Berkshire; Kilsyth, Edinburgh and Motherwell in Scotland; Monmouthshire, Bridgend and Port Talbot in Wales; Belfast and Bangor in Ireland are mentioned. From further afield there are reports from Holland, Switzerland, Sweden, Egypt and from Barratt on his way to India.[23]

Just a year later many of the same places were still sending news, and to them were added Bombay, Germany, Liberia, Winnipeg in Canada, and several places in Australia.[24]

It is beyond the scope of this study to chart this correspondence in detail, but it does indicate the widespread reach of Boddy's magazine within the emerging Pentecostal Movement. His own commitment to an international and ecumenical perspective played a crucial role in establishing the Movement in Britain and elsewhere, and this material is now valued for its light on the earliest days of the global Pentecostal Movement.

The end of Confidence

Confidence remained an important newspaper into the early
1920s. By then Boddy was ageing and beginning to tire, and
Mary was ill throughout her time in Pittington (1922–26).
Donations began to dry up and several times Boddy indicated
that no further editions would be issued until sufficient funds
had been received.

The single-mindedness of Boddy's personal leadership and
editorial control finally became a liability, and other denomina-
tionally based publications from the Pentecostal Movement
began to take the place of his magazine. *Redemption Tidings*
became the outlet for the Assemblies of God, and the new *Elim
Evangel* – the first issue of which Boddy described as 'very
thrilling' – for the Elim churches founded by then by the Jeffreys
brothers.[25] In this way Boddy saw the baton of publishing
passing on to another generation as *Confidence* came to an end.

The Sunderland Conferences and Conventions, 1908–14

The publication of *Confidence* was clearly an important element
in Boddy's guidance of the early Pentecostal Movement. Taylor
stated, 'It is difficult to exaggerate the importance of *Confidence*'[26]
and it was surpassed in importance only by Boddy's leadership
of the Sunderland Whitsuntide Conventions. The two were
intertwined from the start: the magazine made great use of
sermons and lectures given at the Conventions, whilst attendance at the Conventions benefited from the publicity provided
by the magazines.

The Conventions were held in the week after Whitsunday
from 1908 to 1914; subsequently the First World War brought
them to a halt.

Boddy's sense of adventure and confidence in his God-given
abilities, his ease with people from many backgrounds, and his
willingness to learn from other Christians whilst being secure in
his own beliefs, all came to the fore in his organisation and
chairing of these events. Harnessed to his pastoral and
evangelistic concerns from over twenty five years of parish
ministry these qualities were to give the fledgling movement
enough security to become established.

Visitors, attracted by the reports in newspapers, had continued to come to Sunderland after Barratt had left, and they were able to attend prayer meetings held nearly every night in the Vestry.

Quite apart from the concentration of meetings that was to come through the Conventions, by September 1908, the first anniversary of the initial meetings held with Barratt, Boddy claimed to have held more than 500 Pentecostal Meetings, which were additional to the usual Sunday services. On Wednesday evenings there was a 'meeting of those who have received the Baptism of the Holy Ghost with the Sign of Tongues'. There were thirty to forty people from the area, with many more visitors from further afield. This was an opportunity to discuss difficulties, as well as to pray together.

Mention is made of many visitors, including H. Mogridge from Lancashire, and people from Carlisle, London and Scotland.[27]

The news of the impact on such visitors spread quickly, encouraging people in other centres to pray still more fervently. For example, Wigglesworth reported from the Bowland Street Mission in Bradford that 'many receive the Gift of Tongues and Baptism of Power' and that 'We have seen demons cast out, and the very devil of disease rebuked.'[28] The same page of *Confidence* included notice of a Revd C.F. Atherton holding waiting meetings in his Manse, having received baptism (presumably of the Holy Ghost) in Wigglesworth's house. There is a sense that Boddy is quietly showing the transmission of the movement from one person to another.

As a result, invitations to visit and to speak came quickly and Boddy began to travel again.

At the beginning of January 1908 both Alexander and Mary spoke at the Faith Mission, Lochrin Hall, Edinburgh. A few brief details are given in a testimony by a Mrs C. Beruldsen of Edinburgh.[29] For her, these meetings came after a long period of seeking blessing from God and reading about the meetings in Sunderland with some uncertainty. The talks by the Boddys clearly had a significant effect on her for within two days she and her husband had travelled to Monkwearmouth to join in the prayer meetings. By her own account she was 'filled with calm rest and peace' in the prayer meeting on 4 January. Mary then questioned her about her faith in Jesus and her willingness to repent, and she prayed for her very briefly to receive the Holy Spirit. Mrs Beruldsen believed she had been healed from a stomach disorder which had affected her for over six months. In another meeting on 8 January she prayed in tongues herself. The incident demonstrates the rapidity of the growth of the Pentecostal Movement, with the interchange of ideas and people from one place to another.

We know of a second visit to Scotland by Boddy in this period, during the last weekend of March 1908, when he was invited to a Mission Hall in Kilsyth, thirteen miles to the east of Glasgow. Boddy's own report was not dissimilar from those from his travel books, involving descriptions of the place, contact with local people, and now a much greater emphasis on spiritual reflection.[30] He was particularly impressed by the stories of those converted through hearing others speak in tongues and he also recorded seven examples of restitution after conversion or some other spiritual experience. He noted the chain of influence from Sunderland to Dunfermline and thence to Kilsyth, though without mentioning the names of the people concerned.[31]

This remarkable weekend help to establish an influential Pentecostal assembly, which is still in existence as an independent church.[32]

First Conference, 1908

Contacts such as these and the desire to encourage what would have been quite small groups of people led to the first Conference in Sunderland from 6 to 11 June 1908.[33] Publicity was given through the new magazine, with the inside front page of the first issue of *Confidence* giving a general invitation to 'all who have received their "Pentecost", or who are seeking it'. Visitors were required to make a signed declaration on the (free) admission tickets: 'I declare that I am in full sympathy with those who are seeking "Pentecost" with the Sign of Tongues. I also undertake to accept the ruling of the Chairman.'[34]

From his own experience of the previous autumn in Monkwearmouth Boddy was aware of the potential for controversy. He had described the Kilsyth meetings as looking disorderly and he was aware of speakers who might bring reproach on the Movement. In his instructions about the meetings he encouraged prayer and praise, and punctuality to allow quiet or silent prayer before the meeting started. It was the leader's role to start choruses, and in case of difficulty his rulings were to be accepted promptly.

The published timetable allowed for three meetings each day: at 11 a.m., 3 p.m. and 7.30 p.m., with a variety of prayer meetings and opportunities for discussion and teaching. In his publicity Boddy gave prominence to Sunday Church of England services, including Holy Communion; on this first occasion there were Sunday services of Holy Communion at 8 a.m. and 10.30 a.m. and by 1912 an additional service at 7 a.m.

As was to happen in succeeding years, a full report on the Conference was given in *Confidence*, along with extensive articles based on the talks given by the range of speakers. This provides a valuable resource for understanding the developing theologies of Pentecostal leaders in the UK and Europe, as well as the organisation of the movement. We shall concentrate our description on the first Conference since the others followed similar patterns, and then note some of the features which arose in the later conferences.

The third issue of *Confidence* in June 1908 was almost entirely taken up with reporting the Conference, and the details that follow are from that edition.[35]

Boddy's initial intention had been to hold a Conference in September 1908 as the anniversary of the first outpouring, but he followed a suggestion to make it the more 'appropriate season of Whitsuntide'.

Conference preparation

Before the Conference proper there were preliminary meetings in the parish, including time for prayer and fasting. Among the early visitors were the wife of Barratt and others from Christiania (Oslo), Norway, and Pastor Gerrit Polman and Brother Kok from Amsterdam, previously known to Boddy by correspondence only.

At prayer on Thursday 4 June Polman was described as 'blessedly baptized' when hands were laid on him. Thursday evening was taken up with the regular feeding of 300 unemployed men in the Church Hall, with the added attraction of Polman and Kok singing in Dutch and English. An 'after meeting' was held, and Boddy's pastoral concern is once again evident in his description of 'many sad lives' and 'very bitter experiences'.

By Friday 5 June many visitors had arrived, and Boddy singled out for mention a group from Kilsyth. A 'powerful Vestry Prayer Meeting' was held that night, with Mary Boddy as the speaker, on a text from 1 Corinthians 1:10, emphasising the need for unity of purpose. Andrew Murdoch from Kilsyth and Mrs Beruldsen also gave testimonies about the benefits of the Pentecostal experience. It is clear that even before the Conference had started Boddy was making effective use of his network of likeminded people.

The Welcome

The opening Welcome Meeting was held on the Saturday evening in the church itself, partly because there were too many people for the large Vestry. Boddy thought it worth highlighting that this first meeting of a Pentecostal Conference in England took place in a church of the Church of England, perhaps because it was unexpected, but also perhaps because he wanted to show the respectability of this movement and to encourage its growth within the Church of England.

It was a sober occasion, with the people singing on their knees the Trinitarian hymn of Bishop Heber, 'Holy, holy, holy, Lord God Almighty'. The welcome was given both by Boddy and the local Salvationist, James Techner, who was to speak at later Conferences. Even that night a prayer meeting was held in the Vestry, which apparently was memorable for some who attended.

'Ever since 1892, Whit-Sunday has been a very blessed day at All Saints, Monkwearmouth, but no Whit-Sunday has been so wonderful as that of 1908.' Thus began Boddy's account, under the quotation, 'When the day of Pentecost was fully come' (from Acts 2:1 in the Authorised Version). Immediately one is linked into Boddy's own experience of the Spirit in 1892, with the implication that he had connected that experience to Whit Sunday for some fifteen years, as well as given a connection to the first Christian Pentecost as recorded in the Acts of the Apostles.

Boddy recorded that large numbers responded to the invitation to the Lord's Table (terminology and action both indicative of his evangelical theology) at both 8 a.m. and 10.30 a.m.

At Evensong Boddy preached on 'This is that' (Acts 2:16), the beginning of Peter's quotation of the prophet Joel. Boddy found himself at one point speaking in tongues, but restrained himself. Once again he emphasised the remarkable nature of the event for the established church, commenting there were 'more who spake in "Tongues" than ever were gathered in an Anglican church before'; this may indicate that his belief at this time was that speaking in tongues was a necessary sign of baptism in the Spirit. A busy day was filled out with meetings in the Parish Hall at 3 p.m. and 8 p.m., both involving women speakers from abroad, and three events for children and young people, again using visiting speakers.

The Conference pattern

This busy weekend was only preparation for what Boddy then called the Opening Meetings of the Conference on Monday, 8 June. They held a discussion about the Waiting Meetings and Boddy emphasised the importance of keeping close to Scripture. It is worth noting that the only other two speakers he quoted in *Confidence* were women, and that in all four women (including Mary Boddy) and six men took part in the discussion, a gender balance not often noted in the deliberations of the church generally, though more common in the Salvation Army at that time.

Meetings for prayer and praise were held on the Monday evening and Tuesday morning, with a brief mention of casting out demons from a soldier, and notes from a sermon given by Mary on the text from John 7:38–39.

A change of rhythm was provided on the Tuesday afternoon with a social gathering, though it still included singing and testimonies. Boddy drew particular attention to the unity given by the Spirit, mentioning the attendance of 'Anglicans, Methodists, Friends, Salvationists, Congregationalists, Mission members, etc.', an unusually comprehensive coming together of Protestants for the early twentieth century, especially in its inclusion of Salvationists.

In addition he noted the presence of people from several nationalities, specifically English, Scottish, Welsh, Irish,

Norwegian, Danish and Dutch, and he had also named a few American visitors elsewhere. His key theological phrase for this was being 'one in Christ Jesus'. His own gregarious nature was expressed in his instructions to people to 'change places often, and so seize the opportunity of meeting many friends'.

Following the Social Gathering they held an open-air meeting no more than fifty yards away, with singing and the giving of testimonies. Boddy's evangelistic motivation was behind this brief but significant episode, and one story was recorded of a news reporter being convinced of the spiritual reality spoken of.

Subsequent meetings included teaching on 'the Nine Gifts' (a reference to 1 Corinthians 12:7–10), the giving of tithes (to do away with Bazaars and Sales of Work), and prophetic messages and their testing. This last topic was recorded in some detail in the magazine, and shows real awareness of the danger that speakers could consciously or unconsciously manipulate messages to their own ends.

On the Wednesday evening the topic was the Near Coming of the Lord, introduced by Boddy reading Luke 12:32–40 and with sermons by Miss Barbour of Wimbledon and Miss Sisson of the USA. Both spoke of an imminent return of Christ.

The first meeting on Thursday, 11 June covered the need for morality to safeguard the work. The second was on the issue of Divine Healing; there was teaching by Boddy on the basis of the instructions to the elders of the church in James 5:14–16 – a favourite text of his – and advocating a holistic understanding of healing, in body, soul and spirit. He also recognised the temptation to exaggerate in testimonies, and advised care. This was followed by a string of testimonies from Monkwearmouth and elsewhere. A show of hands demonstrated that a large number believed that they had been healed personally.

In reporting the last night of the conference Boddy referred to his own comments that the Conference had been held to glorify Jesus, and not to boast of tongues. There is a hint of the perception that this was a movement about tongues, a perception Boddy was anxious to refute. More than two hours of testimonies followed, with just a few recorded in the magazine. Although this was the end of the official programme Prayer Meetings were held in the Vestry through the Friday with visitors who lingered, among them Mrs Beruldsen and Agnes

Thelle from Norway, who had given a number of prophetic messages during the week.

Boddy's assessment of the Conference

Besides his very detailed description of the Conference Boddy also wrote two pieces of assessment in this Conference edition of *Confidence*, the first acting as an introduction, the second as an editorial. In the first piece he picked out six key phrases about the Conference which were important to him: strengthening, fellowship, brotherly love, real joy, solemn time, and teaching. These phrases provided an interpretative grid through which Boddy wanted to demonstrate the breadth of the events and their biblical orthodoxy. Explicit biblical references were given for some parts of the discussion. Under 'fellowship' he mentioned that the number of visitors from elsewhere was about 120 – perhaps an allusion to Acts 1:15 – and picking up a phrase from Acts 2:1 (without citing the reference) he wrote, 'we were all with one accord in this one place'.

In all he believed that some 500 people had attended some part of the Conference. He was also emphatic in the section on teaching that 'We are learning to put the Gifts in their right place. To look to the Giver far more than to His gifts. To honour Jesus, to keep closer and closer to His Word.'

The editorial emphasised the guidance of the Holy Spirit in controlling the Conference, and described the greatest blessing as 'the vision and reality of the glorified Christ.' His evangelical convictions are clear in the centrality of his Christological statement, and the subsequent comments that touched on the value of the Atonement, the Word of God, and the overcoming of temptation from Satan.

This last point acted as a bridge for him to comment on the fear that many Christians had felt about this movement, a reminder of the opposition that he and the other Pentecostal-minded leaders faced. More specifically Pentecostal concerns were prominent in the remainder of the editorial, namely healing, discernment as a spiritual gift, the testing of messages, and the right use of tongues.

His comment on this last topic exposed a problem he had presumably found amongst some people: an expectation that one might receive 'a message in "Tongues" for details of daily life and guidance'. Boddy was robust in refuting this idea, citing St Peter, and looking for a spirit of love to solve difficulties. At this early stage in the development of the Pentecostal Movement here is further evidence of Boddy's guidance as he sought to provide reflection on the remarkable events experienced by many people and to deal with possibly irresponsible interpretations and understandings.

Assessment by other people

The issue of *Confidence* in the following month of July was much shorter, perhaps because of the financial burden of the June issue, but it did include further reflections on the Conference from other people.

The first came from Pastor Jeffreys of Waunlwyd, South Wales; he was grateful for the sense of peace and of fellowship found at the Conference. He also commented that prophecy was becoming more common amongst his group.[36]

The second article was by Mrs Barratt, translated from Norwegian. She mentioned Alexander and Mary together, and noted that they were having the same difficulties as they had had in Norway. She was struck by Mary's teaching on unity and by Alexander's leadership and willingness to reach across denominational barriers. She was saddened that there were few pastors or leaders from the churches present, but was very supportive of Boddy's leadership. He was the leader at all the meetings, but in her estimation 'took up very little time. It was the visitors (brothers and sisters) who took most part in meetings.'[37]

The third item was a letter of testimony by a Signora Malan of Turin, Italy. She gave a long account of her search for 'complete deliverance from sin and self', a search which was frustrated by illness and doubts, but finally realised, she believed, when Mary Boddy prayed for her and anointed her with oil.

Her letter is notable for the inclusion of her own written version of some of the words she spoke with the meanings she understood them to have. For example, she gave her first word in tongues as *katakuma* with the meaning 'buried' from Colossians 2:12.[38]

Boddy's motive in printing these items was not explicitly stated, but given that the only other pieces in this issue were a letter from Toronto, Canada and a testimony from a workman in Scotland, he seems to have been wanting to promote a sense of a worldwide movement, in which Sunderland played a key role.

This was a reasonably accurate picture: the Pentecostal Movement was already spreading in several parts of the world, and Sunderland was becoming a key centre, both through the magazine and the Conferences that had begun. The meetings at the 1908 Conference were well organised and led to six more. Their successful organisation owed much to Boddy's efficiency and his ability to bring together people from very different backgrounds.

The Later Conferences

The themes of leaders, the crossing of barriers, divergence and the effect locally are used here, in order, to describe in a relatively brief way the development and impact of the Sunderland Conferences. The teaching ministry and the use of spiritual gifts, including healing, will be discussed in chapter eight.

Leaders

During the course of the seven Conferences virtually all the contemporary Pentecostal leaders of Britain and significant numbers of the future leaders and of overseas leaders attended too. Some received a personal baptism in the Holy Spirit there, as evidenced by the gift of speaking in tongues. It seems from the annual reports in *Confidence* that most of those mentioned attended each year once they had started.[39]

In the 1908 Conference British leaders of Pentecostal groups included Andrew Murdoch, Kilsyth; Smith Wigglesworth, Bradford; H. Mogridge, Lancashire; T.M. Jeffreys, South Wales; and Miss Barbour, Wimbledon. Foreign leaders mentioned included Miss Sisson, USA, and Pastor Gerrit and Mrs Polman from Amsterdam. (Polman had previously been a Salvation Army officer under Arthur Booth-Clibborn.) From Norway came Mrs Laura Barratt, wife of T.B. Barratt, Agnes Thelle and Dagmar Gregersen.

In 1909 specific meetings for leaders were included in the programme as the Movement became more organised, and

Boddy himself believed this was likely to be among the most fruitful elements of the Conference. About fifty leaders were mentioned as having attended, though only a minority were recorded by name.[40] An important British attendee was Cecil Polhill, one of the Cambridge Seven missionaries – an influential group of young evangelists from Cambridge University in the 1880s, and one of the founders, with Boddy, of the Pentecostal Mission Union (see chapter seven). Arthur Booth-Clibborn, the son-in-law of William and Catherine Booth, the founders of the Salvation Army, was helpful as a translator from German and Dutch, and a speaker himself, and was a regular attendee apart from 1912 and 1913.

The overseas contingent of leaders was even more impressive, and provides substance to Boddy's assessment of the lasting significance of the meetings of the leaders. This time T.B. Barratt was able to join his wife. From Berlin, Germany came Pastor Paul and Mrs Paul, with Pastor Paul speaking on the need for discernment when the unconscious mind was influencing people. Daniel Awrey of Oklahoma, an early American friend of Boddy, spoke on the necessity of good leadership in providing proper direction. Other leaders included Mr and Mrs Montgomery (California, USA) and Pastor Meyer of Hamburg, all of whom became firm friends of Boddy's, and Mr A.H. Post of Los Angeles. The Polmans of Amsterdam returned and again were prominent in the meetings.

In each of the following four years new speakers and leaders came from the USA, German, and Russia, as well as from other parts of Britain. An exact estimate of numbers is not possible, since Boddy included details of testimonies from named people who usually should not be regarded as leaders.

On a conservative estimate there were twenty-three named leaders from Britain during the seven years of the Conventions and forty-two from other countries, many returning each year, testimony to the positive sense of fellowship and to the leadership exercised by the Boddys. For both British and foreign leaders roughly one third of those named were women. Another ten or so new leaders came each year, an indication of the travelling undertaken by the Boddys, and it was only in 1914 that this dropped to just three new people being named.

The largest group was from the USA, including Levi Lupton and Pastor Frank Bartleman, a key reporter from Azusa Street in

1906. In 1911 Pastor and Mrs Kellaway came from Los Angeles, USA, providing another personal link to Azusa Street. Boddy recorded their comment, 'But now what we want at Los Angeles is just such teaching as you get right here', but sadly was not more specific.[41]

Pastor Joseph H. King from North Carolina was a key speaker at the 1912 Convention. Dr Florence Murcutt, also of Los Angeles, came in 1913 and 1914 and spoke prominently on healing.

German pastors were the next largest group, and Boddy developed close relationships with Jonathan Paul, B. Schilling and E. Humberg through their membership of the International Pentecostal Council. This Council also included Barratt, Polhill, Polman of Amsterdam and J.H. King of USA (in 1912 only).[42]

Among British leaders who should be noted, besides Smith Wigglesworth and Polhill, there were Stanley Frodsham, Bournemouth; Thomas Myerscroft, leader of the PMU training school; and Stephen and George Jeffreys of Wales, who attended in 1913, with George leading a number of Bible studies. The Jeffreys brothers went on to lead the Elim churches in the UK.

In 1912 Howard Carter, who went on to lead the Assemblies of God in the UK, attended the Conference with his brother and mother.[43]

At the last two Conventions Dorothy Kerin was a major speaker, describing her own healing and speaking on the subject on healing.

Her attendance was sufficiently conspicuous for the national newspaper, the *Daily Mirror*, to comment adversely: 'The Convention has, as usual, been marked by a great deal of hysterical behaviour on the part of the congregations.'[44]

This brief description of the leaders at the Sunderland Conventions serves to highlight the significant role played by women in the early leadership of the Pentecostal Movement. Diane Chapman has examined *Confidence* and other records with this feature in mind and – rightly – concluded that '[d]uring the Sunderland Conventions men and women ministered with complete equality'.[45] She sees the roots of this in the key roles women had in the Holiness movement, the way in which women were often the first to experience speaking in tongues, and Boddy's own encouragement of women in ministry.

In discussing influences which helped to release women's ministry she begins with the work of Boddy, 'Facilitator of Women's Ministry',[46] before describing Pentecostalism as egalitarian and a revival movement. Even when having women in leadership became more controversial in the Movement,[47] Boddy remained supportive and Chapman concluded: 'Without such a charismatic figure as Boddy . . . one wonders whether women would have had such freedom.'[48]

Boddy's success in drawing the leading members of the Pentecostal Movement to Sunderland repeatedly, and in attracting new leaders in significant numbers virtually every year, establishes his own position in its forefront nationally and internationally. There were other Conventions, many of which he himself attended, but there was a real sense in which this was the leading Convention in Europe, and significant leaders wanted to be there.

Crossing barriers

Boddy was very conscious of the way in which the Pentecostal experience broke down barriers. He referred to this in a number of contexts, including barriers of gender, denomination, social class, nationality and skin colour. He wrote a particularly animated editorial after the 1909 Congress, which is worth quoting at length:

> Pentecost has girdled the world. There were over 300 delegates, and they came from the east and from the west, from the north and from the south. The fire has touched every land. Germany, Holland, France, Italy, Russia, Norway, Sweden, USA, Canada, Ceylon, India, and the four sister states of Britain, were all represented . . .
>
> The Power of Pentecost . . . is sweeping through all the earth, breaking down every barrier of race, language, custom, or creed . . .
>
> No racial antipathies here! Without there may be war-scares, but here perfect brotherhood amongst all the different tongues and kindreds. Those beloved German brethren! Our hearts went out in extra yearnings of love towards them. No denominationalism! Anglicans, Lutherans, and every kind of Nonconformist, all assented in a common "Yea and Amen" to

the Bible faith which has been once for all delivered unto the saints. Here is the witness to the world, that Pentecost is of God. Its perfect peace and concord stamp it with the hall-mark of heaven. "By this shall all men know that ye are my disciples, if ye have love one to another." Nothing has ever so united the children of God, scattered abroad, as this blessed experience.[49]

Such comments by Boddy were not unusual: in his tours of the USA he was concerned about racism amongst Pentecostal groups, and his consistent support for women in church ministry has already been alluded to.

On the other hand, he did retain fairly traditional ideas about his role as head of his household – his daughter Jane remembered that he never offered to help with domestic matters[50] – and when it came to the 1914–18 war he was a strong supporter of fighting against Germany, despite his many friendships with German pastors and considerable anguish over the matter.

His vision of the church was largely Protestant, though when travelling in foreign lands he was happy to share fellowship with Roman Catholics and with the Orthodox.

In short, he was serious about the overcoming of barriers by the gospel and the experience of the Spirit, but like most of us he was also constrained by his upbringing and social expectations.

Divergence

Just as it is important to understand Boddy's commitment to the overcoming of barriers and to unity of purpose through the Spirit, so we also need to acknowledge that there was a variety of views on a number of issues. As the years went by these became more substantial: four issues that were especially problematic were baptism, the leadership role of women, the significance of speaking in tongues, and the desirability or otherwise of creating a new church.[51]

It is noteworthy that in 1911 Barratt wrote an article in *Confidence* under the heading 'An Urgent Plea for Charity and Unity';[52] in it he wrote how diversity of opinion was carried over from denominational differences:

At the commencement of the Revival this was scarcely noticed, but many who formerly were Lutherans, Methodists, Baptists, Quakers, and so on, *still retain their old views* regarding various important questions. The Revival has *not* changed this. The *object, value, time* and *method* of observing *water-baptism* is still a matter of discussion, likewise the *necessity, meaning* and *importance* of *the Lord's Supper*, and the proper method for conducting it. Besides this, there are other questions on which many do not agree. Even in the matter that interests us all so greatly – *the tongues*, there is some difference in the way in which their value and importance has been stated by teachers within the Revival.[53]

1. Baptism

The issue of water baptism was certainly controversial, even though Boddy did not include the details of the discussion in *Confidence*. We have just a hint of it in the above quotation – 'still a matter of discussion' – and slightly stronger in the second part of the article when Barratt wrote: 'Neither do the different opinions concerning *tongues* need to cause any ill-feeling amongst us, or *any other question*; but it does seem that when we come to the subject of WATER-BAPTISM the case is different.'[54]

There appears to have been no resolution of the issue, and at the later Sunderland Conventions several people were baptised in the sea at Roker. It began with a single candidate in 1912, which Boddy did mention very briefly in *Confidence*[55] in a section based on press reports. Even this small-scale ceremony was reported in the *Newcastle Daily Journal*.[56] The following year Smith Wigglesworth baptised three unnamed women and two men from Gateshead, Tom James and Tom Knight, the latter man later becoming a minister in the Assemblies of God.[57]

This ceremony was clearly an embarrassment to Boddy, who did not include it in his reports in *Confidence*, most likely because it involved what he would have regarded as rebaptism.

But if he ignored it, the national press did not: *The Daily Mirror* made it front page news, with four photographs and inside the headline 'Converts Icy Bath', while *The Daily Sketch* focussed on the blue pyjamas worn![58]

Nonetheless, Boddy continued to print articles by Wigglesworth and to remain friends with him.

In 1914 there were further baptisms, this time by a Mr C.W. Longstracth, a missionary from South Africa, which again attract-ted the attention of the national press, with a report and pictures.[59]

2. The role of women
Differences over the role of women came to the fore at the 1914 Convention. Boddy chaired the debate from which he recorded the remarks of six other men and just one woman, Mrs Polman of Amsterdam. The foremost speaker wanting greater restrictions was Pastor Paul: he was not against women teaching or prophesying, but believed that a woman should not be the leader of a Christian community – 'he did not find anywhere in the Bible that a sister should be bishop of the assembly' and 'He was sorry when he found a lady directing alone.'[60]

Other speakers were more obviously positive about women speaking, but it tended to be in the context of a smaller assembly, a special conference and not the church itself, while several made positive remarks about married couples working together. Thus Boddy wrote: '[W]here the husband and wife worked in harmony there was little or no difficulty, for they two were one.'[61] The impression given is that Boddy continued to be happy to see women ministering quite publicly but that other (male) leaders were becoming less convinced.

As the Movement became more institutionalised so more traditional readings of Scripture were favoured, and the leader-ship of the Movement became more clearly male in the years after 1914, a sociological phenomenon seen after other revivals, such as the Wesleyan and the Primitive Methodist revival

3. Speaking in tongues
The issue of speaking in tongues was mentioned by Barratt as one of 'some difference' between the 'teachers within the Revival' and we shall return to this subject in chapter eight.

4. Forming a new church
The fourth important issue discussed on a number of occasions was the desirability or otherwise of forming a new church.

Barratt first wrote about this possibility in his double article of February/March 1911,[62] but had already considered presenting it at the first Hamburg Conference in December 1908. Boddy and Paul had dissuaded him at the time.

By 1911 Boddy was prepared to publish Barratt's proposal, which was to establish new Christian communities where 'the older Christian communities . . . *shut out* the fresh glorious flow of Revival, grace and power.' In fact, Barratt acknowledged that during 1910 three Pentecostal Centres had been established through his own ministry in Copenhagen, Gothenburg and Christiania (Oslo).[63]

Boddy himself remained convinced that the way forward was renewal for individuals within existing churches, not a new organisation. In an editorial entitled 'Unity, not Uniformity' he wrote about the spirit of the first days of the Movement: 'Christians of many kinds came and went; most of them returned to their own churches. Differences existed as before, but they were never emphasized.' He went on to explain his own thinking and offered a warning:

> The Editor of "Confidence" does not feel that the Lord's leading in these days is to set up a new Church, but to bless individuals where they are. There is just as much danger, sooner or later, for a "Pentecostal Church" (so-called) as for any of the churches that hare risen and fallen.[64]

Boddy and Barratt were to persist with their views, with Barratt again making the case at the International Pentecostal Consultative Council at Amsterdam in December 1912 for a more formal alliance, or even for the formation of churches.

In contrast, Paul was not happy even with the term *Movement*, preferring to see it as a Gift of the Holy Ghost and an 'Organism'.

The advisory council of leaders tended to agree more with Paul and Boddy (the two of them had generally been the chairmen of the meetings) and the final declaration included the phrase 'Not a unity in which uniformity prevails' and to speak of 'unity in spirit and fraternity'.[65]

This was the last occasion on which Barratt attended the leaders' meetings. In 1913 he was baptized by immersion and left the Methodist church. In effect he organised his own church from this point, with baptism by immersion a condition of membership.[66]

Boddy continued with his own, different, views, but apparently did not allow the divergence between him and Barratt to end their friendship and association – Barratt remained 'our beloved brother' in Boddy's memoir of 1914,[67] and he continued to print news about Barratt in *Confidence*. Nevertheless, the subsequent, less frequent, items imply that the relationship was continued only by letter.

(a)Local effects
Boddy's long ministry in Sunderland gave respectability to what could otherwise have been seen as a very extreme movement, and the evidence of his own reports suggests that hosting the Conventions and the Pentecostal experience more widely had a very significant impact on his parish ministry.

The Evidence of the Visitation Forms

It happened that Bishop Handley Moule required his clergy to fill in a Visitation form in July 1908 and the tone of Boddy's reply is very different from those of other clergy, even though he does not directly mention the Convention recently held.[68] For example, like other clergy he found that people would not attend Morning and Evening Prayer held during the week, but 'almost Daily Prayer is held in our Vestry, as numbers of earnest Christians gather with me – both Church people and non-conformists and pray down blessing on God's work.' In commenting on the canonical requirement for clergy to say the Daily Office apart from 'reasonable hindrance' he mentioned 'the constant pressure of other spiritual opportunities'.

Sermons were no longer described as following the liturgical seasons or particular courses (as he had said in the Visitation of July 1904), but instead he replied: 'The preaching of a Victorious Christ-Victory over the works of the devil through the Cross proves to be the most attractive.'

Asked about anti-religious sentiments, socialism and spiritualism, he responded: 'The preaching of Christ in the power of the Holy Ghost seems to me to be better than evidential addresses of necessity adverting these errors', apparently not convinced by what would now be termed apologetics.

He was also much more positive than in previous returns about the quality of the lay-help he received, making optimistic remarks about people working with children and other events: 'The summer school grows in spiritual power. Many of the

Teachers are much nearer to their Lord both in life and in teaching than they were some time ago'; and also, that lay help is found in 'Open air preaching and helping in children's services and in prayer meetings. I may say that in the goodness of God very vigorous (spiritual) lay-help is given.'

A more specific account was written by Boddy on the first anniversary of the visit by Barratt under the title 'A Year of Blessing'.[69] He particularly mentioned that the 'Pentecostal Prayer Meetings (full of power and almost nightly) have gone on all the year round', a contrast to previous attempts to encourage prayer. The special Wednesday evening meetings 'of those who have received the Baptism of the Holy Ghost with the Sign of Tongues' were mentioned previously. Filling out his comments in the diocesan return, he was particularly pleased with the impact on young men and women, who were prepared to speak at Open-Air Meetings, and on Sunday School Teachers, who were seeing conversions in their classes. He went on: 'there is among the young people a genuine earnestness rising higher than ever in one's ministry of nearly 24 years in this Parish.'

Boddy noted that all nine gifts of the Spirit from 1 Corinthians 9 had been manifest 'in some measure', and that God had 'allowed a great stream of information, of praise and testimony, to go out from this place all over the world'. This was built on his parish work, both the familiar services and other activities, and the more than 500 Pentecostal Meetings held in addition.

Thus, even while he continued faithfully to hold the required Prayer Book services it is evident that the Pentecostal Movement had a major impact on the use of his time and his ministry in the parish.

Edith Blumhofer is right to point out that '[t]here is no evidence that Boddy introduced Pentecostal practices into his regularly scheduled Anglican services',[70] and to emphasize his loyalty to the Church of England. She has, however, perhaps missed the apparently changed nature of his preaching within such services which would have supported the additional, more overtly Pentecostal meetings.

Boddy's continued work as a parish priest gave him a base lacking for many other Pentecostal leaders in Britain and elsewhere, not least the USA, where itinerant ministry became the desired pattern for a time. It gave him credibility in his leadership of the Movement, even if it was harder for him to go the other way by introducing Pentecostal ideas to fellow Anglicans. There are very few Anglican ministers reported as attending the Conventions or other meetings, rather more from Non-conformist churches. Opportunities to speak were mostly in Non-conformist venues, though he did print a substantial article on speaking in tongues, based on a talk given in the nearby evangelical parish of St Gabriel's Bishopwearmouth.[71]

The Convention week grew in its impact and by 1910 numbers were such that people were forced on to the streets and there was some national press interest, with a brief report in *The Times*[72] and photographs in the *Daily Mirror*.[73] In 1911 the reports mentioned that some local ministers were attending. By 1912 the Convention was given civic status when it was opened by the Mayor of Sunderland, E.H. Brown, in his chain of office; he had previously attended as a private individual.

Bishop Moule's Attitude

It would be good to know what Bishop Moule thought of it all; certainly he must at least have tolerated Boddy's ministry, and he is quoted on several occasions in *Confidence*. However, we have no direct knowledge of how he regarded the Pentecostal Movement in one of his parishes. His own book on the Holy Spirit, *Veni Creator*, originally published in 1890, is a rounded discussion of the doctrine and work of the Holy Spirit as found in Scripture, yet it contained no mention of the gifts of the Spirit.[74] It may be that his thinking did move on, for we have already noted his positive remarks about the Welsh Revival.

The last occasion on which Boddy quoted Moule is perhaps the most significant, not just for its length but also because it was based on a talk given by the Bishop at All Saints Church in the summer of 1919, under the title 'The Hope of the Approach of the Lord's Return – And its Influence upon Life'. The subject of the second coming of Christ was one which was important to them both, and in it Moule referred to his own belief in predictive prophecy – in foretelling as well as forthtelling, as he put it.[75] It seems reasonable to conclude that he was more supportive than some other Keswick Convention leaders might have been, and that Boddy was fortunate – blessed, he would have said – in having Moule as his bishop throughout this period, probably the most sympathetic diocesan bishop of the time.

• The Final Convention

Arthur Booth-Clibborn wrote what was intended as (merely) a sketch of the latest Convention after the 1914 gathering but now seems a moving epitaph for all the Conventions under the heading 'Ripening for Rapture'. He was very positive about the tone of the meetings, the number of people attending and what he saw as the wider significance of the Conventions:

> Those who have attended the convention year by year agree that the light, the life, the love, and the (true) liberty have steadily risen, and have come to highest expression in this the Seventh. The new and well filled gallery showed how the attendance has also risen.
> There was a distinct ripening visible in the Convention and its attenders. The writer, not having been present at the last two, had perhaps on that account a better perspective. There was a deeper colour, so to speak, such as one sees on the cheek of an apple just before it falls.[76]

He went on to apply this illustration in a somewhat confusing manner to a vision he had previously received; the conclusion he came to was that the ripeness of the Convention seemed to be another sign of the approaching rapture or second coming. There was no intimation of the wider catastrophe about to engulf Europe; what he called the 'incomparably grave character of the present time in world history' referred to the impending rapture.

In a more homely postscript Booth-Clibborn described seeing Boddy immediately taking up his parish duties as the Convention ended, as he led a 600 strong procession of Sunday School children, parents and friends on the annual Sunday School Treat:

> It is interesting and typical of the practical character of this movement to see the Vicar of the Parish actively engaged in his parochial duties a moment after the closure of the Conference. The sound of the cheering of those children lingers in one's ears as the train moves away.[77]

Here was a man approaching sixty years of age, with half of those years having been spent living next to a smoky ironworks, full of enthusiasm for the youngsters of his parish as soon as a demanding and draining international Convention had ended. This vignette speaks loudly of Boddy's energy and commitment, and perhaps of why so many people responded so positively to his leadership by example.

The Strain Begins to Show

By 1914 the Conventions were an important event in bringing together and encouraging the early Pentecostal Movement in Britain and indeed Europe, and we will look at Boddy's international work in the next chapter. However, we have also seen how the growth in the Movement was putting strain on Boddy's leadership and the way in which problems of discipline began to emerge more explicitly. Most obviously the success of the meetings was generating more emotion and expectation and in 1913 and 1914 in particular there were breakdowns in order and outbursts of speaking in tongues with which Boddy was not happy. He was keen to keep things orderly because of the number of newspaper reporters now present, a feature of Boddy's reaction to the publicity surrounding the initial visit by Barratt in 1907.

Even more significantly for the future there was a build-up of Pentecostal practices and assemblies independent of other church groups. Although Boddy himself wanted to see the Pentecostal Movement work within the existing churches, this did not happen in most places and younger leaders grew up and began new groups.[78]

As baptisms became more frequent it was clear that Boddy's leadership of the Conventions and within the Pentecostal Movement as a whole would have been considerably strained and weakened even without the devastation of the First World War.

The Historians' Perspectives

In summarising the lasting importance of the Sunderland Conventions it is worth hearing the voice of two Pentecostal historians.

The British Pentecostal historian, Donald Gee, wrote that these Conventions 'must occupy the supreme place in importance' in the early life of the Pentecostal movement in the British Isles.[79]

The most recent British Pentecostal historian, William Kay, endorses Gee's view and adds his own positive assessment of Boddy himself:

> The conventions were held in Boddy's parish and he was their dignified and respected chairman. To Sunderland came many of those who were later instrumental in the founding of the Pentecostal denominations studied in this book.[80]

Notes

1 The availability of these magazines has been greatly increased by their publication on CD-ROM by the Assemblies of God Flower Pentecostal Heritage Center

2 Though they are undated publications, the twelfth is a reprint of a letter from Smith Wigglesworth to the Boddys, dated 5 November 1907. The titles are listed in the Bibliography

3 There is no date on copies of the document held at Mattersey Hall, but he wrote at the start: 'For more than four months we have been learning by experience'

4 *The "Pentecostal Baptism"*, 4

5 *Morning Leader*, 3 October 1907

6 *Confidence*, April 1908, 21

7 *Confidence*, April 1908, 5

8 *Confidence*, April 1908, 3

9 *Confidence*, January 1917, 12

10 Hudson, *Earliest Days*, 53

11 *Confidence*, May 1908, 19

12 *Confidence*, January 1910, 12

13 These details in *Confidence*, August 1911, 192

14 *Confidence*, June 1909, Supplement, 5

15 *Confidence*, April 1908, 13

16 Hudson, *Earliest Days*, 54 gives details of these and other authors, and also the histories of the magazines described below

17 *Confidence*, March 1910, 61

18 There is a useful short biography of Polhill: Hocken, 'Cecil Polhill', *Pneuma* 10, 1988, 116–40

19 Taylor, *Publish and be Blessed*, 115

20 See Taylor, *Publish and be Blessed*, 142, 161 for the contributions of Polhill

21 *Confidence*, April 1922, 29

22 *Confidence*, May 1925, 166

23 *Confidence*, April 1907, 5–16

24 *Confidence*, April 1908, passim

25 *Confidence*, May 1925, 162

26 Taylor, *Publish and be Blessed*, 119

27 *Confidence*, September 1908, 4–5

28 *Confidence*, April 1908, 7

29 *Confidence*, April 1908, 11–12

30 *Confidence*, April 1908, 8–11

31 Hudson gives some details of the chain, particularly mentioning Victor Wilson of Motherwell, known to Boddy as the contact in Motherwell. See Hudson, *Earliest Days*, 64 and *Confidence*, April 1908, 11

32 The website for Kilsyth Community Council includes a somewhat disparaging reference to this revival, the last of four such events, the others being in 1742, 1839 and 1905. {http://www.kilsyth.org.uk/religion/kilsyth_revival.htm} accessed 15 March 2005

33 This first event was termed a Conference, the second in 1909 a Congress, while the others, from 1910 to 1914, were termed Conventions, usually International Pentecostal Conventions

34 *Confidence*, April 1908, 2

35 *Confidence*, June 1908, 3–22

36 *Confidence*, July 1908, 3

37 *Confidence*, June 1908, 5

38 *Confidence*, July 1908, 5–7. It is incorrectly cited as Col 2:2 in the article

39 Further information about some of the earliest attendees can be found in Hudson, *Earliest Days*, 61–66

40 *Confidence*, June 1909, 130

41 *Confidence*, June 1911, 129

42 See the signatories on the statement of 31 May 1912. *Confidence*, June 1912, 133

43 Whittaker, *Pentecostal Pioneers*, 100–30

44 *Daily Mirror*, 15 May 1913; there were further negative comments the following year, 3 June 1914

45 Chapman, *Rise and Demise of Women's Ministry*, 218

46 Chapman, *Rise and Demise of Women's Ministry*, 234

47 See the important debate 'Woman's Place in the Church' at the 1914 Convention, recorded in *Confidence*, November 1914, 208–09, 212–14

48 Chapman, *Rise and Demise of Women's Ministry*, 236

49 *Confidence*, June 1909, 127f

50 Jane Boddy, *A.A. Boddy*, 4

51 These and other issues are also discussed in van der Laan, 'Proceedings of the Leaders' Meetings'

52 *Confidence*, February 1911, 29–31

53 *Confidence*, February 1911, 31. Emphases as in the original

54 *Confidence*, March 1911, 63. Emphases as in the original

55 *Confidence*, June 1912, 135

56 *Newcastle Daily Journal*, 1 June 1912, 7

57 Discussed in Cartwright, *Smith Wigglesworth*, 58

58 *Daily Sketch* 'Baptized in pale blue pyjamas', 6; *Daily Mirror*, 1; and 'Converts Icy Bath', 5, all on 16 May 1913

59 *Daily Mirror*, 4 June 1914

60 *Confidence*, November 1914, 209

61 *Confidence*, November 1914, 213

62 *Confidence*, February 1911, 29–31 and March 1911, 63–65

63 *Confidence*, February 1911, 30

64 *Confidence*, March 1911, 60

65 *Confidence*, December 1912, 284 and 277

66 Van der Laan, 'Proceedings of the Leaders' Meetings', 47

67 *Confidence*, February 1914, 25

68 All responses from Durham Diocesan Visitation Returns, All Saints, Monkwearmouth, 1908

69 *Confidence*, September 1908, 3–5

70 Blumhofer, *Alexander Boddy*, 32

71 *Confidence*, May 1910, 99–104

72 *The Times* 18 May 1910, 4

73 'General Booth's Brother-in-law at the Pentecostal Convention', 8 June 1911, 6

74 Moule, *Veni Creator*

75 *Confidence*, July 1919, 39-43, 45. The remark about predictive prophecy is on p. 40

76 Both extracts from *Confidence*, June 1914, 104

77 *Confidence*, June 1914, 106

78 Robinson's study of Boddy, *The Charismatic Anglican*, makes much of this by comparing Boddy and Michael Harper, and the different courses of the Pentecostal and charismatic movements.

79 Gee, *Wind and Flame*, 37

80 Kay, *Pentecostals in Britain*, 12

Seven

Leadership Exercised: A Heart for Mission and Travelling

So far we have concentrated on Boddy's ministry in Sunderland and Britain, but even that has hinted at his wider influence. Boddy had been a great traveller in his younger days, and this now gave him the impetus to take the Pentecostal message abroad, not just in written form but personally. In addition to the international circulation of *Confidence* Boddy kept a global perspective through his encouragement of overseas missionary work and his key role in the European Leaders Meetings, which became known as the International Advisory Council. Partly in connection with those meetings Boddy made six trips to Europe in the later part of each year from 1908 to 1912. He also made three visits to North America: in 1909, 1912 and 1914.

Organising for Foreign Mission

Boddy had a longstanding interest in overseas mission: he often linked with missionaries in his travels in the 1880s, and in his parish sought to encourage parishioners to take magazines and contribute financially. The manner in which Pentecostalism spread internationally from the very beginning encouraged its adherents to think globally. A conviction that the return of Christ was imminent added to the pressure for mission, especially in areas with little or no previous missionary activity. The discussion early in the history of the Movement about the possible use of speaking in tongues in foreign missionary work is a good indication of the desire of many to engage in such work.

The first tangible sign of explicit missionary activity was the setting up of the PMU in January 1909. The prime mover was Cecil Polhill, who had previously worked with the China Inland Mission (CIM); he became the secretary and treasurer. The PMU was set up on 'faith lines' modelled on the CIM, so its missionaries were not guaranteed support, and were expected to rely on God in a direct sense. Polhill's financial support was crucial in sustaining the PMU for many years, until it eventually became the missionary wing of the Assemblies of God when this denomination was formed in 1924.

The PMU was also very dependent on Boddy's encouragement: the first council meeting was in the All Saints vicarage and Boddy became the editorial secretary. From the formation of the PMU, publicity for it came out through virtually every edition of *Confidence* until the penultimate issue in 1925, when a truncated report, though still substantial, was given on missionary work in Central Africa. Reports from the PMU then moved to *Redemption Tidings* in line with the adoption of the PMU by the Assemblies of God.[1]

The formation of the PMU in 1909 made clear the dominance of Polhill and Boddy: besides the two of them the only people present at the meeting of 9 January were Andrew Bell of Dunfermline and Harry Small of East Wemyss, Fifeshire. Three other men, already becoming known in the Pentecostal Movement, were also named as part of the PMU council, namely T.H. Mundall, a solicitor from Croydon, Victor Wilson from Motherwell, and Andrew Murdoch of Kilsyth. The fledgling council felt able to ask other Pentecostal centres to send representatives and names of candidates for foreign service, as well as offerings to finance the work. The intention to provide training for missionaries was there from the beginning, though salaries were not guaranteed. Candidates needed to 'have received the Baptism of the Holy Ghost themselves', to 'be sincere believers in the Atonement through the Blood . . . and . . . in the infallibility of the Holy Scriptures'. They also needed 'fair knowledge' of the Bible and 'accurate knowledge' of salvation and sanctification. (The exact difference between fair and accurate knowledge was not specified!)[2]

The first group of missionaries went to Western China and Tibet under the guidance of Polhill. Some sixty people – thirty-six women and twenty-four men – were trained and sent out by the PMU by 1925: just over half to Yunnan province in Western China, and others to India (from 1909), the Belgian Congo (1913) and South America (1917).[3] Boddy regularly printed letters from these missionaries in *Confidence.*

The setting up of the PMU illustrates two significant points: firstly, that the reputation of Boddy and the Sunderland Conference (there had been only one at this stage) was already such that they could unselfconsciously assume the leadership of the Pentecostal Movement; and secondly, that Boddy had no desire to create a Pentecostal denomination, even though the existence of the PMU showed his ability to set up a national network centred on Sunderland and using the magazine *Confidence.* Just a little later, in the context of the formation of a PMU for the USA, he wrote:

> The Writer has felt strongly that it is a mistake to form another home organisation, which soon may become another 'church', and follow the fate of so many before it. Union for the purpose of sending out and helping and advising Pentecostal Missionaries in the dark places of Heathenism, is to his mind, the great need today.[4]

Boddy's main contributions over the years to the PMU would seem to be his initial support of Polhill's vision and then giving continuing publicity through *Confidence.*

From 1909 the Sunderland Conventions were known as the International Conference and they included time to discuss PMU business. By the time of the First World War, when Boddy was sixty, his involvement gradually diminished, though Polhill remained fully involved. It was after that war that Polhill came to have less influence as younger leaders from less aristocratic backgrounds took over in Pentecostal assemblies.

Despite his encouragement of the PMU and his desire to see foreign mission flourish, Boddy's main personal contribution to the spread of the Pentecostal message came through his links with and visits to mainland Europe and North America. All the energy expended in his earlier travelling days was now devoted to sharing the gospel and supporting Pentecostal groups.

Europe

Martin Robinson's study of Boddy's travelling ministry suggested that his international trips were more significant than his British ones, and that his visits to mainland Europe were more focussed on pastoral and theological issues, whilst his visits to North America were more evangelistic, more concerned to spread the gospel and the Pentecostal Movement.[5]

The distinction should probably not be pressed too sharply, but Boddy's own reports do suggest that there is something in it. For example, he recognised that there were differences between the North American and British contexts:

> Of course one is not able, as a resident in the old country, fully to appreciate the difficulties of Pentecostal brethren in U.S.A. and Canada, both in guarding against impostors, and in providing for those practically turned out of their churches.[6]

Boddy had wanted from an early stage to travel to Amsterdam to enjoy fellowship with Pastor Polman and the Pentecostal group he led, and this became possible in September 1908, when he had about ten days there. He employed his travel-writing style once again, describing the journey vividly and giving thanks to God for protection when a pane of glass very nearly fell on him in an art gallery. The new element in his account was the far greater attention now given to spiritual matters. In this case there were meetings with the Pentecostal Brethren, who were 'wonderfully alike everywhere'. Details of testimonies, his talks and a Conference in Amsterdam all followed. Amongst other contacts Boddy also had the opportunity to meet with a Pastor de Wilde of Sneek, Holland, who had returned from seeing Pastor Paul in Germany. In such ways the personal links between the leaders of the Pentecostal Movement were strengthened, and by recording them in *Confidence*, Boddy spread an awareness of these links widely, reinforcing the impression of a growing network for his readers.[7]

In each of the next three years Boddy visited Continental Europe on three-week visits at the request of the leaders he knew. So in September and October 1909 he went to Germany, Switzerland and France, following an invitation from the German Brethren.[8] Even on the train journey through France he took the opportunity to give away copies of the Gospels in French, and in his report told his readers how to obtain the tracts from the Scripture Gift Mission.

The main purpose of the 1909 trip was to speak at the third German Conference held at Muhlheim-Rhor, where he joined with Paul, Polman and Barratt. This was a well-attended Conference of some 2,300 people, and Boddy had the honour of giving the closing address, which took the theme of being bearers of the water of life to others.[9]

More opportunities for travel writing and the giving of Gospels (this time in German) followed as he went to Zurich to speak at a Pentecostal Mission. After a brief call in Geneva the final leg of his journey took him to Paris, where he sought to give encouragement to the small group of Pentecostals.[10] Ever active, he found time to speak at a Breton Mission Hall in Le Havre before catching the ferry to England.

A journey to Denmark, Germany and Holland in September and October 1910 presented further occasions for encouragement and for greeting friends old and new. In particular he spent a week living and ministering with his friend Pastor Paul in Berlin. On the return journey he stayed with his other good friends, Pastor and Mrs Polman in Amsterdam, again ministering with them and visiting the sights. He was delighted to be able to report that on successive Sundays he had worshipped with Danish, German, Dutch and English congregations, making the point that this work of God was international, making them 'all one in Christ Jesus'.[11]

Boddy's third and final trip of this kind occurred in November 1911, and once again it was to Germany. His reports in three editions of *Confidence* (November 1911 to January 1912) are characteristically full of travel detail, but also include interesting information about the development of the Pentecostal Movement in Germany (and especially in Silesia), where he was able to meet his daughter Mary, who was staying in Germany at the time. His visit began in Berlin, where he spent a weekend with Pastor Paul, his family and congregation.

From Berlin he travelled another 500 kilometres (so he recorded) eastwards to Kattowitz; it was close to the then Russian border, and, like Sunderland, an industrial town which had developed rapidly in the second half of the nineteenth century. Close to the meeting point of the German, Russian and

Austrian empires, it was where Boddy met up with Mary and they stayed in a Christian guest house.[12] Boddy was intrigued by the proximity of the borders and visited the border posts with Mary, hoping – unsuccessfully – to be allowed into Russia on the strength of his membership of the Imperial Geographical Society of St Petersburg. He also had the opportunity to address the local Pentecostal group on three successive evenings at the invitation of Brother Kaper, whom he had met in Berlin the previous year.

After a few days together Mary returned to Hermsdorf and her father stopped at Brieg in Silesia for further meetings, this time at the request of Brother Edel. Edel was the editor of *Pfingstr-grusse*, a Pentecostal paper for Germany similar to *Confidence*, and would later visit the Sunderland Convention, in 1913. Boddy again preached on one of his favourite topics, 'The Coming of the Lord', reporting that it 'proved to be a message which He [the Lord] has intended I should give'.[13]

The final leg of his visit to Silesia was to the capital, Breslau, where lived Pastor Regehly, who had been in Sunderland at the 1910 Convention. He wrote that he was warmly received, despite anti-British feeling in a recent political gathering. Indeed, he began his article by referring to the strained relations between Britain and Germany and the importance of Christians creating kindly feelings; he had been published in the 'English Secular Press' in this vein, and urged prayer for peace.[14]

The report ended with some reflections on the progress of the Pentecostal Movement in Germany. In a letter from an unnamed friend we learn about the Gemeinschaft movement, which had begun thirty years earlier after a revival, leading to meetings in simple Mission Halls similar to the early Methodist meetings in England. These proved strong recruiting grounds for the Pentecostal Movement, though not with 'richer and more influential people'. The author believed the Gemeinschaft movement had enabled more rapid spread of the Pentecostal message than in England.

Boddy also wrote about the importance of good leadership, mentioning Pastor Paul first, but also naming ten leaders in ten towns – an indication of his excellent links with and knowledge of the German leaders. He drew attention to the fact that only Paul, Voget and Gensichen were Pastors, as clergy of the state church, whilst the others were 'Predigers' – preachers or evangelists. His final assessment was suitably positive: 'In

Germany to-day the Pentecostal visitor from England will find much to strengthen his faith, and to encourage him in his conviction that the Movement is from the Lord. Hallelujah!'[15]

Boddy also had two other visits to the Continent to take part in international leaders' meetings. The first of these was to Hamburg, Germany, just three months after his first visit to Amsterdam in 1908. This was a follow-up meeting to one for German pastors the previous year in Barmen, held this time with leaders from other countries, with Boddy and Polhill as the British representatives.[16] About fifty pastors from Germany attended, headed by Meyer, Paul and Voget, together with Barratt from Norway, Polman and Kok from Holland, and others from Switzerland and Sweden. Boddy, Barratt and Paul were the main contributors, with both scriptural addresses and reflection on the emerging practice of their Pentecostal groups; Polhill spoke on the importance of foreign missions, with support from Barratt.

Though it seems from elsewhere that Boddy generally preached through an interpreter, he was proficient in conversational French and possibly German too. Polhill had learnt German as a young man during a two-month stay with his Catholic uncle in Stuttgart in 1883.[17] Their sense of confidence in leadership was enhanced by their ease with travel and foreign languages and this enabled them to become prominent in the international gatherings. Their prominence was further consolidated by the decision to hold leaders' meetings at the Sunderland Whitsuntide Conventions. Barratt has rightly been described as the apostle of the Pentecostal Movement in Europe by reason of his priority in time and the length of his ministry.[18] Nonetheless, Boddy's continued links with Barratt seem to have been crucial in developing Barratt's own understanding and in creating a European network of Pentecostal leaders. Within this network Boddy was something of a spiritual father figure. These men – there were no women in the group – formed the nucleus of the International Advisory Council.

The International Advisory Council

The International Advisory Council found itself tackling three main issues: the significance of speaking in tongues, organising the Pentecostal Movement, and providing sound counsel to counter extremists.

The significance of speaking in tongues was repeatedly discussed by these leaders, at meetings held in Sunderland and at others in Germany and Holland. Over time it became clear that Barratt saw speaking in tongues as *the* sign of baptism in the Holy Spirit, whereas Boddy and others could not make such a complete equation of the two phenomena, even when that had been their own experience. Along with the differences over organisation discussed in the previous chapter, when Boddy's view prevailed at the International Advisory Council meeting of 1912 in Amsterdam, this led to Barratt's leaving the leadership group in 1913.

All the leaders were agreed in wanting to guard against what they saw as extreme teaching, though of course the Pentecostal teaching was itself seen as extreme by other Christians. Boddy's pastoral approach tended to hold sway in the statements issued by the group. Good examples of this can be seen in the final declaration from the 1912 Amsterdam meeting. There was just one reference to speaking in tongues, and it read somewhat negatively:

> We do not teach that all who have been baptized in the Holy Ghost, even if they should speak in Tongues, have already received the fulness of the blessing of Christ implied in this Baptism. There may be, and in most cases will be, a progressive entering, in of the believer into this fulness, according to the measure of faith, obedience, and knowledge of the recipient.[19]

Boddy's influence can also be detected in the comments about motivations for seeking this baptism, in the light of his frequent comments on the priority of the facts of the gospel even over faith and feelings:

> While we encourage all believers to seek the same full Baptism as recorded in the Acts of the Apostles, together with its manifestations, yet we would earnestly warn against merely seeking soulish experiences or fleshly demonstrations, which not a few have mistaken for the work of the Spirit.[20]

Although these meetings had limited influence after the First World War they were of great importance in setting the tone of much of the European Pentecostal Movement up to 1914.[21] Boddy's long pastoral experience, and his desire to see the historic churches renewed, were crucial elements in the agreements reached, and helped to develop a slightly different flavour from that of the Pentecostal Movement in North America.

North America

Boddy made three visits to the USA and Canada in the period before the First World War, apparently at the invitation and financing of American friends.[22] The first, in 1909, lasted four weeks; the other two, in 1912 and 1914, were for nearly three months. He travelled widely in that time, meeting old friends and making new ones, visiting many denominational churches, especially the Episcopal sister churches to the Church of England, as well as Pentecostal assemblies, both black and white. On one occasion he went to Azusa Street, Los Angeles.

In continuity with his earlier life he wrote extensive travelogues, not in book form, but in the pages of *Confidence*, and no fewer than nineteen editions have some part of the continuous narrative he produced about these three visits. From this wealth of writing I have mostly selected themes which recur, rather than attempt to describe his detailed itineraries.

The traveller returns

On his visits Boddy was ready to travel long distances, especially to see friends he had made. The visit in 1909 saw him away from home for four weeks, with just over two spent in Camp Meetings near Toronto in Canada and Alliance in Ohio, with briefer visits to Chicago and New York. As always, he was curious to see the sights, and on this trip he was pleased to revisit Niagara Falls, this time in heat – twenty years earlier it had been icy.[23]

The visit of 1912 was arranged around an invitation to conduct a mission in Winnipeg from 28 September to 8 October, but Boddy used the opportunity to visit New York, Washington

DC and New Orleans, to go west to Arizona and Mexico, to visit the Grand Canyon, to see friends in California as well as at the Azusa Street Mission, to conduct the mission in Winnipeg, and to return via Chicago. He provided a map of his journey in North America, showing his near circumnavigation of the USA by train as he passed through half the continental states. He reckoned to have travelled 10,000 miles overland and a further 6,000 miles across the ocean.[24] His final transatlantic trip in 1914 was structured around four Camp Meetings where he was an honoured speaker: three in the east in Massachusetts, Philadelphia and Atlanta, and one on the west coast at Cazadero, North California. Although this trip was cut short by the outbreak of war in Europe it still lasted for nearly three months and involved a total of 14,000 miles of travelling and frequent ministry – a real feat of stamina for a man in his sixtieth year.[25]

Friendships

When Boddy visited other European countries it was generally at the request of his friends amongst the leaders there, and the same pattern was true in North America. A full list of people he met and corresponded with would be very lengthy. Clearly wherever possible he sustained relationships over time and distance, and that he met or wrote to many of the leading figures in the North American Pentecostal Movement.

The very first Camp Meeting he attended at Stouffville, near Toronto, came through his contact with Daniel Awrey, who had attended the Sunderland Convention earlier in the same month. This meeting was the first Pentecostal Camp Meeting held in Canada, and had its origins in the Mennonite church. Other invitations, such as one to speak at a Camp in Alliance, Ohio, seem to have come about through knowledge of his work in *Confidence*, but his lifelong capacity for building friendship served him well, and he made many new friends and contacts through that meeting in June 1909, including his namesake Pastor J.T. Boddy.[26]

One of the first pastors he met at Alliance was William Hamner Piper of the Stone Church, Chicago, editor of 'the best printed Pentecostal paper I have seen, "The Latter Rain Evangel."'[27] It is likely that Boddy also met David Wesley Myland, a layman at the Stone Church and author of *The Latter*

Rain Covenant, since he wrote an Introduction to this important book, described as 'the first definitive Pentecostal theology that was widely distributed'.[28]

Piper's death at the end of 1911 was reported in *Confidence*.[29] However, Boddy's fellowship with the Stone Church was continued through Piper's widow, Lydia, when he returned in 1912. On this visit he certainly spent time with David Myland.[30] Boddy and Myland had much in common in their teaching and experience, not least a desire for unity which overcame doctrinal differences and a readiness to accept different descriptions and patterns of spiritual experience.

Pastor Joseph H. King of the Pentecostal Holiness Church had attended the 1912 Sunderland Convention as part of a two-year world tour, and travelled across the Atlantic with Boddy later that year. This, too, was a significant relationship, for King was a highly respected leader and theologian, in the holiness Pentecostal strand. The friendship was renewed in 1914 at the Atlanta Camp Meeting, and Boddy commended him, writing, 'There is no one with a truer heart in Pentecostal circles.'[31]

Another notable friendship was the one Boddy developed with the Revd A.B. Simpson, president of the Christian and Missionary Alliance, an organisation with hundreds of missionaries preaching the fourfold gospel of regeneration, baptism of the Holy Ghost, healing of the Body, and the coming of the Lord. This friendship began in June 1909 and was continued on Boddy's other visits. It is notable because Simpson was a significant figure in the Protestant church in the USA and though he showed sympathy towards Pentecostal ideas he did not associate himself with them. Boddy was very happy to develop the friendship, despite some theological disagreements, and he was able to accept Simpson's invitation to preach on Divine Healing in July 1914.[32]

Boddy's friendship with Mr and Mrs Montgomery of Oakland, California, gave him access to the West Coast. The Montgomeries had been present at the 1909 Sunderland Convention and Boddy visited them in both 1912 and 1914. Mr Montgomery was a mine owner, whose wife Carrie Judd was commended by Boddy as the 'able Editress' of 'The Triumphs of the Faith' for thirty years. Boddy had a high regard for them both; in his report on what transpired to be his last Camp Meeting in the USA, at Cazadero he wrote, 'Mrs Carrie Judd

Montgomery's name was a guarantee against fanaticism or wild fire, and the meetings were controlled by the Spirit.'[33]

One final indication of the importance of friendships to Boddy is given by his 1,000 mile 'detour' to Winnipeg to be with a number of people he had known in Sunderland. Some were emigrants; others, like Mr and Mrs S.V. Carter and Mr and Mrs Lockhart, had visited Sunderland, and Boddy was pleased to renew the friendship. In his initial remarks about them, he recorded that the Carters worshipped both at St Luke's, an Anglican church, and at Pentecostal gatherings.[34]

He later emphasised that a 'Professor Baker, of St John's College (Anglican), is in full sympathy with the Pentecostal blessing', that some ordinands had received the blessing, and that Archdeacon Phair of Winnipeg continued to stand firm on the blessing. News that the Archdeacon had received 'Pentecost with the Sign of Tongues' had been brought during the visit of a Mr Gibson from Winnipeg to the first anniversary Vestry meeting in Monkwearmouth, resulting in Hallelujahs and delight that such a prominent church man was involved;[35] Boddy had also printed the testimony of Archdeacon Phair to 'speaking in an unknown tongue' soon after that.[36] This friendship with fellow Anglicans was especially precious to him, no doubt helping to authenticate his own commitment to the Pentecostal blessing within the Church of England.[37]

Unity

As with the Pentecostal Movement in Europe Boddy was very concerned to promote the unity of the church, and particularly of those who testified to Pentecostal experience. Not least he believed that lack of unity would undermine the Pentecostal witness to the gospel. In his report on his 1912 visit he gave his most extended exposition of this theme, based on talks he gave at the Colegrave Camp Meeting, four or five miles north of Los Angeles.

> The theme which the Lord brought me back to each time ere I closed my addresses, was the hope that the sad divisions among Pentecostal people here in the United States, and especially in Los Angeles would be healed up by a Baptism of Love. I pleaded with them to allow others to be fully

persuaded in their own minds. I pleaded with them also to bear when spoken against, to be silent and not to answer back again, and to pray for the other side lovingly, whichever side they belonged to.

On the Sunday morning, when kneeling in one of our Episcopal churches in Los Angeles, the Lord had given me, I felt sure, words I must place before these brethren. It took the form of a resolution which the meeting endorsed most cordially. The resolution was this:-

> "RECOGNISING THE GREAT NEED OF UNITY in the Body of the Lord (see Cor. *(sic)* xii., 25 and xi.,30-31), and noting the opportunities Satan is getting through sad divisions – *We*, by the help and grace of our Lord, do undertake individually and collectively, to refrain from condemning one another in the matter of the question known on the one hand as 'THE SECOND WORK OF GRACE,' and on the other as 'THE FINISHED WORK OF CHRIST.'
>
> We also undertake to do all we can, in love, to dissuade our beloved brethren and sisters in Pentecost from giving way to a spirit of harshness in these matters, but allowing each one to be fully persuaded in his own mind."

I was thankful that such a glad endorsement was given to it here and elsewhere.[38]

The clear implication of his appeal is a lack of unity amongst the Pentecostals, and that harsh words had been used against others. The specific issues he picked out were differences over 'The Second Work of Grace' and 'The Finished Work of Christ'; the former position was the earlier one amongst Pentecostals, and drew on the holiness tradition. It emphasised the need of three spiritual experiences: justification, sanctification and baptism in the Spirit. The latter position was a recent innovation in 1912, developed by the dynamic young preacher William Durham. He advocated that two distinct experiences were necessary, namely regeneration and baptism in the Spirit. The conflict was especially marked in Los Angeles, since Durham had set up his own mission there in 1911 and made it his base until his premature death the following year.

Boddy's own position was closer to the former doctrine, and it was ably defended by his friend J.H. King; but as so often his instincts were for unity. Once again Boddy's Anglicanism comes through, as he adds the detail that these words came to him 'when kneeling in one of our Episcopal churches in Los Angeles': his desire for unity was expressed through his attendance both with the Pentecostal believers and at the church of his denomination, as well as in the statement above. Sadly unity was not forthcoming.

He was pleased to commend the unity of the believers in Winnipeg, who came together during his visit after having been separated by doctrinal differences. At the conclusion of his account he reported: 'Several letters have reached me since I have returned home expressing great thankfulness for my messages advocating unity and love between the brethren.'[39]

It is tempting to generalise from these remarks to assume that Boddy felt this way about the church throughout the USA, and he has been cited in that way.[40] Certainly he does refer to divisions in the USA, but the remarks here should be read in the light of the intensity of religious life in Los Angeles at the time, in which groups 'fought each other almost to a standstill'.[41] There were other occasions when Boddy was very warm about American groups. For example, reflecting on three nights of ministry at a coloured people's Mission in Indianapolis he wrote: 'I do not remember in all my journeyings to have been among a more lovely people in the Pentecostal work.'[42]

The 'colour' question

Boddy was very struck by what was known as 'the colour problem' in the USA, and he hoped that Pentecostal witness might overcome such divisions, along the lines of the hope at Asuza Street in 1907 that the baptism of the Spirit would overcome barriers of colour. There are references to 'coloured people' in each of his three accounts, most notably in his 1912 account, when he spent longer in Southern states.

He was frequently aware that his needs were being met by coloured people, such as waiters and train conductors. So he held 'helpful talks' with a waiter at Niagara Falls; in Spartansburg, South Carolina, he had a conversation with another waiter about salvation, to their mutual agreement; and he had fellowship with a coloured porter on a train heading across a desert.[43] A century later the language he used might seem patronising, but his willingness to speak with all manner of people was evident in his earlier life (think back to the women on the Russian barges, or the traders of North Africa) and his attitude of acceptance is consistent throughout his life. Unlike some of his contemporaries Boddy seems to have had no problem in recognising 'coloured people' as fellow believers, with an equal claim to salvation through Christ.

He regularly sought out 'coloured churches' on his visits: on his first Sunday in the USA in 1912, 11th August in Washington DC, he attended the early Communion service at Trinity Episcopal church. He then found St Luke's Colored Episcopal church, where he met the minister, Mr Brown; and later he went into a coloured Baptist Mission Church because of the energetic preaching.[44]

In Atlanta he noted that coloured people were in the majority on the streets and tram cars and there was separation of races in public transport. A white man could preach in a black church but not go to the home of the coloured pastor. He recorded an account of a lynching of six Negro men, noting the lack of any proper trial. He went so far as to say that to him as a Christian visitor 'the negro folk seem an attractive, happy people, childlike in their love of strong colours and strong statements' but that '[o]nly a few white people has one heard speak kindly of the black people'.[45]

At the Azusa Street Mission in Los Angeles he was delighted to pray with the wife and mother of William Seymour, referring to the 'two coloured friends and a white brother [himself]'. He was pleased to find that the Sunday congregation still included white and coloured people. In his brief remarks about Azusa Street he mentioned that the many religious people who had come made a difficult crowd for a coloured preacher to handle.[46] This could be a downplaying of Seymour's abilities, but it could equally be a recognition that the social conventions of the context were against him.

Unfortunately, the Pentecostal Movement as a whole did move away from the ethnic idealism expressed at Asuza Street in 1907 and still there in Boddy's practice and thinking. From the beginning there were racist attitudes amongst some influential leaders – Charles Parham was one such. As time went on, social pressures led to increasing segregation, and there was little thought-through opposition to it.[47] Boddy's own comments tended to assume the rightness of his own position, without his feeling any need to provide biblical or theological arguments in its favour.

Critical comments

Boddy was prepared both to congratulate and to criticise where he believed it necessary, and in addition to the 'colour question' he was critical of two other aspects of Pentecostal practice that he encountered in the USA. His remarks about money-raising tactics were expressed in the context of a visit to a church in New Orleans where he encountered a variety of fundraising efforts:

> How the dear people of this church and many other churches need true Pentecostal teaching, and complete separation from worldly methods. Wherever I went it was money, money, much more than Christ, with the honourable exception of the P.E. Church I mentioned in my last letter. There it was Christ only; and no reference to money-making.[48]

This makes clear that he found the problem of money wherever he went. He also criticised the church in England for its methods of raising money.

The only other occasion in his North American accounts that he discussed money specifically was in the wider context of the supposed healing ministry of a Dr Yoakum. Yoakum worked in the Pisgah suburb of Los Angeles, running a home for down-and-outs, a tabernacle for preaching, the Ark for reclaimed girls and women, and best known for faith healing. Boddy's description is headed, unusually,: 'Appreciation and Candid Criticism'.[49] Boddy described him as a man of God and saw him behave in loving ways to visitors coming for help. On the other hand, he did not see any miracles of healing, despite claims to many; he disliked the large-scale practice of sending out blessed handkerchiefs; and he repeated the description of Yoakum as having 'optimania' – taking an 'exaggerated or rosy view' of his ministry.

Boddy also reported in detail questions he had put to Yoakum about a questionable investment in a Mexican mine. Boddy felt that Yoakum had made mistakes through impulsiveness and was inclined to believe the best of him; nonetheless he did make suggestions for changes, some of which he believed were taken up.

Boddy also criticised him for being ordained irregularly as a bishop by an irregular archbishop, but his Anglican view on this topic did not prevail with Yoakum.

The final criticism was over the pressure exerted on people to give money:

GIVE AND BE HEALED (!!!).
An offering was made, people coming up and making their gifts. Dr. Yoakum told them emphatically that people were OFTEN HEALED if they gave as the Lord wished them to give. I must confess I did not like this way of appealing for large gifts.[50]

Boddy's conclusion was that Yoakum was genuinely motivated by God's love for the outcast, but was overwhelmed by the needs of people. Boddy's remedy was study and meditation on God's word. His own pastoral sensitivity came to the fore in this series of meetings, a sensitivity to the needs of the people and to the man attempting to minister to them.

Keenness and generosity

It would be wrong to end this brief description of Boddy's engagement with the North American church on a negative note. He wrote his own summary after his final visit of 1914, offering four constructive observations, quoted here:

1. I found the Pentecostal people in USA Orthodox as to the Scriptures, the Atonement, the Coming of Christ, Hell and Heaven, etc. Much apostasy in Christendom, but our people (often called Apostolic Faith or Latter Rain Disciples) always true and loyal to these truths. For this we do thank God.

2. I noticed that in USA there is a love of physical 'manifestations'. Many find them stimulating and strengthening. That which shocks some does not seem irreverent at all to others who wish to be very true to God. There is a great danger in

judging. We know that in suppressing what we think is the 'flesh' there is a danger of 'quenching the Spirit'.

3. . . . there was a loving spirit, there was adoration of the Lamb, and a longing desire to help all into the very highest experience. There is a beautiful desire to help others in spiritual things.

4. The friends in USA are very appreciative and generous. They recognise sincerity and are grateful to the messenger who has a live message. Keenness is a key note in America. Thank God also for those who are keen in serving him.[51]

His own standards of orthodoxy are of course evident, as is his aspiration to think the best of people. He knew that the American way of religion was not always to his taste, but he was willing to work with others whenever possible; in this way he endeavoured to live out his call for unity. He disliked most of what he saw by way of money-raising, but he was the product of an established church which still was able to draw on considerable historic resources. In his thankfulness for friends' generosity to him perhaps there was some recognition that church life truly was different in the USA.

Travelling Reflections

There is no doubt that Boddy's travels abroad were an important part of his ministry and cohered well with his work through *Confidence*. The travelling reinforced the personal bonds between leaders in the Pentecostal Movement, and gave its members a sense of belonging to something wider and bigger than their local assembly. Wacker has commented on the 'exceptional geographical mobility' and 'underlying assumptions about personal autonomy' of many early Pentecostal leaders, beginning his case with Boddy.[52] While it is true that Boddy did travel widely, the criticisms seem overstated in his case at least, with a careless conflation of Boddy's travelling career of over thirty years into the period of his Pentecostal experience.

Boddy was probably a little sensitive about such charges at the time, and he made an implicit defence on one occasion, when leaving for Germany and to see his daughter Mary, in November 1911:

> A long-delayed opportunity for a little change had come to the Editor of "Confidence". He was able to leave Sunderland on the 2nd November for a rather late "summer" holiday. The Annual Parish Gathering on All Saints' Day (November 1st) had taken place, and after it the Vicar felt that he could be spared awhile, and that other voices might be heard in All Saints' Church.[53]

It is important to keep the time spent on these trips in perspective. From 1908 to 1914 Boddy spent approximately 41 weeks out of the UK, an average of less than six weeks per year. More than half this time was concentrated into the two lengthy trips to North America in 1912 and 1914; in 1913 he had no foreign trips. He did also travel about the UK, but again, these were fairly short visits for conferences. In all, he was probably not out of his parish in Sunderland for much longer than any modern parish priests taking their holiday entitlement and going on retreats and to occasional conferences. He had a succession of reliable curates working with him, and he was assiduous in his parish duties and acknowledgement of episcopal authority.

Boddy's wider ministry, through organising mission and travelling himself, played a key role in the development of the Pentecostal Movement in Europe and North America. He was far from being alone, but his influence was substantial in holding people together, especially in Europe. His work as a minister in a State church was noted by others, such as Barratt, and gave some credibility to the movement. There was also mutual benefit for ministers who could bring to their own churches ministers from other parts of the world, a phenomenon still encountered today by white ministers in some African contexts. All these reasons will have played their part in stimulating travel between the various Pentecostal centres.

Notes

1 *Confidence* 1926, 8
2 The details in this paragraph are in *Confidence*, January 1909, 13–5; the report is preceded by the words 'VERY IMPORTANT'
3 For details and discussion see Kay, 'Pentecostal Missionary Union', 90
4 *Confidence* August 1909, 175
5 Robinson, *The Charismatic Anglican*, 79
6 *Confidence*, August 1909, 175
7 *Confidence*, September 1908, 6–9, 11–12, 16–17
8 *Confidence*, October 1909, 223–7 and November 1909, 245–48
9 *Confidence*, November 1909, 245–16
10 *Confidence*, November 1909, 263
11 *Confidence*, October 1910, 243
12 *Confidence*, November 1911, 261
13 *Confidence*, December 1911, 282
14 *Confidence*, January 1912, 3 and 5
15 *Confidence*, January 1912, 6
16 *Confidence*, December 1908, 24 and Supplement
17 Hocken, *Cecil Polhill*, 117 and 130, fn 87
18 E.g. Bloch-Hoell, *Pentecostal Movement*, 75 citing also David du Plessis and Donald Gee
19 'Declaration' *Confidence*, December 1912, 277 item 3
20 'Declaration' *Confidence*, December 1912, 277 item 5
21 Van der Laan, 'Proceedings of the Leaders' Meetings', 49
22 *Confidence*, April 1913, 70 gives a clear reference to such funding for his 1912 trip
23 *Confidence*, September 1909, 198
24 *Confidence*, April 1913, 70
25 *Confidence*, December 1914, 226
26 *Confidence*, August 1909, 172
27 *Confidence*, September 1909, 198
28 Robinson, 'Myland', 632. Boddy reprinted his Introduction and an extract from the book, though he called it *The Latter Rain Pentecost* (*Confidence*, November 1911, 258). On Myland, see also the useful biography and assessment in Jacobsen, *Thinking in the Spirit*, 110–33
29 *Confidence*, February 1912, 43
30 *Confidence*, January 1913, 16.
31 *Confidence*, September 1914, 13. For more on King see Jacobsen, *Thinking in the Spirit*, 164–93
32 *Confidence*, September 1909, 199; October 1914, 183
33 *Confidence*, December 1914, 224
34 *Confidence*, August 1912, 182
35 *Confidence*, September 1908, 6

36 *Confidence*, December 1908, 12–13
37 *Confidence*, January 1913, 15
38 *Confidence*, November 1912, 246
39 *Confidence*, April 1913, 70
40 E.g. Wacker, *Heaven Above*, 79
41 Bartleman, the first historian of Azusa Street, cited in Wacker, *Heaven Above*, 79. Bartleman had attended the Sunderland Convention in 1910, and his views would have been known to Boddy
42 *Confidence*, January 1913, 17
43 *Confidence*, September 1909, 199; September 1912, 208; December 1912, 282–83
44 *Confidence*, September 1912, 203
45 *Confidence*, September 1912, 208
46 *Confidence*, October 1912, 232
47 Jacobsen, *Thinking in the Spirit*, 260–62
48 *Confidence*, October 1912, 223. The P.E. Church mentioned seems to be a Cathedral on 120th Street, New York
49 There is a substantial account in *Confidence*, November 1912, 248–51; 255–58 printed in small type
50 *Confidence*, November 1912, 256
51 *Confidence*, December 1914, 226–27
52 Wacker, *Heaven Below*, 214
53 *Confidence*, November 1911, 258

Eight

Leadership Exercised: Developing Pentecostal Theology

As we have seen, Boddy was primarily a pastor who desired to help people encounter God through Christ in the power of the Holy Spirit. He did not set out a systematic theology in his writing, though he did write quite extensively about some issues, notably spiritual gifts. In what follows I seek to set out the main theological issues of significance to Boddy himself, briefly locating his views in the context of his own time.

Some indication of Boddy's influence in the English-speaking world is given in a recent *Reader in Pentecostal and Charismatic Studies*: this book provides nearly one hundred extracts from writers in English throughout the twentieth century from the Pentecostal and charismatic movements globally. Very few writers have more than one contribution; Boddy is top of the list with four extracts, and there are another five from *Confidence* by other authors. Given the wide-ranging nature of the Reader this is an extraordinary total from one source.[1]

For six years, from April 1911 to January 1917, Boddy printed a short statement about the magazine at the front of each edition of *Confidence*. This included some history of the Movement, especially the Whitsuntide conventions, and also the following statement of key beliefs.

"Confidence" advocates an unlimited Salvation for Spirit, Soul, and Body; the Honouring of the Precious Blood; Identification with Christ in Death and Resurrection, etc.; Regeneration, Sanctification; the Baptism of the Holy Ghost; the Soon-Coming of the Lord in the air (1 Thess. iv., 14); Divine Healing and Health (Acts iv., 13) . . . His [the Editor's] desire, and that of his helpers, is that ever in this Paper "He (Christ Jesus) may have the pre-eminence."[2]

We shall therefore look at these issues, given their importance for Boddy, and also his ecclesiology and his understanding of sacraments, both of significance for him as an Anglican.[3] He was always a pastor more than a systematic theologian; there is, for example, no use of historical criticism of the Bible in his writings, though he does make use of older, more conservative scholarship. His beliefs are revealed at least as much by his practice as by his words, so his theology should be read in the light of his pastoral concerns.

The Centrality of Christ and the Passion

The Honouring of the Precious Blood; Identification with Christ in Death and Resurrection, etc. "He (Christ Jesus) may have the pre-eminence."

From first to last Boddy believed that the Pentecostal blessing was *from* Christ and *to glorify* Christ. He never varied from what is often regarded as a key evangelical tenet, that Christ must be central. Thus in 1922, in the last edition of *Confidence* Boddy produced in Sunderland, he included a long article headed simply 'A Personal Testimony'. We have used this article in previous chapters because it contains personal information about his own life and developing theology. It is significant, then, that he ended the piece with a description of how the Holy Spirit had led him to see the central place of Christ '[f]or He has taught me not to place Him – the Holy Spirit – in the place of Christ, but to allow Him to glorify Christ in us and through us. It is Christ alone Who saves.'

In a statement wholly in line with the Holiness movement he went on to emphasise union (elsewhere termed *identification*) with Christ as the key to victory over sin: 'The Holy Spirit has led me to see, and therefore now to teach, our Union with Christ in His Death, Resurrection, and Ascension, with its victory over sin and disease.'[4]

In the same issue he wrote an article setting out the familiar evangelical doctrine of new birth, with a total commitment to

Christ as the Saviour, to whom Christians are united by faith. It is the role of the Holy Spirit to make that union real in the experience of the believer, he wrote, and went on to rejoice that there may be a time of 'rapturous joy'. However, Boddy clearly stated that the Christian should follow this order in both belief and practice: first fact (meaning the fact of salvation in Christ revealed in Scripture), then faith, and then feeling, a point he made on several occasions in connection with both salvation and baptism in the Holy Spirit. He warned that new believers are frequently tempted to reverse the order, and so become discouraged in difficult times.[5] Here is the voice of the evangelical pastor devoted to Christ.

The same emphasis on Christ was there in the very first issue of *Confidence* in 1908: the first theological article in this first magazine was written by Mary Boddy and headed 'His Own Blood'. The article set out their key beliefs in the power of Christ's blood, shed on the Cross, to give 'Perfect Victory over sin, disease, and all the powers of darkness'. The final section of the article had the subheading 'It is all Jesus Christ' and made clear their belief in the centrality of the Cross of Christ in Christian living and the role of the Holy Spirit:

> The Triune God, quickening our mortal bodies, all our faculties vitalized by the Life-giving Spirit into such an apprehension of the risen and glorified Christ that, as we "stand fast in this liberty," walking by faith and not by sight (or feelings), the Holy Ghost can manifest Himself as He wills through us to the building up of His Body and the edifying of His Church. Glory be to Jesus.[6]

The 'pleading of the Blood' was a common feature of evangelicalism of the time, and the Boddys continued to emphasise it. In the second issue of *Confidence* it begins with what were described as 'Verses given by the Spirit – 7th May 1908 – M.B. [Mary Boddy]'. These included the lines:

> But fears will often come; dear Lord,
> Lest Satan should deceive;
> "Fear not, my child, for thou art safe,
> My Blood doth shelter thee."[7]

The verses were followed by an article by Alexander, 'Our Faithful God', which referred to the cunning of the devil in creating fear over 'Baptism of the Holy Ghost', and again advocating 'pleading the Blood' and concentrating on Christ:

> The Blood of the everlasting Covenant is sufficient to overcome the Enemy to-day. We are safe under the Blood. The pleading of the Blood in the power of the Holy Spirit will put to flight all the powers of darkness. Best of all, let us magnify Jesus until he is so great as to completely shut out the Devil from our thoughts.[8]

These quotations must suffice: virtually every edition of *Confidence* continued in similar language, and the views expressed by both Alexander and Mary were consistent throughout this time.

Salvation, regeneration, sanctification

> . . . *unlimited Salvation for Spirit, Soul, and Body;* . . . *Regeneration, Sanctification*

Developing the theme of the centrality of Christ, we note the emphasis placed by Boddy on *unlimited* Salvation, this being the first item in his list of doctrines. In this he was following the main lines of the teaching of the Keswick Movement, which, if not outrightly Arminian, was certainly not high Calvinist. The absence of limit, then, is primarily a belief that all people are potentially in the scope of salvation, in contrast to the Calvinist belief in double predestination.

We should probably find a secondary referent for *unlimited* in the phrase *for Spirit, Soul, and Body*, with the concept that salvation affected every part of a person. It was spiritual first, but also had implications for healing, as we shall see in the section on Divine Healing. Boddy began his Roker Tract 'Health in Christ', reprinted in *Confidence* in August 1910, with a discussion of the meaning of salvation in the New Testament:

> Our Lord is a "Saviour" because He SAVES. Now when we read in the Acts of the Apostles (xvi., 30), "Believe on the Lord Jesus Christ and thou shalt be saved," we must not forget

what this glorious word "saved" can include if we do not limit our faith in Him who is the Life. The Word "Saved" is rightly translated "made whole" in St. Luke viii., 48 – "Thy faith hath made thee whole," and in the preceding chapter at the 50th verse, exactly the same sentence is translated, "Thy faith hath saved thee." The Greek verb "save" (sozo) is rendered "make whole" in about eleven passages in the New Testament.*
*See Grimm and Thayer's Lexicon of the Greek Testament.

Here was Boddy's basis for a holistic view of salvation, which led him to advocate and practise healing through prayer well before his Pentecostal experience of 1907, and possibly as early as 1892.

A two-stage experience of God was also taught by the Keswick Movement, with both regeneration and sanctification being by faith.[9] Boddy taught these doctrines, describing them as the work of the Holy Ghost:

> We know that it is the Spirit of Christ, and we realise that we are one with Christ in a new and increasingly real manner. We begin to understand more fully, more experimentally, that we were on the Cross in Christ, and that in Him we buried self and "Sin" in His grave, and with Him have already risen to "Victory" in the Heavenlies. For the Holy Ghost has come to guide us into all Truth and to glorify Christ. (John xvi.,13–14.)

> As Jesus of Nazareth was empowered by the Holy Ghost to live the "Wonderful Life," and to have constant victory over the Devil, so this same Holy Spirit is the *power*, and the only power, in which we may live out Christ's Life on Earth, and ever gain the victory over His enemy and ours. He makes the indwelling Christ very real to us (Ephes. iii., 17).

He continued later in the article:

> By trusting the Redemption through His precious Blood, we become partakers of the Divine Nature . . . The Holy Ghost is the Divine Friend who brings this about. We are born of the Spirit.

> We are in Christ. This is Birth from above or regeneration. Christ is now in us, and this leads on to 'Holiness' or 'Sanctification.'

This is His aim – 'That He might sanctify the people with His own Blood, He suffered without the camp' (Heb. xiii., 12).[10]

Even in the extreme conditions of the First World War he did not compromise his belief in the necessity of salvation through Christ alone. In 1915 he reprinted a tract on salvation, 'The Sin against the Soldier and the Saviour', he had distributed in northern France. 'The sacrifice of these human lives is set forth as being sufficient to merit heaven without the atoning work of Christ. What an awful departure from the truth of God is this!'[11]
 However, Boddy did not stop at salvation and regeneration, as the next section will show.

Baptism in the Spirit and Spiritual Gifts

 . . . the Baptism of the Holy Ghost . . . Divine Healing and Health (Acts iv., 13).

Boddy was among the group of teachers and pastors who had enormous influence on the development of the understanding of baptism in the Spirit and spiritual gifts in the twentieth century. William Kay's scholarly history of British Pentecostalism begins its theological survey of spiritual gifts with Boddy and the Sunderland Conventions. In assessing current Pentecostal beliefs about vocal spiritual gifts he concludes that 'the main outlines of understanding have remained largely intact' from those of the Sunderland Conventions.[12] The importance of the healing ministry to Boddy is apparent from its specific inclusion in the list of key beliefs, and its contested status indicated by being one of just two items in the list with a reference to Scripture.[13]

Baptism of the Holy Ghost

Theological understanding of the entry into Pentecostal experi- ence was varied in the earliest years of the twentieth century as writers in various parts of the world struggled to describe in words what they took to be a divine encounter – mystical experi- ence has always been difficult to verbalise. There was no uniformity even regarding the appropriate shorthand phrase that should be used, with *Baptism of the Holy Ghost, Baptism in the Holy Spirit* and *Fullness of the Spirit* being three of the more common terms used. Similarly, there was considerable debate about the relationship of this experience with those of regeneration and sanctification.

Boddy himself took the view that there were three events that God had for people, namely regeneration, sanctification and baptism in the Spirit. A hint of this was contained in the first edition of *Confidence*, where he wrote about the Pentecostal assembly at Kilsyth, and their leader 'Bro. Murdoch . . . [who] . . . is scarcely equalled in his loving guidance of souls into salvation, sanctification, and the Baptism of the Holy Ghost.'[14]

He put it more clearly in his report of a discussion on speaking in tongues at the Pentecostal Conference in Hamburg, Germany in December 1908:

> Thus we see three steps :-(1) Justification through the Blood, (2) Sanctification by union with Him in Death and Burial, and (3) the Baptism of the Holy Spirit with this helpful sign as a divine encouragement.[15]

Boddy's fullest statement on this issue was in his 1912 article 'The Holy Ghost for us' discussed above in connection with regeneration and sanctification. This was a more systematic article than some he wrote, and he made clear his acceptance of the well-worked Wesleyan Holiness theology of regeneration and sanctification. This he set out in six points. In his seventh he went on to state: 'But there is a greater work still which He [the Holy Ghost of God] can do. He can endue us with power to witness for Christ. This is through "Baptism" into the Holy Spirit.' He linked this event with the prediction of John the Baptist in Matthew 3:11 ('He shall baptize you with the Holy Ghost, and with fire'), and with the sign of Tongues on the Day of Pentecost (Acts 2) and again at Caesarea (Acts 10) and Ephesus (Acts 19).[16]

This belief in three spiritual experiences was in keeping with Boddy's background in the Holiness tradition. His friend J.H. King became one of the foremost exponents of this view in the USA, articulating this clearly in response to the two-stage 'Finished Work' theology of W.J. Durham.[17] Boddy did seek to hold together Pentecostals holding both views, as we saw in the previous chapter, but his own view was similar to King's. In all forms of Classical Pentecostalism the doctrine of 'subsequence' has been taught, that is that the baptism in the Spirit is subsequent to conversion; the debate about two or three events is now less pressing, with recent scholarship mostly suggesting that Christian initiation is a one-stage but complex event with various facets, including repentance, water baptism, and baptism in the Spirit.[18]

Boddy and King expressed their beliefs as the clear teaching of Scripture, and there is no reason to doubt their sincerity. However, there were and are other interpretations made of the same passages.

In addition to their involvement with the Wesleyan Holiness tradition – King joined a Methodist church after his conversion at sixteen – they both describe a gradual and developing experience of the Holy Spirit. Boddy dated his first experience to 1892 and spoke about seven occasions when the Spirit had seemed especially powerful to him. King understood his religious experience to be 'one of slow progress in faith punctuated by various crucial, and often mystical, moments of advance'.[19] It seems plausible that their similar spiritual experiences led Boddy and King to form a similar theology. Their friendship and mutual respect will have reinforced this, along with their desire to work with existing church structures and to seek unity.

As the third event in this sequence baptism of the Holy Ghost was primarily believed by Boddy to provide power for witness and Christian living. Within this scheme spiritual gifts were both evidence for the baptism and the means by which spiritual power was exercised. The fullest discussions of spiritual gifts in the pages of *Confidence* are found on the topics of speaking in tongues, prophecy and healing, and all were discussed at the first Convention.

Speaking in Tongues

It is often assumed that Boddy changed his views on the relationship between baptism in the Spirit and speaking in tongues, thus Allan Anderson is not unusual when he wrote: 'He appears to have shifted his position from an "initial evidence" position to a more flexible view of Spirit baptism.'[20] In his very helpful essay on the early twentieth-century history of speaking in tongues Neil Hudson sees Boddy as changing his mind when he 'argued that tongues did not indicate the Baptism of the Spirit, if love was not present in the believer's life'.[21]

So what *did* Boddy teach?

Boddy's first printed comments on speaking in tongues occur in his series *Leaflets on "Tongues"* from the end of 1907. The first leaflet mentioned his visit to Oslo in March 1907, and provided the main biblical references from Mark 16:17, Acts of the Apostles and 1 Corinthians 12–4. His main concern was to claim this as work of God and to ask Christians not to disparage it. Subsequent leaflets were mostly testimonies of various people, with very limited theological reflection.

In the first issue of *Confidence* Boddy wrote about speaking in tongues under the heading '"Tongues" as a Seal of Pentecost'. The phrase *seal of Pentecost* seems to have been coined by Boddy himself, with *seal* being more or less synonymous with the term *sign*. After again attacking those who disparaged this gift or sought to frighten God's children he expressed his own thanks to God for this gift as a supernatural sign of his baptism in the Holy Ghost. On the basis of 1 Corinthians 12:29 Boddy distinguished between speaking in tongues as a definite sign for those who claimed to be baptized in the Spirit, and 'a *continuous* Gift of tongues'. He expected there to be fruit as a result of this experience in the form of whole hearted love for 'the Blessed Lord'. Finally, note his careful distinction between what he believed was right and how others saw the matter. These are his words in full:

5. Let us each for ourselves keep as near as possible to what we see in the Scriptures when seeking the Baptism of the Holy Ghost, and then let us make all allowance for others who seem to act somewhat differently in detail.

6. Our kind Heavenly Father makes great allowances for the honest mistakes of His children.

7. One is often asked, "Do you think anyone can have had the Baptism of the Holy Ghost and not have had the Sign of Tongues?" I cannot judge another, but for me, "Pentecost means the Baptism of the Holy Ghost with the evidence of the Tongues."[22]

Here Boddy expressed what became known as the doctrine of 'initial evidence' or 'consequence', and which has remained a key tenet of Classical Pentecostalism since. However, in characteristic twists he also wanted his readers to allow for differences, at least 'in detail', and he also was careful to state that this was his position – 'for me'. His eirenical nature and desire to be inclusive wherever possible manifested itself even over this distinguishing issue.

Pressure to examine this belief came from supporters and from critics, from letters from Britain and in discussion at Conferences abroad. Thus the European leaders used a substantial portion of their time at Hamburg in December 1908 to discuss the issue of speaking in tongues. Boddy was questioned on the first morning about their experience in Sunderland, and in response to a question about tongues replied: 'in this movement we have only called that a "Pentecost" which was attested by the speaking in Tongues.' He also emphasised his teaching that 'entire Sanctification' was a precondition of receiving this Sign.[23]

Two days later came a discussion on whether or not tongues was a necessary sign of baptism in the Holy Ghost. Boddy was asked to lead this, and gave his testimony as part of the report. He made clear his own commitment to the necessity of this Sign, but added the important rider: 'With the sign of Tongues has always come something from God, and generally a great gift of Love, as one would expect.'[24]

His expectation that divine love would be shown in the person's life as a result of the Pentecostal blessing was constantly expressed. This expectation was there in Mary's initial testimony in 1907 when she put the stress on asking for the Holy Ghost rather than tongues and 'the Power to love and believe and witness'.[25] Boddy mentioned it in the first edition of *Confidence*, and repeated it at the 1908 Hamburg Conference. He included it in an editorial of November 1910, with the subtitle 'Love: The Evidence of Continuance' and written in response to many letters he had received. He described this editorial as 'very much what the Editor of "Confidence" has written before' and set out his desire, again, to be as inclusive as possible with all who owned Christ as Saviour:

The writer feels that we can have the closest fellowship in Christ with many who differ with us on these points. Some think that they go further than we do, and some think we go too far. We may not be one in our explanation of Pentecostal Truth but we have one Lord Jesus, one Saviour, and can joyfully meet in Him.[26]

He accepted as difficult questions the cases of those who had unworthy motives, or were brought to the baptism prematurely by 'methods', and he would not say that all who had not spoken in Tongues had not been 'Baptized into the one Body', refusing to push the logical conclusion of his commitment to necessity of the Sign of Tongues. In fact, as a result of his 'Pentecostal fellowship with many at home and abroad', he put more emphasis on the value of seeing divine love. His conclusion was that '"Tongues" are a sign of His mighty entrance, but Love is the evidence of His *continuance* [original emphasis] in controlling power.'[27]

An indication of the interest in the subject is seen a little earlier in the same year (1910) when Boddy printed his address 'Speaking in Tongues: What is it?' It was given to a Men's Service in St Gabriel's Church, Bishopwearmouth, Sunderland, and in it he explained the use of tongues in prayer and adoration.[28] He went through the scriptural passages relating to tongues and gave present-day examples. He also reported five effects he commonly observed:

1. Wondrous joy. that the Spirit has thus sealed the believer unto the day of redemption. It is something very real.
2. An increase in the believer's personal love of the Lord Jesus.
3. A new interest in the Word of God. The Bible becomes very precious and its messages very real.
4. A love to the souls for whom Christ has died and a desire to bring them to Him.
5. The soon coming of the Lord is now often laid upon the believer's heart.[29]

Throughout the article he did state the value of tongues, but emphasised the greater importance of exalting Jesus and following him. 'To me personally the chief thing is not the Speaking in Tongues, but the Baptism of the Holy Ghost, of which it is a sign.' On this occasion he described the gift of tongues as a 'confirmatory token' of the baptism in the Holy Ghost, a potentially valuable phrase which he does not seem to have used again. As in his paper *'The "Pentecostal Baptism"'*, he felt the need to state that in the New Testament passages this gift was not given for missionary purposes, though he also said the bestowal of the gift for mission had been known in recent times, and gave a couple of examples.[30]

Soon after these items Boddy published 'The Pentecostal Baptism: Counsel to Leaders and others' based on his experience and, of course, the Scriptures. This article began with guidance on the use of speaking in tongues, based on his understanding of 1 Corinthians 14, with criteria which were very similar to those used later in the century by Pentecostals and charismatics: no more than three such messages in a public meeting, and then only with interpretation, otherwise the gift is to be used privately.[31]

In June 1912 the main leaders at the Sunderland International Convention made a brief statement on the baptism of the Holy Ghost, stating it 'is always borne witness to by the fruit of the Spirit and the outward manifestation, so that we may receive the same gift as the disciples on the Day of Pentecost.'[32]

This view was reiterated by the International Advisory Council of December 1912 (it was, after all, nearly the same group of men meeting as had met six months earlier).

They also went on to state their belief that there was more for the believer to receive of 'the fulness of the blessing of Christ implied in this Baptism', even after speaking in tongues. Whilst this statement was not Boddy's alone it coheres well with the teaching Boddy gave, both on speaking in tongues and on other issues.[33] It is possible that Barratt was less committed to this view of tongues, but he did sign the whole statement. It appears to be the last occasion on which he attended the self-appointed International Advisory Council, but the issue that stands out as causing division was not glossolalia but the creation or not of new churches or organisations.[34]

In 1914 there appears to have been some controversy over the use of tongues as a continuing gift: was it for private use only, or was it for use in public gatherings for worship?

The former view was put with some passion by H. Mogridge, leader of a Pentecostal group in Lytham, Lancashire, at the Whitsuntide Convention. Boddy chaired a discussion in which his own views were clearly to the contrary, and a number of other leaders responded to Mogridge, among whom were Polhill and Paul, who continued to believe in the use of tongues in public settings.[35]

That this was an issue at the time is perhaps confirmed by another article which Boddy reprinted from Frodsham's magazine, *Victory*. This was an extract from a historical novel by the deceased Dean Farrar of Canterbury which gave a description of tongues in worship, based on scriptural and early Patristic evidence, but not contemporary experience. The author of the article was struck by the parallels between this historical description and their present Pentecostal experience, even though the Dean had died before the 'present Revival'. At least one reason Boddy included this was its support for the use of tongues in public worship.[36]

Boddy's understanding of this gift was consistent throughout the written teaching we have, allowing for some variety of emphasis as circumstances required. He was definite in believing that this was a necessary gift as the initial sign or seal of baptism in the Holy Ghost, but with two caveats: first, a subsequent manifestation of love was more important than continuing to speak in tongues, valuable though he found this spiritual experience to be; and second, he was unwilling to unchurch sincere believers who had not had this experience themselves.

Prophecy

As with the gift of speaking in tongues, the gift of prophecy was discussed at the first Sunderland Conference in 1908, with an opening address from Boddy himself, and then comments from four other named speakers, significantly at this first Conference all of them women: Miss Schofield and Miss Sisson from the USA, Miss Scott of Sunderland, and Dagmar Gregersen from Norway, whose compatriot Agnes Thelle gave a prophecy which was printed.[37]

The teaching Boddy gave at this stage on prophecy did not greatly vary over time: the impression on this and on tongues was that even by the first Sunderland Conference he had thought very carefully about his views, and any changes were more a matter of emphasis than of substance. He wanted potential prophets to have letters of commendation from well-known leaders to avoid 'unsuitable persons', which suggests he was alert to possible problems and was in accord with his general concern that the Pentecostal Movement be as well received as possible.[38] Slightly incongruously he moved on to the giving of a tithe in order to receive blessing, thus doing away with the 'need for Bazaars or Sales of Work'!

From the beginning he made use of 1 Corinthians 12 and 14 to justify the earnest coveting of the gift of prophecy. He even used a distinction familiar in equivalent teaching today, that prophecy is as much forth-telling as fore-telling. He was clear that messages in tongues and prophecies were not to be expected to give guidance in everyday life, though 'at any crisis . . . God can and does give a special message'.[39] Guidance came about through 'common sense' under God's control. He saw dangers in messages which were specific about dates or names.

Miss Schofield drew on her American experience to tell the gathering that besides the Holy Spirit and possibly unholy spirits the unconscious mind of the speaker could also influence what was said, as in a recent case of a 'prophecy' of a gift of $1,000. Miss Scott referred to the subtle danger of the speaker continuing to speak 'in the flesh'.

Miss Sisson spoke about the call of missionaries in response to possible prophetic messages, and also about a prophecy of the San Francisco earthquake of 1906.

Dagmar Gregersen's contribution conflated thoughts about prophecy with the gifts of interpretation and discernment.

The tone of the discussion was generally measured, realistic about some of the problems which could result from encouraging people to prophesy, and intimated that the speakers already had considerable experience to draw on, as well as reflection on their interpretation of Scripture.

There was less continuing discussion of prophecy in the pages of *Confidence* than there was of speaking in tongues: prophecy was not given the same evidential status as glossolalia, and so it was less controversial inside the Movement.

On other occasions in 1908 there was reference to not using prophecy or interpretation of tongues as a substitute for guidance. For example, Mary Boddy wrote: 'Nowhere can we find in the Word of God, in *this* dispensation, any suggestion, that guidance in the affairs of daily life for ourselves, and especially for others is to be given thus.'[40]

In the same edition of *Confidence* Barratt was reported as supporting this view, saying quite specifically that he had not been guided in his travels by 'Messages'.[41]

Boddy had to repeat the same advice of 1908 as part of his Counsel to leaders in January 1911; his words suggest that there were still people responding without thought to over-specific messages, and undertaking 'long, fruitless journeys ... [resulting in] God's money spent in vain'.[42]

The positive place of prophecy was expressed in terms of St Paul's words in 1 Corinthians 14:3, which identified edification, exhortation and comfort.[43]

Later in the year the Thursday morning session of the Leaders Meetings at the Sunderland Convention was devoted to the topic of 'Prophetic Utterances and Interpretations: their Value and Place'.[44]

Notes from talks by George Berg of Bangalore, South India, and Jonathan Paul of Berlin were published later in the year. Berg's main point was to emphasise that any purported prophecy should be given in charity (cf. 1 Corinthians 13) and the best check on its origin was its 'harmony with the Word of God'. He also commented that God would give 'you enough time to deliver [a message]'. He, too, spoke against 'an idea in some places that nothing can be done unless it comes through a message'.[45]

Pastor Paul agreed with the need for conformity with the Word of God and, like Boddy, referred his listeners to 1 Corinthians 14:3. Edification meant bringing the hearers of a prophecy to focus on Jesus. Exhortation, he explained, needed to come from 'a clean man or woman', but no further detail was given. Comfort was associated with love for people: 'You cannot comfort others if you don't love them.' This ruled out judging others, and he repeated the injunction to follow the way of charity.[46]

In all these cases there is an undercurrent of awareness of the dangers of allowing prophecy to take place. It was all too easy to manipulate others, to judge them or to obstruct the believers from encountering their Lord. The more apocalyptic conception of prophecy as foretelling is notably absent in these discussions.

The need to guard against prescriptive personal messages was repeated in several of these articles from 1908 to 1911, and came again in an even more extended form in a talk given by Mrs Polman of Amsterdam at the London Conference in early 1912. Her impassioned talk was printed at length in *Confidence*, a sign of concern over the extent of the problem.

The Apostolic Faith Church led by William Hutchinson represented a more extreme version of Pentecostalism: a few years later, in 1915, Hutchinson's son-in-law wrote: 'If it is the Word of God, whether it be written or spoken, it cannot be anything else but God's Word and therefore in that sense it is the same identically.'[47]

Mrs Polman's forceful message was quite the reverse: 'I tell you that the work in England will be much better if you do not listen to personal messages. Your little circles will be more blessed if you put them out.'[48] She went on to give an example of trying to rebuke someone with such a message: 'On another occasion there was another sister who told us she had a personal message, and we warned her and told her to be silent, and now they are both gone. They have ruined two homes.'[49]

The problem here appears to have been the break-up of two marriages because of a personal message. In other instances the problem was an overzealous desire for missionary work.

In endorsing Mrs Polman's words Boddy gave these examples:

One brother travelled half round the world to preach the Gospel at a village in Palestine, and found ruins only when he got to that place. A sister travelled with her husband many many thousands of miles, and was not permitted to land, and had to return sorely burdened and saddened.[50]

A different aspect of the gift of prophecy was discussed in connection with the ministry of women at the Sunderland Convention of 1914. The mainly male participants – the only woman recorded as speaking in the discussion was Mrs Polman – wrestled with biblical texts which referred to women prophesying, women keeping silent, and their experience of women prophesying. As hinted in chapter six above, there was some retreating from the more egalitarian stance of the earliest days of the Pentecostal Movement. The general conclusions were that women could prophesy in smaller gatherings, distinguished from the church assembly, and that it should be carried out under the authority of a male pastor.[51]

Healing

If the gift of prophecy was less controversial, that of healing was far more controversial, and the space devoted to the topic in *Confidence* reflects both this and the Boddys' interest in it.

In one of his final editions of *Confidence*, which had something of a theme of healing, Boddy explained the healing ministry he had continued 'since about 1892', the time of his first experience of the work of the Holy Spirit in his life. Boddy did not change his views on healing significantly after his baptism with signs in 1907 and this article of 1922 gave a feel of how he had practised this ministry for some thirty years.[52] Because it was his continuing practice we shall look at this article more closely, and summarise the later material.

The heading was not 'Healing', but 'Anointing with Oil', because Boddy's scriptural basis for the healing ministry was James 5:13–16, the anointing of the sick by the elders. He recognised that for some people to have this service in a church building could be helpful and mentioned a 'rather long' service written by Bishop Packenham Walsh, Bishop in Assam, India. For Boddy, however, it was 'Not in Church. No robes. Generally (if the sufferer is able) in the Vicarage.' It was still a formal occasion, but less churchy, with the sick person kneeling, accompanied by others, whilst the 'Elder' stood, ready with olive oil. After a prayer for guidance he was to read 'very deliberately and sincerely' James 5:13–16. The opportunity was then given for oral confession, and he stated, 'In one case as the confession was made the trouble instantly disappeared.' After confession the patient must pray, surrendering to Christ.

Next was the turn of the Elder to '"rebuke" the sickness, the pain and all the evil powers behind the disease'. This was related to Luke 4:39, where Jesus rebuked the fever of Simon Peter's mother-in-law. This was to be done 'in the Name' of Jesus, and placing 'the sufferer under the Precious Blood for cleansing'. Then the person was ready to receive 'the Lord, and Giver of Life and Health' (clearly based on the Credal affirmation), of which the oil was 'a channel of spiritual blessing . . . a symbol of consecration . . . and a token of the coming of the Holy Ghost'.

The anointing itself was done in a very specific manner:

With a finger of his right hand dipped into the oil, he touches the fore-head in the 'Name of the Lord,' and then in the full name of the Trinity, placing his left hand with the oil in it on the head of the sufferer, with such oil as remains.

This was to be followed by the laying on of both hands, as in Mark 16:18, first on the head, 'and then, if wise and convenient . . . on the seat of the trouble'. The service was to conclude with the patient giving thanks to God and, whilst the patient was still kneeling, the Elder giving a blessing, based on that in Numbers 6:24–26.

Boddy's brief commentary was that it was the prayer of faith which saved the sick, and so the Elders should be 'men of faith, and faith in this particular'. His testimony was that in many cases healing came gradually.

In final words that are echoed today he advised that 'the believer should seek for the touch of Christ, which brings blessing.' For '[s]ome at this service have received a Baptism of the Holy Ghost, when they came for healing.'

Although this article was written in 1922 these themes recur consistently in Boddy's teaching on the subject. Faith in Jesus, prayer, a quiet, unemotional approach, being open to the Holy Spirit – all these are mentioned by him again and again. It illustrates most effectively how Boddy's theology and pastoral practice were interwoven.

The healing of Mary Boddy from asthma in 1899 was crucial in opening them to Pentecostal phenomena more generally, a prompting that occurred to other evangelicals in the late nineteenth century, among them Carrie Judd Montgomery, later a close friend.[53] Mary's own healing seems to have arisen from her reflections on Scripture while she was laid up, for in her testimony she wrote:

> I was willing, if it were God's will, to be an invalid – not having heard of Divine Healing. I began to search the Scriptures on this point, relying on the Holy Spirit to teach me . . . After many months of prayer, God *spoke* to me from John v.39–40, on the 23rd of February, 1899, and as I believed the Word and *received* Jesus to come into me as my physical life, He did so, and I was made whole.'[54] [original emphases]

Following this Mary discovered she had a gift of healing and would regularly lay hands on people. In Kay's assessment the many years of experience gained by Alexander and Mary ensured a reality about claims for healing and their balanced view on healing was most helpful in the development of Pentecostal thinking.[55]

The first volume of *Confidence* included a brief mention of victory over disease through Christ's atonement,[56] and the second an overview article by Mary on 'Health and Healing in Jesus'.[57] Mary expressed a fuller theology of healing here, based primarily on the atonement: 'For on Calvary the cry, "It is finished," proclaimed to the whole world the fact that the whole of the Curse had been done away with.' She believed that the Redeemer had fulfilled the Scriptures by bearing human sin and sickness. She also mentioned her own and others' healing as an encouragement to the readers to believe that they might be healed.

At the first Conference Boddy led a session on Divine Healing, teaching from James 5:14–16, and giving practical advice. It is virtually identical to that in the article of 1922 already discussed. In 1908 he also referred to the possibility that God would raise up female elders, and the importance of not exaggerating testimonies of healing: 'In order to give God glory, His people sometimes may be tempted to go a little beyond their experience.'[58]

By 1910 it would seem that Boddy's healing ministry was attracting attention, and certainly there were numerous testimonies declaring healing in the pages of *Confidence*. That year he printed three major articles, two based on talks he had given to groups of Anglican clergy who were nearly all not part of the Pentecostal Movement.

He spoke in Durham on 'Faith Healing' on 13 January to the Junior Clergy Society, the topic proving of interest to more senior clergy too.[59] He sought to deal with the charge of 'mind-suggestion' and discussed three theological strands from Scripture: the redemption won by Christ on the Cross (Isaiah 53:4; 1 Peter 2:24), the charism of healing located in elders (James 5), and the power of the Holy Spirit (Luke 4:38; Acts 10:38). He identified negative and positive aspects to healing: the negative involved overcoming the devil, in the form of casting out demons associated with sickness; the positive was the filling of the person with the life of the Lord. As we saw in his views on salvation he was explicit that salvation was for the body as well as for the soul and spirit, a holistic view which continues to find resonances.

His clerical audience may have been less happy with his strong words about their shared church:

> The Church of today with its formalism, its love of dignity, its unapostolic methods of raising money, has need to confess that it is poor and blind and naked. It has endowments, and cathedrals, and costly churches of stone, but when a sick one would send for the elders of our Church to come with the prayer of faith that shall save the sick, he cannot find such.

Nonetheless, in his conclusion he asserted he had seen a change over the ten years he had sought to trust God for healing, saying that 'today, Bishops and Christian Leaders are sympathetically examining into it.'

Soon after this paper he gave another entitled 'The Missionary's Supernatural Outfit' for the Sunderland CMS clergy, of whom he was one.[60] He reminded his mission-minded hearers of the works of Jesus in healing (Matthew 11:5) and the promise of Jesus that believers would do greater works than his (John 14:12). Therefore in his view the missionary societies needed to send missionaries open to supernatural signs, including the casting out of demons and healing the sick. This represented a confluence of his views on the gifts of the Spirit, mission and healing.

In these papers and that published in August 1910 he was ambivalent about the place of doctors and nurses: on the one hand he expressed gratitude for their work. On the other, he expounded the view that there was no actual commendation of the medical profession in Scripture, and pointed out that Jesus and the early apostles did not hand out medicine. However, he always accepted that only a small minority of believers would go entirely without medical aid, and when Mary became ill again the 1920s she went for convalescence, and had a nurse living in. In a related discussion he refuted the teaching of 'so-called Christian Science' that 'all pain and disease is unreal – you are to believe you have not got it and it will go'. This was to ignore both 'the power of Satan and the work of the Atonement'.[61]

It was no doubt with some satisfaction that he was able in October the same year to print, without any commentary, a short piece under the heading 'The Bishop of Durham on Faith Healing'.[62] Bishop Moule had given a devotional address to the Church Congress in which he tentatively connected the health of body and soul: 'I for one cannot doubt that normally the soul's health is at least friendly to that of the body, which, glorified at last, is to be its inseparable partner and vehicle for ever.' Though not an outright endorsement of Boddy's theology it did provide some comfort to Boddy that his 'father in God' did at least have a similar holistic view of salvation to his own.

There was one final paper on healing by Boddy, again delivered to fellow clergy, this time the South Shields Clerical Society on 1 December 1913.[63] It is evidence that his teaching continued to be consistent, drawing on the same scriptural passages, making similar theological points, and even using the same illustrations, though with more recent ones added. He was very explicit in this talk about a link between sickness and evil: 'SICKNESS IS GENERALLY FROM SATAN. Supernatural healings are to be sought because sickness is *generally* from Satan or his emissaries' [original emphases].

He also attempted some systematising of types of healing, identifying five, and giving examples of each. Using his language, these were:

1. by God's sovereign grace.
2. as a result of earnest believing prayer.
3. through the laying on of hands.
4. through the laying on of a handkerchief over which very special prayer has been offered.
5. through the prayer of faith, with the anointing of oil.

This was not a full systematic theology of healing, but it shows Boddy continuing to reflect on the ministry in which he was engaged and seeking to be careful in the examples of healings that he provided.

Of the many testimonies he printed the most prominent was the case of Dorothy Kerin. Dorothy was aged twenty-two and had been seriously ill since the age of fourteen, bedridden for the previous two years. She was regularly prayed for by the clergy and parish of St Paul's Herne Hill, but appeared to be dying. Her healing was the example Boddy used for his first type: God's sovereign grace. She had a vision, which she described as being of an angel, calling her to get up and walk, which she did to the astonishment of those by her bed. The reports were first printed in national newspapers and taken up by Boddy for *Confidence*.[64] Boddy was able to meet with her soon after this event and referred to her testimony at the 1912 Sunderland Convention.[65] According to his daughter Janie's testimony Dorothy came to stay with them, 'the beginning of a long friendship'.[66] Miss Kerin then visited the Convention in both 1913 and 1914 to give her testimony, attracting the attention of the national newspaper *The Daily Mirror* on both occasions. Her picture was printed, with a heading in 1914, 'Miracle girl at the Convention'.[67] Boddy printed a full account of her testimony as recorded in the paper *North Mail*.[68] Nonetheless, although she gave the testimony several times Boddy was restrained in the use he made of her case, a feature of his pastoral concern and friendship.

Taylor's much longer discussion of Boddy's role in the healing ministry concludes with three points: first, that the printing of testimonies in *Confidence* inspired and encouraged others to seek healing; second, that the magazine acted as a publicity agent for those engaged in healing, giving them a much higher profile than would otherwise have been the case; and third, that Boddy's balanced views counteracted the temptations to exaggeration and distortion.[69]

Taylor also identifies five theological points in which Boddy and other contributors to *Confidence* influenced subsequent Pentecostal thinking:[70]

1. the denial of sense perception, distinguishing the actual disease from its symptoms.
2. healing is found in the atonement of Christ, with a corollary that spiritual healing is the highest form of healing.
3. a link exists between demonic activity, not possession in the case of Christians, and sickness.
4. Christians can take authority over sickness, rebuking it.
5. the disparagement of medicine, with some shift to a more accommodating view as circumstances changed.

Boddy was very committed to the ministry of healing and sought to explain it from Scripture. His desire to be true to

Scripture and to the lived experience, positive and negative, of the people he knew and loved meant that he was kept from more extreme views on the subject, though always believing that healing was a present possibility.

The Second Coming of Christ

'the Soon-Coming of the Lord in the air (1 Thess. iv., 14)'.

As an evangelical, Boddy held an apocalyptic view of a kind common at the time. He had a strong sense that Christ could return soon, a view which predated his Pentecostal experience. So when preaching in Jerusalem in the 1890s he concluded his sermon with reference to the second coming of Christ, which, again like others, he believed would take place on the Mount of Olives.[71] Receiving the baptism of the Holy Ghost reinforced this belief, and he included it in his opening statement of key doctrines at the front of *Confidence*.

The first article reprinted in *Confidence* in April 1908 was 'The Bridegroom Cometh', expressing a belief in the imminent return of Jesus.[72] The article made much use of the Early Rain, Latter Rain typology in use at the time; indeed the movement was often called the Latter Rain Movement. The rainfall in Israel was divided into 'early rain' at the time of planting crops and 'latter rain' just before harvest, which swelled the grain and fruit. This typology was much used at the beginning of the twentieth century and the author of the article was able to use it and apply it to the Pentecostal outpouring of the Spirit without much explanation; Boddy himself used the term in an editorial of June 1908, again without explanation.[73] The giving of the Spirit was regarded as an unprecedented sign of the second coming: 'each year speeding more intensely towards the predicted consummation'.

At the first Whitsuntide Conference Boddy introduced the topic of 'The Near Coming of the Lord', and allowed Miss Barbour (Wimbledon) and Miss Sissons (USA) to be the main speakers.

Miss Barbour made three points in support of a 'near coming', the first being a calculation of biblical dates of the 'times of the Gentiles' and suggesting a return might be in 1914. The second was the large numbers of Jews returning to the Holy Land. The third was the direct revelation by the Holy Spirit to believers. These themes were to recur in such teaching, with a variety of dates, though that of 1914 was to have particular significance in the light of the deadly 1914–18 European 'Great War'.[74]

This belief in the second coming, or parousia, is threaded through the testimonies recorded in *Confidence*, and Boddy went so far as to see it as a common sign that someone had received the gift of speaking in tongues: 'The soon coming of the Lord is now often laid upon the believer's heart.'[75]

Guided, as so often, by the Anglican liturgical year Boddy focused on 'The Two Advents' in *Confidence* for December 1910. So in addition to reflections on the first Christmas, which he based on his time in the Holy Land, he printed an anonymous piece, 'How He may come', based on a particular view of the Rapture, rather like the *Left Behind* series of our own day.[76]

He also included a long article, also unsigned but from internal evidence almost certainly his own, on 'Seven Signs of His Coming'.[77] The first two signs were extended versions of Miss Barbour's first two. His other five signs explored further scriptural passages and themes: Daniel 2, linked to a schematic, dispensationalist interpretation of history; 2 Thessalonians 2:3 and 2 Timothy 3:1-5 to discuss apostasy; the number of earthquakes, discussed in the light of the Noah story (with Matthew 24:7 not cited but in the background); the preaching of the gospel to all nations (Matthew 24:14); and finally, the outpouring of the Latter Rain, in both a literal sense in Palestine, and a spiritual sense in the giving of the Holy Spirit. The theme was rammed home with another article on 'The Day of the Lord', setting out a detailed timetable for that day, and in a devotional Christmas message by Mary.

This belief in an imminent parousia gave urgency to missionary work – a feature of many revivals and especially of the Pentecostal Movement. In Boddy's case this was an extension of his long-term support for mission work, mainly through CMS, and now channelled through the PMU. It made an interesting inversion of the argument that preaching to all nations was a sign of the imminence of Christ's return.

He returned to this subject in *Confidence* July 1911, this time including a story by Harriet Beecher Stowe and addresses from the Whitsuntide Convention. Among these were 'The Final Great Rejection' by Arthur Booth-Clibborn, 'The Bride and her

Heavenly Bridegroom' by Jonathan Paul, and 'The Coming Rapture' by Mary Boddy. An editorial by Boddy was titled 'The Coming of the Lord'.

Boddy regarded this as 'a very profitable subject', for it roused people to good works and useful lives. In introducing the various articles he also gave three comments of advice, 'only needed by *some*, but it is needed in the case of some of the Lord's most earnest and devoted children.' First, 'however near we may believe that the Coming of the Lord may be . . . (k)eep to your business!' and he quoted Jesus: 'I pray not that Thou takest them out of the world' (John 17:15). Second, 'some highly strung temperaments' could 'live in an unwholesome state of panic' if they thought about dates of the Coming of the Lord. Third, the Pentecostal blessing reminded people to be ready, while still doing 'our daily duty well'.[78]

The advice was undoubtedly good, but in part undermined by the very magazine articles themselves, especially over the detailed calculations of dates for 'the times of the Gentiles'. Boddy was wise enough to recognise the difficulties this doctrine could cause sensitive or over-earnest souls, but was so committed to it as an essential part of Christian doctrine in the form with which he was familiar, that perhaps he inadvertently sustained the problems he advised against.

There was some ambivalence in Boddy's approach to the giving of dates for the second coming. His first published comment on the outbreak of war in 1914 hoped for a quick end, and speculated, 'It may be by His coming in the air for his own.'[79]

The same month the editorial was by Mary on the war: she saw the war as a spiritual one, with the outcome sought in the appearing of Christ: 'We now look for the glorious appearing or manifestation of our Lord and Saviour, Jesus Christ' and she hoped for 'the final and complete overthrow of the Antichrist'.[80]

Boddy was well aware of the text, 'But of that day and hour knoweth no man' (Matthew 24:36), but his publishing of detailed timetables and his comments that the war was a sign of the 'end times' could give a different impression.

In January 1915, hearing of an earthquake in Rome, he headed a short item in *Confidence* with Luke 21:10–11.[81] Later in the same issue Mary wrote: 'The end of the age is at hand' and described the signs of spiritual conflict which were the evidence. The following month a long article on the war began with a discussion of Armageddon and interpreted the declaration of war by Turkey, with soldiers marching across Syria, as at least a possible sign of a fulfilment of Revelation 19:19.[82]

Though not discussing it in as much detail as the use of spiritual gifts Boddy was typical of the Pentecostal Movement in seeing the war as a sign of the end times, the 'Latter Rain'. The imminent second coming of Christ had always been part of his creed, and its importance was strengthened by his personal experience of the Holy Spirit, giving a sense of the closeness of God, and then by the trauma of the 1914–18 war which was reminiscent of the apocalyptic visions of the New Testament.

Other Topics

That completes the topics listed at the front of *Confidence*, but there are two more theological topics important to Boddy – in a sense he was so close to them that perhaps he did not need to mention them: his ecclesiology and his understanding of sacraments. He had been instructed in the Church of England Articles of Religion in his Licentiate at the University of Durham, and although he does not quote from them he was well aware of their teaching: every time he or one of his many curates was licensed by the Bishop they had to recite the articles publicly. For this reason, in some of the discussion below I refer to the Thirty-Nine Articles in the 1662 *Book of Common Prayer* familiar to Boddy to supplement the discussion of his practice and the relative lack of explicit teaching by him on these topics.[83]

'One, Holy, Catholic and Apostolic Church'

'One, Holy, Catholic and Apostolic Church' is the current translation of a line of the ancient Nicene Creed. The versions of the Apostles' and Nicene Creeds in the *Book of Common Prayer* supply the same four adjectives about the church. They provide a good framework within which to summarise Boddy's view of the church, and indeed much of his theology and practice.

1. One
Boddy retained a very high view of the whole church throughout his life, always seeking fellowship with other

Christians, and unity in witness. Article 19 sets out just two marks of the church: 'the pure Word of God is preached, and the Sacraments be duly administered'. Boddy put most emphasis on the first of these marks, and this enabled him to accept Christians of many denominations as part of the one church. When the Pentecostal outpouring first occurred in his parish in 1907 he saw it as a renewal movement and regularly spoke against forming another organisation.

In this commitment to his existing denomination he was helped enormously by having a relatively sympathetic bishop in Handley Moule. Although Moule did not specifically support him in public there was a shared background in evangelicalism and the Keswick Holiness Movement. It is quite possible that with any other bishop Boddy would have been pressurised to leave the Church of England.

The view that Pentecostalism was a renewal movement within the existing churches was held by other European leaders, such as Jonathan Paul and Gerrit Polman, in the early stages of the Movement. Barratt was the first major figure to depart from this consensus and in the years before the 1914 war this led to some disagreement between them. But for Boddy the interdenominational nature of the Pentecostal Movement was evidence that it was of God.[84] His important editorial of 1911, 'Unity not Uniformity', drew attention to the various denominations of people involved in the movement, and concluded: 'The Editor of "Confidence" does not feel that the Lord's leading in these days is to set up a new Church, but to bless individuals where they are.'[85]

In practical terms it meant that Boddy sought to encourage people to know Christ in the power of the Holy Spirit, but he did not expect them to leave their churches, nor did he suggest that only Pentecostals were Christians.[86] In his own parish, Pentecostal prayer meetings were held on Friday, Saturday and Sunday evenings for a number of years, but they were not the only activities and they were not held with any exclusive intent. He sought normal relationships with other local clergy, and to present Pentecostalism in favourable light, and occasionally he was able to speak at local churches, usually the more evangelical ones.

On a number of occasions he mentioned the predominance of 'church people' at his meetings in Monkwearmouth, not in an exclusive spirit, but to encourage other Anglicans to take this movement seriously.[87] Where possible he highlighted the involvement of other Anglican clergy, so the Revd Clement Dickinson, Curate of Ferryhill, just south of Durham, had his testimony printed in 1908 under the heading 'Testimony of a Clergyman', as well as two songs he had composed in 1909.[88] At least once Boddy engaged in open-air preaching on a summer Sunday evening, 'join[ing] forces with a neighbouring church and its Vicar'.[89] In the discussion about tongues at the Sunderland Convention of 1914 an unnamed clergyman from Bristol spoke of his experience.[90] There are few other references to other clergy, though, and their paucity suggests that Boddy did not have much success in involving them. Boddy's care in recording such details can be seen in his report of a London Conference of 1912, when he mentioned two clergymen who spoke, but who were 'not in the Movement'.[91]

2. Holy
Boddy had had his early Christian life revitalised by going to the Keswick Convention (which, as we saw in chapter two, was the central gathering in England for the Holiness Movement), and his Pentecostal experience built on that earlier period of his Christian life. He certainly believed in personal holiness, to be achieved by pleading the Blood for sin and for victory over disease, and demonstrated in the fruit of love,. We noted earlier his criticism of the church for its 'formalism' and its 'unapostolic methods of raising money': he wished to see his church living out its calling to be holy. In his own parish he listed among his blessings 'church and parish funds all in a satisfactory position, through the systematic contributions of those who love their privileges'.[92]

More than that, he saw holiness in a wider context: the social holiness advocated by Wesley. Boddy had been prepared to work for and with poor working people in his parish and on his journeys before his Pentecostal experience. Later when travelling in the USA he was troubled by the materialism and racism he saw and spoke against both, looking for Pentecostals to set good examples over these issues.

For Boddy holiness was not confined to personal piety but had a corporate outworking. In his own mind at least his support for the war effort was based on his view of the correctness of supporting helpless Belgium in the face of German militarism. For example, 'Belgium had been guaranteed protection. She was cruelly invaded and ravaged, contrary to treaty. England was compelled, in honour, to do all she could.'[93] Given that, he still looked for the war to bring purification to church and to Empire. The church that was holy was not the visible organised church or churches, but the real people of God.

3. Catholic

With his positive remarks about believers from many lands and denominations, Boddy exemplified belief in the church as a worldwide, universal body. His travels throughout his life brought him into contact with a great variety of Christians and churches and he sought to learn from them, even while being confident of his own beliefs. Article 34, 'Of the Traditions of the Church', allows for diversity of practice in different nations, and Boddy exemplified that tolerance in good measure. It was this openness that was so helpful in his acceptance of the Pentecostal message, and that enabled him to provide leadership of the Movement when other Anglicans were unable to do so.

4. Apostolic

Boddy was certainly committed to the church as apostolic in the scriptural sense of its continuing apostolic or missionary task of preaching the gospel. In this he was true both to his Anglican heritage – 'Holy Scripture containeth all things necessary to salvation' (Article 6) – and to the Holiness Movement.

This apostolic preaching began with Faith in Christ (Articles 11 and 18), but, of course, for Boddy the work of Christ came alive to the believer through experiencing the baptism of the Holy Spirit.

Throughout his life he was ready to witness to his belief in Christ, and held regular parish missions. He was a great supporter of CMS, both when he was abroad and through parish support groups, the 'Gleaners' being a favourite. His promotion of the PMU with Polhill was very important to him and a significant outworking of what it meant for him for the church to be apostolic.

The more usual Anglican interpretation of *apostolic* at the time was in terms of the three-fold order of deacons, priests and bishops, legitimised by properly ordained bishops, that is, in the apostolic succession, passed on through the laying on of hands.[94]

Of this Boddy did not write. However, he implicitly accepted it: we know he celebrated the anniversary of his own ordination each year at least until 1892. He had a very high regard for his bishops, especially Lightfoot and Moule. His criticisms of the church were its 'formalism' and its 'unapostolic methods of raising money', but not its ordering of ministry. The proper authorisation of leaders was a regular theme in his writing, as a safeguard against extreme and unorthodox ministry. Throughout this time he was given curates by Bishop Moule, an indication of his relative acceptability, and of his own readiness to work within the given structure. This acceptance of Church of England governance was important in enabling him to remain within the denomination, but it was also to lead to strains with other Pentecostal leaders from non-Anglican backgrounds.

Sacraments

Connected to Boddy's ecclesiology was his understanding of sacraments – their being 'duly ministered' is the second mark of the church in Article 19. He retained his evangelical Anglican stance on Baptism and Holy Communion throughout his life (Article 25 recognises 'two Sacraments ordained of Christ'), a fact which caused some conflict within the Pentecostal Movement.

Differences of opinion over the baptism of infants were recorded in *Confidence*, with Barratt moving from his Methodist roots to repudiating the practice, while Boddy retained it. Although Boddy himself did not want the issue to be a factor in the gradual separation of Pentecostals from the existing churches, it seems to have become that. His support for infant baptism remains somewhat sensitive to Pentecostals; for example, an Elim author, Richard Bicknell, has written of 'the sacramentalist position of the early "fathers"',[95] clearly including Boddy in this assessment.

It is also clear from his practice that Boddy took Holy Communion very seriously. The programme for the first Whitsuntide Conference in 1908 included two celebrations of Holy Communion on Whitsunday,[96] and in 1912 there were three services, beginning at 7 a.m., which many of the Conference participants attended.[97] He was grateful for '[a]n increasing roll of communicants'.[98] Furthermore, his earliest conscious experience of the Holy Spirit in 1892 occurred at an early morning service of Communion to celebrate his ordination on St Matthew's Day.

If anything, his wife Mary put even greater theological emphasis on Holy Communion, for she made use of the Communion service theologically at least six times in her articles, where Alexander never did so.[99] So, for example, in 1915 she wrote, '[i]n order that our body though mortal may become holy and whole, we eat of His flesh. In the Holy Communion we participate of His flesh and of His blood, we feed on Him by faith.'

However, there is nothing within Boddy's writings to suggest that his views on the sacraments were significantly different from those of other evangelical Anglicans. The differences with other Pentecostals arose mainly because of the previously held beliefs of each party.

Although not a dominical sacrament, confirmation was part of the Church of England's provision from the sixteenth century and was given greater prominence by the bishops of the latter part of the nineteenth century. In chapter four we discussed Boddy's short book, *Laying on of Hands*, written in 1895 for young confirmation candidates. At that stage he was very supportive of confirmation, and instructed his readers in its supernatural nature, in the gift of the Holy Ghost. There is nothing to suggest that he significantly changed from this position, for it was consistent with his teaching about baptism in the Holy Ghost.

A glimpse of Boddy's continuing desire to work with the grain of his Anglican tradition and to emphasise the value of confirmation can be caught in the way he reported the telling by Smith Wigglesworth of his life story to the church at Monkwearmouth:

> To us it was interesting to hear how the first touch of Divine power he received was at his Confirmation as a "Church" boy in a Parish Church in Yorkshire. As the Bishop laid hands on him, the same divine power of the Holy Spirit, which he now experiences in a fuller measure, came upon him, and went through his whole being.[100]

What is of note here is the prominence Boddy gave this in his report, and the way he picked up on an item which might give some support to his own practice.

Summary

Boddy was not an exceptional theologian, but primarily a pastor who thought about his ministry and also enabled other people to express their ideas. However, in his reflections on speaking in tongues and on the ministry of healing he did make some more substantial contributions to later thinking. Furthermore, he did seek consistency in his practice and theology, building on the evangelical and Anglican framework in which he had been nurtured.

Although his theology was lost for a time it was partially recovered in the 1960s by Michael Harper and it remains significant as the first attempt to reconcile Anglican teaching and practice with Pentecostal experience and teaching.

Notes

1 Kay and Dyer, *Pentecostal and Charismatic Studies*, passim
2 *Confidence*, April 1911, 75 and subsequent editions
3 Taylor makes a similar decision to use this statement as the appropriate theological grid, though with a slightly different grouping of themes and no mention of ecclesiology or sacraments. Taylor, *Publish and be Blessed*, 177–78
4 *Confidence*, October–December 1922, 56
5 *Confidence*, October–December 1922, 54–56
6 *Confidence*, April 1908, 4
7 *Confidence*, May 1908, 3
8 *Confidence*, May 1908, 4
9 There is a concise discussion in Bebbington, *Holiness*, 73, 77, 87–89
10 *Confidence*, January 1912, 19, 20
11 *Confidence*, August 1915, 148
12 Kay, *Pentecostals in Britain*, 79–80
13 The reference to Acts 4:13 is not the most obvious choice to support a ministry of healing, but since he does cite Acts 4:10–12 in December 1913 in this connection perhaps it should be regarded as including the preceding verses. Was this an allusion to both the asserted boldness and ordinariness of the apostles Peter and John?
14 *Confidence*, April 1908, 10
15 *Confidence*, February 1909, 33
16 *Confidence*, January 1912, 20–21
17 See Jacobsen, *Thinking in the Spirit*, chapter 3 for a detailed comparison between Durham and King

18 There is a helpful summary of the early positions and the more recent debate since Dunn's book in 1970 in Anderson, *Pentecostalism*, 190–95. See the discussion in Turner, *Baptism in the Holy Spirit*, especially the summary, 17–19

19 Jacobsen, *Thinking in the Spirit*, 169

20 Anderson, *Pentecostalism*, 91

21 Hudson, 'Strange Words', 9, based on *Confidence* (November 1910), 261. Hudson's essay was kindly made available to me before its publication, but at a late stage of my own writing

22 *Confidence*, April 1908, 18

23 *Confidence*, January 1909, 5

24 *Confidence*, February 1909, 33

25 Mary Boddy, *"Pentecost" at Sunderland: the Testimony of a Vicar's Wife*, 6

26 *Confidence*, November 1910, 260

27 *Confidence*, November 1910, 261

28 St Gabriel's is still an active Evangelical church in the Church of England.

29 *Confidence*, May 1910, 100

30 *Confidence*, May 1910, 99–104

31 *Confidence*, January 1911, 6. Kay, *Pentecostals in Britain*, 56–57 also makes this point

32 *Confidence*, June 1912, 133

33 *Confidence*, December 1912, 277

34 *Confidence*, December 1912, 284

35 *Confidence*, December 1914, 233–36; January 1915, 12–4. Robinson, *The Charismatic Anglican*, 115 suggested that Boddy's influence was waning by this point; I take the view that Boddy chaired this debate of international leaders in June 1914 precisely because he was still pre-eminent. It was his response to the outbreak of war that led to a more rapid decline in his influence

36 *Confidence*, May 1912, 85–89

37 *Confidence*, June 1908, 15–17

38 *Confidence*, March 1908, 15

39 *Confidence* , March 1908, 13

40 *Confidence* , December 1908, 14. Quite why she emphasised '*this* dispensation' is unclear

41 *Confidence*, December 1908, Supplement, 3

42 *Confidence*, January 1911, 6

43 *Confidence*, January 1911, 6

44 *Confidence*, June 1911, 127

45 *Confidence*, November 1911, 248

46 *Confidence*, November 1911, 249

47 J. Dennis-Hutchinson, 'A talk on the written and spoken word of God', *Showers of Blessing*, April 1915, 4. I owe this reference to Hudson, 'Strange Words', 15

48 *Confidence*, February 1912, 32. The full article covers pp. 30–33
49 *Confidence*, February 1912, 32
50 *Confidence*, February 1912, 33
51 *Confidence*, November 1914, 209, 212–14
52 *Confidence*, April 1922, 21–12
53 This point is made by Taylor in his long and helpful article 'Divine Healing', 55 and 71. The article goes into more detail than is possible here, and I have drawn on Taylor's conclusions
54 Mary Boddy, 'Testimony', 2
55 Kay, *Pentecostals in Britain*, 82
56 *Confidence*, April 1908, 4
57 *Confidence*, May 1908, 16–17
58 *Confidence*, June 1908, 18
59 *Confidence*, January 1910, 8–11, 14–15
60 *Confidence*, March 1910, 69–72
61 *Confidence*, August 1910, 175–79
62 *Confidence*, October 1910, 236
63 *Confidence*, December 1913, 231–36
64 *Confidence*, March 1912, 70–71
65 *Confidence*, June 1912, 131
66 Jane Boddy, *A.A. Boddy*, 5
67 *The Daily Mirror*, 15 May 1913, 9; 3 June 1914, 8
68 *Confidence*, June 1913, 111–13
69 Taylor, 'Divine Healing', 72–73
70 This paragraph summarises Taylor's points. Taylor, 'Divine Healing', 75–77
71 *Days in Galilee*, 343
72 *Confidence*, April 1908, 19, reprinted from *Trust*, Elim House, Rochester, New York
73 *Confidence*, June 1908, 13
74 *Confidence*, June 1908, 17–18
75 *Confidence*, May 1910, 100
76 *Confidence*, December 1910, 278–81
77 *Confidence*, December 1910, 281–83, 287–88
78 *Confidence*, July 1911, 156
79 *Confidence*, September 1914, 163
80 *Confidence*, September 1914, 171
81 *Confidence*, January 1915, 8
82 *Confidence*, February 1915, 26
83 The 'Articles of Religion' can be found at the back of any copy of the 1662 *Book of Common Prayer*. Their numbering is, of course, consistent in the multitude of editions; for this reason I have not given page numbers.
84 *Confidence* June 1908, 9; May 1910, 103
85 *Confidence* March 1911, 60

86 See also Robinson, *The Charismatic Anglican*, 116

87 *Confidence* May 1910, 103

88 *Confidence* May 1908, 7–8; April 1909, 79; May 1909, 103. As so often, Boddy sustained the friendship over a long period of time; in 1919 he printed Dickinson's request for prayer in his lonely missionary work in Assam (*Confidence*, July 1919, 49). Dickinson was in India from 1914 to 1920, returning to England through ill health and dying in about 1924 in his late 50s. *Crockford's* 1923, 1924

89 *Confidence* August 1912, 182

90 *Confidence* December 1914, 235

91 *Confidence* February 1912, 37

92 *Confidence*, April 1912, 88

93 *Confidence*, October 1915, 191

94 This is not found in the Thirty-Nine Articles but in the Preface to the Ordinal, what the *Book of Common Prayer* called 'The Form and Manner of Making Ordaining and Consecrating of Bishops, Priests and Deacons'

95 Bicknell, 'The Ordinances' in Warrington (ed.) *Pentecostal Perspectives*, 214

96 *Confidence*, May 1908, 2

97 *Confidence*, June 1912, 126

98 *Confidence*, April 1912, 88

99 *Confidence*, July 1910, 163; January 1914, 11; August 1914, 150; December 1914, 232; August 1915, 151; February 1916, 30

100 *Confidence*, March 1912, 64

Nine

War and Withdrawal: Boddy's Later Years

Boddy's three-month trip to the USA immediately following the 1914 Whitsuntide Convention in Sunderland may be seen as marking the high point of his leadership in the Pentecostal Movement. The trauma of the First World War irrevocably changed much in Europe; the churches were not immune and it can be no surprise that the Pentecostal Movement was transformed. From the whole panorama of this destructive war we shall pick out Boddy's reactions to it, and its effect on the Pentecostal Movement. That will lead us to consider his gradual withdrawal from wider ministry in his final years.

The First World War

Outbreak of war, and prayer

Boddy heard of the outbreak of war with Germany while on a trip to the USA and broke off his visit to the Camp Meeting at Cazadero, California. During his return journey he ministered to a German-English congregation he had visited before, though '[n]ot a word of course about the war'.[1] Like most other people, he had not anticipated the war, and certainly not its duration and ferocity.

Boddy's initial attitude to the war was a complex mixture of heartfelt patriotism, distress at the break in Christian fellowship with other European Pentecostal leaders, and a desire that God would use 'this terrible war' to bring about his peace. It was painful to be separated from Pentecostal friends in Germany, as his first comment in *Confidence* demonstrated:

It is almost unthinkable that our beloved German brethren, such as Pastor Paul and others, should be separated from us by this cruel state of things. May our Lord end it quickly. It may be by His coming in the air for His own.[2]

Even here his hope of the second coming was prominent.

He also printed a prayer he had used during his journey back form the USA. It began with the opening of the *Book of Common Prayer* Collect for the Fourth Sunday after Easter: 'Almighty God who alone canst order the unruly wills and affectations of sinful men' and included petitions for God to bring peace, 'to comfort and heal the sick and wounded, and to draw many to Thyself'. He remembered the dying and those who ministered on battlefields and in hospitals. He also asked for a 'a spirit of intercession' and that God would 'Guide all in authority, and prosper their endeavours to protect the lands from spoliation and cruelty.' Such thoughts were to be expressed again and again by him over the next four years.

On his return to Monkwearmouth he received his copy of the letter Bishop Moule sent to all his parishes in August 1914 two days before war was declared. Moule saw it as 'England's plain duty to defend Belgium, even though such a step would mean declaring war on Germany'.[3] Boddy's own comments on the reasons for the war were similarly based on the need to defend Belgium: 'Why are we at War? We believe that we were forced in honour to keep our promises to Belgium . . . She was cruelly invaded and ravaged, contrary to treaty. England was compelled, in honour, to do all she could.'[4]

In the same edition of *Confidence* he urged all Pentecostal assemblies to hold a night of prayer on 28 October 1914, as he was doing at All Saints. His suggestions for prayer covered 'Militarism', purification of the Empire, acknowledgement of sin, and 'decisive victories':

We British Pentecostal people should pray very earnestly that "Militarism" may come to an end through this war; that our Empire should learn its lessons soon through humiliation and penitence, and come out refined and purified to serve the cause of Christ more loyally than before. We should acknowledge our sins, and earnest prayer meetings should be held, asking God to uphold the right and give decisive victories, if it be His will.[5]

He printed letters from various British soldiers and also from Pastor Voget of Bunde, East Friesland, who saw 'no war in Christ Jesus and in His true Body', but besides unity in Christ also stated: 'We do not hold that true Christianity and true patriotism exclude each other.'[6] At the same time Boddy also reported that he had heard of some forty German Pentecostal workers involved with the war, though not his friends Paul, Voget, Edel or Humberg.

Each edition of *Confidence* included at least some material on the war, though Boddy continued to print his familiar mix of teaching articles, Conference reports, evangelistic encouragement, news items from around the country and the world, and PMU missionary reports. Here we will concentrate on war-related themes.

In January 1915 Boddy reprinted remarks by Moule, calling the war 'a Holy War . . . [to] disarm effectually the Teutonic militarism'.[7]

By February 1915 it was evident that the war was going to be prolonged and bloody. Boddy continued to reflect on its possible connection with the second coming, referring to Armageddon (Revelation 16:16) and the words of Jesus about the trampling of Jerusalem (Luke 21:24). He linked the apocalyptic vision of these passages to the events unfolding as Turkish armies crossed the Holy Land and Egypt; this was to be seen as a sign of the times.[8] His support for the British war effort was not predicated on this interpretation of apocalyptic, however. He also stated very plainly: 'War is terrible, and only can ever be justified when in defence of the helpless, and to prevent oppression.'[9]

Boddy tried to keep open his links with his European friends, including 'Christian brethren in Germany', who he believed were misinformed about the war. He was pleased to be able to print 'a loving letter' from Jonathan Paul. It gave news of Paul's work on a modern translation of the New Testament, of their mutual friends, and of the fact that his 'son-in-law and both my sons are in the army. It was a serious time for me.' He continued to pray for Boddy, his family and fellow believers.[10]

In the same edition came a letter from Gerrit Polman of Amsterdam describing his spiritual work amongst English soldiers.[11]

Once again prayer for a speedy end to the war was requested, clearly identified in three points similar to those above, though this time explicitly mentioning prayer for Germany:

1. Let us pray for the German people; that the spirit of militarism and "Germany over all" may be re-placed by a desire for brotherly co-operation with all nations.
2. Let us pray for Britain and the Empire that we may learn the lessons God would teach us through this time of conflict and suffering, and be obedient to Him as a nation. That all tendency to boastfulness may be removed from us.
3. That if it be His will, very decisive victories may hasten the close of this awful strife, and prevent further suffering. That the war may not be prolonged.[12]

Though there was no doubt about his support for war by Britain, as he saw it as a just war against oppression, his understanding of the gospel and his friendships with German Pentecostals do seem to have saved him from outright jingoism.

The biggest disruption to Boddy's Pentecostal work was the cancellation of the planned 1915 Convention. The Convention was replaced by a small local event over the Whitsun weekend and by a larger Conference at Caxton Hall in London, organised by Polhill and which Boddy also attended. The Convention was moved partly because of fears of an invasion of the north-east coast, and partly because the war effort was important to Boddy – the Parish Hall was being used as a Detention Hospital for wounded fighting men.[13]

After speaking at the London Conference, Boddy visited troops in northern France, acting as chaplain to the dying, and seeking to bring comfort where he could. He was able to do this through the services of the YMCA, and he formed links with many men serving in the Durham Light Infantry: 'My mission seems largely personal encouragement, to do what I can for the men personally as the way opens.'[14]

From his base in Boulogne he was able to travel about, talking with soldiers and offering what help he could. On one occasion he ensured that French gravediggers tidied up graves they had dug for German soldiers, despite '[t]he French Officials [who] thought it rather strange of me to expend money on such an object'.[15] Later he visited Paris and from there he travelled another twenty miles east to the site of the Battle of the Marne, still close to the front line, where he was moved by the awful bloodshed.[16]

Angels at Mons

On his return to England Boddy was in demand to speak about his experiences, and *Confidence* reflected the greater quantity of material he now had, with travelogue-style reports appearing up to the January 1916 edition. The most intriguing item is his fascination with the reports of the 'Angels at Mons', the sightings of angels as the British troops retreated from the battlefield at Mons, northern France. Boddy 'was three times in France during the war, and always was ready to take down any evidence bearing on the subject of the Angels at Mons'.[17] He was aware that that the original story was a fictional account, but printed a list of at least eight soldiers who had spoken of a sighting.[18] The account of an anonymous lance corporal of a sighting around 28 August 1915 was given at some length. The central element was:

> Immediately afterwards the officer came back, and taking me and some others a few yards away showed us the sky. I could see quite plainly in mid-air a strange light which seemed to be quite distinctly outlined and was not a reflection of the moon, nor were there any clouds in the neighbourhood. The light became brighter and I could see quite distinctly three shapes, one in the centre having what looked like outspread wings. The other two were not so large, but were quite plainly distinct from the centre one. They appeared to have a long, loose, hanging garment of a golden tint, and they were about the German line facing us.[19]

The following month he printed a long extract from a book entitled *On the Side of the Angels*, giving supporting material about the soldier who had given this testimony.[20]

He returned to the subject in January 1916, this time with two detailed testimonies: one from Private J. Easy, whose vision was said to be from August 1914, and one from Private Davies, a Pentecostal, who claimed to have seen a host of angels on 7 December 1915 near Ypres. On this occasion Boddy also printed a commentary from another paper intimating that these visions might be connected with the second coming.[21] The following months he was advertising his booklet *Real Angels at Mons*, which contained the testimonies as well as prayers for use by soldiers on active service. He had met with Private Easy, for he also published a photograph of himself with the soldier.[22]

In an editorial of 1916 entitled 'Our Victory over Demons and Disease', Boddy made an explicit connection between these reports and his Pentecostal faith:

> CHRISTIANITY IS A SUPERNATURAL RELIGION. We believe in the "Unseen." There are undoubtedly unseen powers round about us. Good powers and evil powers. There are the Angels – God's Angels.[23]

It gave him the opportunity to refer to some of his favourite passages in Hebrews 1 and Psalm 91, where the angels are described as helpers and guardians of believers.

In his major study of the Church of England during the First World War Alan Wilkinson locates these Angel stories as one element in the widespread superstition quickened by the war. He notes Boddy's promotion of the stories, alongside Bishop Moule's own enchantment with them (without realising that Moule was Boddy's bishop). The Dean of Durham, Hensley Henson, was outspoken in his criticism of the story, and depressed to find Moule 'deeply bitten by the Angelic legend'.[24]

Boddy no doubt heard Moule speak at the 'Town's Thanksgiving' in the Victoria Hall in Sunderland on 12 November 1918, the day after the Armistice was signed. Moule himself alluded to three 'acts of God independent of the co-operation of man', namely, 'the readiness and position of the British Fleet at the outbreak of war, and also during the retreat from Mons . . . [and] a definite answer to National prayer'.[25]

Despite Henson's criticism, and acknowledging the first fictional account, Boddy returned to the story after the war, again finding in it support for a supernatural worldview in a sceptical age.[26] In seeking to harmonise the various stories, and admitting the lies of at least two soldiers, he settled on there having been four appearances, one of which was that cited by Moule in a letter to the *Spectator* magazine. The story was well known independently of Boddy's efforts, but his attachment to it helped to spread it further and it is a reminder of his desire for evidence confirming his understanding of God's activity in the world.

His son shot down

In late 1917 the war came very close to the Boddy family when their son James was shot down over France.[27]

In September 1914, very early on in the war, James had left his university education at Emmanuel College, Cambridge, having been commissioned as a Second Lieutenant in the Durham Light Infantry. He eventually transferred into the Royal Flying Corps in November 1916. On 23 November 1917 he was shot in the head by Manfred von Richthofen (the 'Red Baron') and crashed, breaking both thighs. He was saved by the bravery of Captain Fox Russell, who had himself been injured in a forced landing but brought a rescue party to James under heavy fire. Fox Russell was later awarded the Military Cross for this rescue; James Boddy had a leg amputated as a result of his injuries.[28]

James's wounds were very serious and his father and sister Jane were given permission to visit him in France. Alexander expressed thanks for the prayers offered for James, who had been at death's door at least three times but brought back each time. On a second visit he found James suffering from tetanus, but later notes that he had 'a wonderful' recovery.[29]

James's injuries as a whole remained serious: in July 1918 he was in the London Hospital,[30] and more than a year after the crash, after the end of the war, he was still there, making very slow progress, and not sure of keeping his remaining leg.[31] Jane, who had been working with the YWCA in France in the last year of the war,[32] was now nursing in another London hospital and able to visit James.

During this period James wrote a small volume of poems, mainly on religious themes, reflecting the sadness of the war, but also an evangelical faith.[33]

Eventually recovery did come: in September 1919 Alexander saw him walking on crutches, and hoping to come home.[34]

Boddy's reaction to this traumatic episode underlined his personal commitment to the war, but along with Mary's illnesses also vitiated his teaching on faith healing.

Pentecostal developments

As we have seen, the Whitsuntide Conventions, so crucial to the unity of the British Pentecostal Movement, were moved from

Sunderland to London for all four years of the war. During those years Cecil Polhill was the convenor of the London Conferences, which meant Boddy remained a key speaker. Nonetheless, the move diminished his position and the pre-eminence of Sunderland as the British centre of Pentecostalism. There was a parallel diminution in the role of *Confidence* from 1917, when it had to become first bimonthly and then quarterly. His receding role was not a sudden process, but it occurred gradually, and to some extent was inevitable as he grew older and reached his early sixties during the war.

There were more specific causes of a lessening of his leadership role as a result of the war. Although not as numerous and well known as the Quakers, many British Pentecostals were Conscientious Objectors (COs) to the war, and some were imprisoned for their belief. The conflict within British Pentecostalism about the war and pacifism is reflected in the pages of *Confidence*. For example, Boddy gave a mention to an anti-war book, *Blood against Blood* by A.S. Booth-Clibborn (whom he described as '[m]y honoured brother in the Lord'), but he made it clear that he did not agree with it and recommended F. Ballard's *Britain Justified – The War from the Christian Standpoint* instead.[35]

He reprinted, but without endorsement, a letter from the Dutch Pastor Polman that hinted at his Polman's pacifism and at that of George Jeffreys, Booth-Clibborn, Dr Phair and others. Polman wrote: 'Our part is to do what we can to help the needy ones and bring the gospel of peace to them who are in unrest.'[36] The letter was followed by a short item from 'a Pastor, whose addresses at the Keswick Convention and elsewhere have been so helpful of late', a circumlocution for Bishop Moule. To Boddy's obvious satisfaction Moule had written: 'To say, "War is of the devil, and in principle and practice is entirely anti-Christian," is to take refuge from one's obligations behind a generalisation which is half a truth and half a lie.'[37]

In taking this attitude both Moule and Boddy were entirely typical of the clergy of the Church of England at that time – indeed, older evangelicals were especially noted for their support for the war.[38] As Wilkinson puts it: 'Anglican opinion was almost unanimous in rejecting pacifism.'[39] Wilkinson could find only two cases of pacifist Anglican clergy, ironically one of them in Moule's own diocese of Durham. In a typically pastoral touch Moule commended the courage and tone of the pacifist incumbent's parish letter: 'It should win you nothing but respect for your courage of conviction and balance of expression . . . my warm regard and respect is only enhanced by the "manner" of your letter.'[40]

However much the support of Boddy, and also of Polhill, for the war can be understood as part of their upbringing within the Church of England, it increased the gulf between them and younger leaders of Pentecostal groups. In commenting on the imprisonment of Pentecostal COs, Donald Gee suggested it was seen as persecution for their Pentecostal beliefs, not just as COs.[41] David Allen has pointed out that many of the leaders had difficulty in gaining exemption from military service because they were not part of recognised denominations, and gave the example of Howard Carter, sent to Wormword Scrubs.[42]

Such experiences provided an incentive to create more formal associations and leadership structures, while the shared experience in the context of a nation that was generally unsympathetic to pacifism created new bonds. As an example, meetings of Pentecostal COs in Wakefield prison led to the establishing of an Assemblies of God there after the war.

Pentecostal denominations were not formed in Britain until the 1920s, but there were signs of new groups being formed out of need. For example, in 1917 Boddy mentioned the expulsion of Pastor Saxby from his Baptist church: 'He has suffered willingly for his convictions, and had to leave his church.'[43]

At about the same time separate Elim groups began to grow in Ireland through George Jeffreys, who at the age of twenty-four had been given a prominent role in the 1913 Sunderland Convention by Boddy. In 1915 he created the Elim Evangelistic Band in Belfast, and his evangelistic gifts led to steady growth in the number of adherents and the number of churches.[44]

The shoots of separate organisations were gradually becoming visible, a trend which Boddy had sought to resist, but was now powerless to prevent. Revival within the churches had not happened and pressure was growing for a new direction.

The war highlighted and exacerbated long-standing problems over the leadership within the Pentecostal Movement. The end of the war did not lead to a return to the previous patterns, but instead soon led to new churches being formed.

Boddy's Last Visits

When the war ended, Boddy was still afflicted with concern for his son, and he caught influenza in the pandemic which swept the world in late 1918 and early 1919, being 'laid up for a number of weeks'. The outbreak of flu was severe in Sunderland and Boddy named a chorister and a Sunday School Superintendent from his congregation who died in the outbreak.[45] He did not mention Mary catching the illness, but it cannot have helped her, and it was not long before she became more seriously ill.

There had been three aspects to Boddy's pre-war leadership, his foreign trips, organising the Whitsuntide Conventions and editing *Confidence*. Each of these aspects was adversely affected by the war.

Boddy was not ready to retire gracefully and he accepted invitations to speak in the summer of 1919 at Atlanta and Los Angeles in the USA, and at Winnipeg and London in Canada.[46] Just for a moment it looked as if Boddy might have resumed his transatlantic leadership role, but his passport application was refused because of the post-war lack of shipping accommodation and he did not mention any further invitations to go to North America.[47]

When Polhill decided not to convene the 1919 Whitsuntide Conference the task fell not to Boddy but to Pastor Saxby. Boddy did attend the Conference held at Croydon by Saxby, and he also spoke at the next three London Conferences (1920–22). Polhill was the convenor again from 1920–24, but the break was crucial to Boddy's diminishing position in the Movement. The impression gained from *Confidence* is that Boddy was no longer the key speaker he had previously been and the 1922 Conference was his last. By then fewer of the emerging Pentecostal leaders were attending this Conference as a variety of other conferences became more important.

The London Conferences became less overtly 'Pentecostal': under Polhill's leadership Pentecostal characteristics such as prophecy and speaking in tongues were not banished, but they were restrained. Polhill placed more emphasis on encouraging foreign missionary work through the PMU. Donald Gee tells the story of a PMU missionary interrupting a meeting with a message in tongues: it was listened to but, he believed, with more embarrassment than in a 'more truly Pentecostal atmosphere'.[48] Later Gee was surprisingly acerbic about Polhill, describing him as a 'poor chairman' and noting how 'the audience . . . squirmed with impatience as he inflicted on them his little homilies'.[49]

The third aspect of Boddy's pre-war leadership had been the editing of *Confidence*. The magazine did continue to be published, but it was issued quarterly from 1918 to 1924, with a single issue only in each of the years 1925 and 1926. Material of the same genres continued to be included, but Boddy's own contributions were fewer, with more from long-standing friends such as Smith Wigglesworth, John Leech and Elizabeth Sisson. Among his own articles were some important retrospective pieces which inform us of his life story, and especially of the way he interpreted it as he looked back. The slightly nostalgic feel of these editions is strongest in the few produced after he moved to the country parish of Pittington, as he shared his appreciation of the history of this ancient parish.

It was not all 'change and decay', though, for he continued both to care deeply for the spiritual needs of his parishioners and to travel to spread the Pentecostal blessing. His long-esteemed bishop, Handley Moule, had one last part to play in Boddy's involvement in both these strands. On Whitsunday 1919 Moule spoke at All Saints Church at Boddy's request on 'The Hope of the Approach of the Lord's Return'.[50] Boddy described Moule as 'the saintly man of God they love so dearly', and printed the address at considerable length.

Later in 1919 Boddy was invited to the Anglican chaplaincy in Brussels by the Revd H. Stirling Gahan, a fellow Pentecostal Anglican, and of some celebrity because he had ministered to Nurse Cavell (a hospital Matron who had helped English prisoners-of-war to escape) before she was executed by a German firing squad.[51] Boddy recorded in *Confidence* how Moule, '[m]y beloved Diocesan, the Lord Bishop of Durham had written an all too kind letter of commendation of the writer as mission preacher'. The letter continued with words of encouragement for the congregation in Brussels, and ended with a thought about the gospel: '[t]he Gospel secret is not a thing, but a Person. It is not it, but He. And this, I know, will be the golden burden of your mission message.'[52]

Any doubt about Boddy's appreciation of Moule is dispelled by his warm words after Moule's death in 1920:

On Ascension Day I, with others, filed past a flower-covered coffin! and I said in my heart, "Good-bye, dear Bishop, I owe much to you." When Bishop Handley Moule came into a meeting we felt an uplift. He brought a spiritual atmosphere with him. He was a man filled with the Holy Ghost.[53]

The trip to Belgium gave Boddy the opportunity to visit battlefields in Flanders and he devoted more of his account to this than to the Mission week. His lifelong gifts of making friends and vivid description had clearly not left him:

> Friday, November 7th. As soon as daylight came I was out in the mud of Flanders, making a preliminary survey along the Menin Road, and examining the first cemetery, partly civil, partly military, with a great central Crucifix. One family vault had been burst to pieces by shell fire. Many of our men's graves had been decorated by Belgian people.
>
> The too well-known Casualty Receiving Station stood by the roadside here, and one can still see some of its buildings. What tragic stories could be told of sights and sounds it has witnessed.
>
> A little later I set off to walk on to Hooge. The clouds hung low, the rain drizzled, the muddy road was churned up by motor lorries which still pass over it, some British, some Belgian. Shell holes on either side, and, not infrequently, live shells lying near. "Can I give you a lift, sir?" cried a cheery padre, near "Hell-Fire Corner." It was Major Gibbons, S.C.F., D.A.C.G. in that area. So I got in his motor and we sped along at a better speed, and up the slope towards Hooge . . . Crater Cemetery.[54]

The Mission week itself was not well attended and he gave no accounts of conversions or of people receiving the baptism of the Holy Ghost, but he was cheerful about it, and the opportunity to be with other believers was valuable to him.

Foreign travel had been part of all his adult life, but that was his last trip abroad. However, while living next to the ironworks at Monkwearmouth he still found it helpful to get away for refreshment. When the proposed visit to North America in 1919 did not happen he was able to spend a month giving a preaching series on 'The Larger Life of Christ' at St James, Taunton, while they were without a vicar. In this account, too, there was more space given to the history of the area and his visits by bicycle than to his spiritual ministry, real though it was.[55]

In succeeding years there were similar trips – in 1920 to All Saints, Hoole, Chester,[56] in 1922 to Holy Trinity, Kilburn, London,[57] and in 1924 to St Anne's Soho, London, to preach ten discourses on 'Christ in His Holy Land'. As if to show he was still full of vigour approaching his seventieth year this last series was advertised in *The Times*.[58]

There is no record of any further such visits or series.

Leaving Monkwearmouth

By 1922 Mary's continuing ill health and Alexander's own age meant that a change of parish was advisable. His own account written at the time is worth reading in full:

The departure of the Writer (Rev. A.A. Boddy) from Sunderland has been sudden. It was represented to him that it was the wish of those who had the appointment of the vacant Vicarage of Pittington that he should accept it. "We should all feel happy in entrusting the spiritual interests of Pittington to your care."

For two or three days he was undecided. He loved dearly his people at All Saints', Monkwearmouth. But the position of the Vicarage, where he had lived for 38 years, close to a great ironworks with its smoke and vibrations, had undermined his dear wife's health and probably impaired his own. The winters were very trying for them both so near the North Sea. A home in the country, with more healthy conditions might be God's way of extending the days of their usefulness for Him.

He summoned the members of All Saints' Parish Council to the Vicarage and laid it before them. They were sad but felt that they must not hinder that which might be for the good of their Leader and his wife. So it soon became widely known that their Vicar was about to leave, that his 38 years' ministry was to end in a very few days. The Writer went through such sorrowful scenes as he hopes never to experience again in this world.[59]

Although he is not explicit, Mary was not with him at this farewell, but convalescing at Milford-on-Sea on the south coast of England. That seems to have been the decisive factor for him when he received the unexpected letter offering him the post at Pittington. Reflecting on the parallels with his own father's move more than half a century earlier from the slums of Manchester was a further help:

> More than 50 years ago my dear father, then Rector of St. Thomas's, Cheetham, had a very similar experience to that which I am now passing through . . . he was 60 and the strenuous life among the poor was beginning to tell upon him.[60]

Once the decision had been reached the move was swift. On the following Sunday he invited parishioners to stay after the service to hear him give the story of his time as their Vicar, an account usefully printed in *Confidence*, January 1923. On Sunday 17 December 1922 he held his farewell services. So many people attended the service of Holy Communion, including many Nonconformists, that a second service had to be held.[61] Here was tangible testimony to the long and faithful ministry of Alexander and Mary in this working-class parish.

In his characteristic style Boddy reprinted a report from the *Sunderland Echo* of the farewell gathering held in the Parish Hall at Monkwearmouth shortly after he and Mary had moved to Pittington. The main speaker was the Revd J.O. Aglionby, vicar of the adjoining parish of St Peter's Monkwearmouth. He spoke of Boddy's spiritual power and gave thanks for his long ministry. Looking to the future, '[h]e was sure that no-one who knew how Mr. and Mrs. Boddy and Miss Boddy had laboured in so hard and difficult a parish would say they did not deserve surroundings without steam hammers and belching smoke . . . and incessant noise.'

Boddy's response to the words and presentation was both fond and an exhortation to 'carry on' with God. Sadly, Mary was not with him, and Jane expressed her mother's thanks for the gift of a watch, as well as her own sadness at leaving the people amongst whom she had been brought up.[62]

Pittington

At the age of sixty-eight Boddy was inducted to the parish of Pittington Hallgarth by the Bishop of Jarrow, with the local clergy also in attendance. He was pleased that seventy-three former parishioners also came by charabancs. His first thoughts were on the benefits of not breathing in the fumes of Sunderland, but he also realised the fumes represented work for many, and that the public facilities offered in a town like Sunderland were considerable. He was grateful for the excellent choir in his new church and had already been welcomed 'in miners' cottages and in farm houses'.[63]

Mary was still away on the south coast at the time of the move, but was able to return to Alexander in Pittington with her friend Miss Newton. By April 1923 she was well enough to write again in *Confidence*.[64]

Alexander himself would soon feel the physical benefit of the move:

> For the first time for a number of winters I have not been laid aside with bronchitis and asthma, but have gone on with my duties through these months feeling stronger and better than in those last days beside the ironworks in Fulwell Road, Sunderland.[65]

However, he did not travel that summer, and in any case their eldest daughter Mary married the Revd Reg Taylor in August, about the time when Boddy was often away from home.

Although his health was better than previously, a poignant remark in the Visitation return of June 1924 reveals that he was not as fit as he would have liked. Asked if there was help from lay people in leading services he replied: 'Only if my voice fails, or my strength is not normal, does a licensed Reader read the prayers from the 3rd Collect onwards.'[66] But he was pleased about the 'historic and beautiful Church and its thankful and hearty services: – together with the friendliness between the Non-Conformists and the Church, all help towards unity in this parish.'

His ecumenical spirit remained strong, and in October 1924 he organised an ecumenical week of prayer in Pittington, with meetings held at two Wesleyan Churches, the Primitive Methodist Church and the Salvation Army Hall, as well as at the parish church.[67]

The following year the Parish Week of Prayer came at the end of September and was followed in October by a mission with students from Durham.

In 1926 he sought permission from Bishop Henson to admit Nonconformists to Holy Communion, permission which was readily given.[68]

In other aspects of his parochial work he built up the life of the church community, reintroducing confirmation and developing the choir, as Jane was later to recall.[69] He also wrote a short history of the church. He was assisted in his work by Mary: although she was largely housebound with painful arthritis, she did still manage to run a women's Bible class and continued with her healing ministry.

Family

Jane, now in her thirties, was involved with work amongst young people, and with visiting newcomers and the sick right through her father's time as Vicar of Pittington. In 1932 she joined the Community of the Resurrection as a novice, and was professed as a nun in 1938. As Mother Joanna Mary she became Mother Superior of the Community in Grahamstown, South Africa. She was known to speak in tongues throughout her life, and was a link with the charismatic renewal in that diocese in the 1970s under Bishop Bill Burnett.[70]

During this period their elder daughter, Mary, was mostly stationed with CMS in Mienchow in Western China with her husband Reg and their two children Evelyn and Noel, though there were also opportunities to visit Pittington on furlough. Boddy noted that they received a letter each week from them.[71]

Relations with James seem to have been more distant, with no mention of his marriage to Marjorie D'arcy in 1920, and only two mentions in *Confidence* after that date. The birth of another granddaughter, Sheila Vazeille, daughter to James, came in 1926, but was probably too late to be included in the last issue of the magazine. Sheila was certainly taken to visit her grandparents, for she has photographs of herself as a baby seated on their knees. When Mary died, James attended her funeral, but not his wife.[72] Taylor reports that most of Alexander's papers were burnt after the death of James in 1954.[73] Although James moved away from the evangelicalism of his younger days he remained committed as a Christian and member of the Church of England. He became very involved with the British Legion in Leicestershire, and shortly before his death he was awarded the OBE for that work, in the Queen's Coronation Honours of 1953.

The Pentecostal Movement

Boddy's involvement with Pentecostalism was declining, partly with his age, partly as new leaders came to the fore. Elim churches were being formed through the evangelistic ministry of the Jeffreys brothers, though formal organisation emerged gradually.

In 1924 the Assemblies of God (AOG) was formed to give some cohesion to other scattered Pentecostal groups, and the PMU was soon merged with the new national organisation, becoming its missionary arm. Boddy and Polhill left the council of the PMU.

Apart from the two further editions of *Confidence*, that was the end of Boddy's public involvement with Pentecostalism. In the penultimate issue of *Confidence* he drew attention to the two new newspapers for these groups: he described the *Elim Evangel* as 'very thrilling', while *Redemption Tidings* warranted only information about subscriptions and the fact that it would contain PMU reports.[74] This difference may explained by the warmth of Boddy's long friendship with the Jeffreys brothers, and his dislike of the absorption of the PMU into the AOG structure.

Their last days

Illness finally caught up with Mary and Alexander. In October 1927 Mary became more seriously ill, and eventually she died on 25 April 1928. Alexander lived on a little longer, supported in his ministry to the end by Jane, and still occasionally engaging in a ministry of healing according to his Visitation return made in October 1928: 'I myself believe in the power of the Lord to heal, and occasionally act on the command found in James 5.17.'[75]

Alexander became ill in the summer of 1930 and died on 10 September. He is buried next to Mary in the Pittington churchyard in a grave marked by a simple headstone.

For the graves Jane selected biblical texts: for her mother, 'Blessed are the pure in heart for they shall see God', and for her father, 'As many as are led by the Spirit of God, they are the sons of God.'

The church at Pittington also has a plaque in the chancel commemorating them both. At All Saints Monkwearmouth there are stained-glass windows depicting other very appropriate biblical passages: for Mary there is a pair of windows, picturing the Mary who sat at the feet of Jesus listening to his words; for Alexander, the Good Shepherd carrying a lamb, a fitting image for a man who devoted his life as shepherd to his parish and to Pentecostal people around the world.

Yet these physical memorials are not the only way to remember the Boddys: the Epilogue offers some assessment of their ministry and legacy.

Notes

1 *Confidence*, December 1914, 224–25
2 *Confidence*, September 1914, 163
3 Moule's own description. Harford and MacDonald, *Moule*, 272–73
4 *Confidence*, October 1914, 191
5 *Confidence*, October 1914, 191
6 *Confidence*, October 1914, 191
7 *Confidence*, January 1915, 5
8 *Confidence*, February 1915, 26
9 *Confidence*, February 1915, 27
10 *Confidence*, February 1915, 28–29
11 *Confidence*, February 1915, 29
12 *Confidence*, February 1915, 33
13 *The North Star, Darlington*, 24 May 1915, 2, reprinted in *Confidence*, June 1915, 105–107
14 *Confidence* July 1915, 127–29
15 *Confidence* August 1915, 145–46
16 *Confidence* August 1915, 146–48
17 *Confidence*, April 1919, 22
18 *Confidence*, September 1915, 165–69
19 *Confidence*, September 1915, 166

20 *Confidence*, October 1915, 191–93
21 *Confidence*, January 1916, 5–8
22 *Confidence*, February 1916, 22, 37; March 1916, 55
23 *Confidence*, November 1916, 180
24 Wilkinson, *Church and War*, 194–95
25 Harford and MacDonald, *Moule*, 281–82
26 *Confidence*, April 1919, 23
27 *Confidence*, January 1918, 7. Sadly, the full account is not available in the CD version of the magazine
28 Franks et al., *Guns of the Red Baron*, 160–61
29 *Confidence*, April 1918, 33
30 *Confidence*, July 1918, 49
31 *Confidence*, January 1919, 6–7
32 *Confidence*, July 1918, 55
33 J.V. Boddy, *Afterwards*
34 *Confidence*, October 1919, 56
35 *Confidence*, January 1915, 6
36 *Confidence*, November 1914, 204–205
37 *Confidence*, November 1914, 205
38 Wilkinson, *Church and War*, 9
39 Wilkinson, *Church and War*, 54
40 Harford and MacDonald, *Moule*, 273–76. Discussed in Wilkinson, *Church and War*, 54
41 Gee, *Wind and Flame*, 102
42 Allen, 'The Glossolalic Ostrich', 51
43 *Confidence*, July 1917, 56
44 Kay, *Pentecostals in Britain*, 20–21
45 *Confidence*, January 1919, 7
46 *Confidence*, April 1919, 24
47 *Confidence*, July 1919, 49
48 Gee, *Wind and Flame*, 111
49 Gee, *These Men I Knew*, 75–76
50 *Confidence*, July 1919, 39–43, 45–46
51 Gahan's account is in *Confidence* July 1919, 44–45. Boddy's description of his trip appeared in *Confidence*, January 1920, 3–5, 10–12
52 *Confidence*, January 1920, 11–12
53 *Confidence*, July 1920, 37
54 *Confidence*, January 1920, 4
55 *Confidence*, October 1919, 55–56
56 *Confidence*, October 1920, 58
57 *Confidence*, October 1922, 50
58 *The Times*, 3 July, 2 August 1924 and subsequent Saturdays. *Confidence*, August 1924, 138
59 *Confidence*, January 1923, 64

60 *Confidence*, January 1923, 66
61 *Confidence*, January 1923, 67
62 *Confidence*, January 1923, 72–73
63 *Confidence*, January 1923, 71–72
64 *Confidence*, April 1923, 82–83
65 *Confidence*, April 1923, 86
66 Durham Diocesan Visitation Returns, St Lawrence, Pittington, 1924
67 *Confidence*, November 1924, 150
68 Braley, *Letters of Henson*, 48
69 Jane Boddy, *A.A. Boddy*, 9
70 Information supplied by the Community of Resurrection to the family.
71 *Confidence* May 1925, 162
72 Newspaper cutting and other information supplied by Sheila Harker.
73 Taylor, 'Publish and be Blessed', 112
74 *Confidence*, May 1925, 162
75 Durham Diocesan Visitation Returns, St Lawrence, Pittington, 1928

Epilogue

Assessment and Legacy

Boddy's contribution to the development of Pentecostalism in Britain, Europe and the English-speaking world has not been widely acknowledged until recently. However, it seems that this is beginning to change. Within Sunderland itself there has been some recognition, with a local history published in 1986. The church in the parish of All Saints has had a returning awareness of their own history, partly sparked by the sale of the church hall used for many Pentecostal meetings to the Monkwearmouth Christian Fellowship in 1996.[1] The Fellowship's new notice board keeps the name of the building as 'All Saints Parish Hall' and it states prominently that this is 'The Birthplace of British Pentecostalism'. In the same period a group associated with the Assemblies of God formed the Sunderland Christian Centre, also explicitly drawing inspiration from the ministry of Boddy.[2]

Generations of British Pentecostal historians, beginning with Donald Gee, have given Boddy honourable mention, and this is especially true of the most recent historian, William Kay. As we saw when discussing Boddy's theology, Kay begins his own discussion of Pentecostal doctrines by examining what was written by Boddy and others in *Confidence*. Boddy's trips to the USA to encourage the Pentecostals have not gone unnoticed: the publication of *Confidence* on CD-ROM by the USA's Assemblies of God Heritage Centre is proof of that; the other six items they made available initially on CD-ROM were all US-based materials.

In drawing this biography to a close we can assess Boddy's ministry in the three interlocking areas of leadership, teaching and pastoral concern.

Leadership

It is entirely appropriate to regard Boddy as the spiritual father of British Pentecostalism as a result of his leadership of the movement. He had considerable authority as a leader, quite naturally assuming the position through organising the Conventions and publishing *Confidence*; and the tone of his instructions in the first issue concerning behaviour at the first Conference meetings leaves no doubt as to where the human authority lay. However, it is not correct to describe him as an aristocrat, as Hollenweger does;[3] it would be more accurate to describe him as a university-educated member of the Victorian middle class. He became a solicitor without a law degree, and for his ordination training he did not attend Oxford or Cambridge, because he and his father could not afford the fees.

The other side of Boddy's confident leadership was the difficulty he had in sharing leadership in Britain. He certainly gave pastoral care to many emerging leaders, but his personal control of the Conventions and of *Confidence* did not enable other British leaders to share the task of leadership; even with his European colleagues there was a gradual diminution in the size of the leadership group.

The break in Conventions caused by the First World War probably only hastened the transfer of leadership to a younger generation, it did not initiate it. Furthermore, conflicts over water baptism and the explication of speaking in tongues were growing and would eventually become too great for the different sides to stay together.

Similarly, *Confidence* was not taken on by other people; instead, new journals, *Elim Evangel* and *Redemption Tidings*, were created by the next generation.

It would not be accurate to regard this change in leadership as entirely caused by Boddy's actions. There were other factors in play, including the rejection of Pentecostalism by most mainstream churches and leaders, and the desire of many Pentecostal leaders to create new organisations. Boddy's own vision and theology had always been for Pentecostalism as a renewal movement within the churches. Yet he and Polhill have been criticised by Donald Gee for failing to see that they could have provided leadership to a new organisation. However, this is to overlook what they did provide by way of stability and, in

Polhill's case, finance. It is also to underestimate the emphasis they placed on the importance of maintaining church unity if at all possible. Nonetheless, despite disagreeing in principle with the idea of forming new organisations, Boddy did not speak against the emerging new denominations, and included news of them in the last few issues of *Confidence*.

In fact, he did not seem to want to cling to leadership, and his character is described by those who knew him in his parishes as humble and warm. Even in the 1980s there were people in Pittington who remembered him with affection, and not as a domineering man. The evidence of his travel writing, both in his books and in *Confidence*, is of an assured man, but also one open to learning from others and their circumstances. That combination of assurance and openness was used to the full in his search for holiness of life and his subsequent promotion of Pentecostalism.

Boddy's upbringing in a vicarage and his own parish ministry had given him considerable organisational skills and these were fully used in the running of the Whitsuntide Conventions as other people were drawn in to help with the practical arrangements; for example, the very first Convention secretaries in 1908 were not based at the Vicarage.[4] The relatively smooth running of the Conventions and their regularity for a number of years was a major contribution to the cohesion and development of Pentecostalism in Britain and Europe. There were other gatherings during this period – *Confidence* gave news of many – but it was the Sunderland meetings which were the most important, as later Pentecostals also agreed.

Boddy's sensible leadership is highlighted by the career of William Hutchinson, who led the Apostolic Faith Church. Hutchinson wanted to be seen as leader of the Pentecostal Movement in Britain, publishing his own paper, and in time ordaining other leaders. His increasingly eccentric views on prophecy as providing guidance in daily life were noted in chapter 8.[5] In contrast, Boddy brought care to the interpretation of Scripture and order in worship, without impeding what he saw as good and upbuilding in the development of Pentecostal practice.

Teaching Ministry

Boddy's teachings were disseminated through his Roker Tracts even before his Pentecostal experience of 1907, and with the publication of *Confidence* his teaching went even wider within the English-speaking world. In each issue of the magazine he provided his own teaching and frequently included an article by Mary, but many other people contributed, from a variety of viewpoints, even sometimes not Pentecostal. Despite his patriotism, he did print some articles critical of the war effort.

His teaching was based largely on positions held by other Anglican evangelicals of the time, with the addition of Pentecostal items, notably divine healing, Spirit baptism and the use of spiritual gifts, especially speaking in tongues and prophecy. His move from the more conservative position seems to have occurred through his spiritual experience in 1892 and his wife's healing in 1899, which reinforced the sense of divine activity in the present. The conjunction of Anglican evangelical and Pentecostal doctrines did lead to some tensions in his own teaching.

Tensions

First, there was a tension between his strong desire to promote Christian unity on the one hand and the need to provide clear teaching on Pentecostal phenomena on the other. This was particularly true in teaching about speaking in tongues, with a wide spectrum of views advanced by contributors to *Confidence*. The tension was there, for example, in his laudable attempt to urge unity between Christians in Los Angeles, who were divided by the teaching of William Durham on the 'Finished Work of Christ'. Boddy ultimately had an instinct, still felt by many Anglicans, that unity in love was more important than absolute precision over doctrine. The Nonconformist backgrounds of many of his fellow Pentecostals ultimately pushed them in the other direction.

The second tension occurred in his desire to show the continuity of his thinking, its unity over time. Again, the issue of speaking in tongues shows this tension clearly when he regularly claimed that his teaching was consistent over time, and any apparent change was simply a matter of emphasis. Some commentators have not accepted his own statements, but have suggested that he did change his thinking and teaching. On the whole I have accepted his personal account, in that the various elements of his teaching on this topic can be found at different dates. Of more significance was the fact that on the whole he was not enthusiastic to appear to be changing his mind: this was most likely linked to his view of Scripture as infallible and therefore leading to changeless doctrine.

A third tension can be found in his teaching on faith in God and its outworking in the areas of money and of healing. He spoke against the methods of raising money he saw in the churches of both England and the USA; in setting up the PMU on the same faith basis as the China Inland Mission he showed how he believed it was right to finance projects. However, he experienced problems in running *Confidence* magazine this way, and the magazine and the PMU were kept viable only through the outstanding generosity of Polhill. Theologically there need be no embarrassment about this if one accepts that Polhill was God's instrument in this provision, but Boddy never put that into writing, perhaps because Polhill wanted anonymity. It does, however, leave us with a curious look to Boddy's teaching and practice on money: on the one hand a childlike trust in God's provision, on the other the need to accept very large subsidies from one benefactor. His experience of finance in the Church of England with its unique level of inherited wealth at that time will have skewed his own thinking, since he was not dependent on the direct giving of his congregation for his own support.

A fourth tension in his teaching related to healing. His view on trusting God for healing was dependent on his own and Mary's experience of God's grace. There was enough realism in his teaching through his life to recognise that not everyone would be able to live as they did. However, he gave the impression that prayer and anointing would be sufficient for those who had the faith. Mary's long illnesses, his own after the First World War, and their son's horrific injuries all contributed to an acceptance of medical help, despite his earlier objections that this was not the best way to find healing.

A change in thinking by the whole family can be seen in the willingness of both daughters, Mary and Jane, to take up nursing posts. The weakness was not the eventual acceptance of medical help, but that his theological framework was not quite flexible enough to cope. Sadly, there is only limited integration between his approach to faith healing and medical care in his final years, though he sustained both.

For all these tensions, though, the teaching that he gave and promoted is traceable down to the present day, as William Kay has shown in *Pentecostals in Britain*. This fact alone would have given him a prominent position in the history of Pentecostalism. He was working as a pioneer within Anglicanism when he sought to harmonise his Pentecostal understandings with his Anglican upbringing, and as such was effective in helping to make sense of the powerful experiences he and many others were having. His commitment to the Bible means that his teaching remains accessible for similarly committed people today. His illustrations may seem quaint, and the lack of engagement with critical scholarship could make him sound naive, but his pastoral wisdom frequently shines through.

Pastoral Concern

Boddy brought a very strong sense of caring for people to all his ministry, and almost everything he wrote expresses his concern for their well-being – spiritual, physical and social. We have heard of his care for his parishioners and his involvement with people from all social classes on his travels. When it came to Pentecostal experiences he was firm in insisting that the use of spiritual gifts was for the upbuilding of the church and the good of the people. Any attempt to manipulate people was frowned upon, and his care can be seen in the meticulous recording of who had experienced what. He did not want to exaggerate the effects of the Movement and played down the more extreme manifestations associated with revival meetings, but nor did he want to 'quench the Spirit'.

In this context it is especially worth noting his efforts in the USA to help American Pentecostals overcome the 'colour problem'. While his language about black people would be considered rather patronising today, in his own day he was a liberal on the issue of colour. He spoke at black as well as white churches, and rejoiced in fellowship between black and white Christians. He did not have a revolutionary social agenda, but given his background as a conservative evangelical Anglican he was quite radical in his understanding of the social implications of Christianity. For example, he saw very clearly the implications of Christian fellowship for breaking down barriers between nations, cultures and different Christian traditions.

Boddy was well aware of the need to evangelise within Britain as well as overseas. His own parish work in Monkwearmouth had required a major evangelistic and pastoral effort. It was a typically Anglican vision of evangelism largely through pastoral care. In a relatively settled community such as Monkwearmouth became, and in the context of a long pastoral ministry (remember Boddy was there from 1884 to 1922), such a vision was possible.

However, the antagonism between most Pentecostal leaders and those from the historical churches was such that the Pentecostals almost inevitably started to create their own assemblies and to engage in forms of evangelism which had neither the advantages nor the disadvantages of being in the established church. If more leaders in the mainstream churches had embraced Pentecostalism, then Boddy's vision might have worked. Some sixty years later, from the 1960s onwards, the charismatic movement within the historic churches went a long way towards Boddy's vision, though the growth of the new churches outside of the historic and the Pentecostal churches is an indication of the ambitious nature of the vision.

One way in which Boddy's leadership and pastoral visions may have weakened the initial development of Pentecostalism in Britain was his and Polhill's policy of sending leaders to the overseas mission field. On the positive side this made a major contribution to overseas Pentecostal work, but another part of the motivation may have been to remove potential leaders from Britain. The PMU struggled throughout its existence despite Boddy's and Polhill's backing and Polhill's financial support. While the urgency of mission was felt by all Pentecostals there is a serious question as to whether Boddy's and Polhill's approach was the most helpful.

Overall, though, Boddy was remembered as a truly pastoral man, who was interested in everyone he met. His writings are richly peopled with miners and ironworkers, housemaids and mothers, peasant women and monks in Russia, fellow travellers and railwaymen, the English abroad and foreign visitors to

Sunderland, nearly of all them named and given life in a few words of description. His ability to make friends quickly was important in both his parish and his wider Pentecostal ministry. It brought him love in his parish and enabled a disparate group of European Pentecostal ministers to gel and support one another; without Boddy's sheer friendliness that support would have been much less possible.

Boddy's Legacy

For all that Boddy's vision of a renewed church had apparently failed even before the end of his life, he has left a legacy in other ways. In the mid 1970s Martin Robinson wrote a helpful comparison of the ministries of Boddy and Michael Harper, an evangelical Anglican priest at that time promoting charismatic renewal in the Church of England. Like Boddy, Harper found himself a pioneer in a new movement and this makes it instructive to begin with Robinson's assessment and to reassess it thirty years on.

Robinson believed that Harper had picked up three elements of Boddy's vision,[6] coincidentally, though Harper did know something of Boddy's story.[7] Robinson identified these common elements as:

1. 'The Pentecostal experience is a gift from God to the whole church.' For Boddy and for Harper, unlike for most Classical Pentecostals, this meant embracing 'the risk of taking Pentecost to the churches as they are'.
2. 'The Pentecostal outpouring is intended to draw together rather than force apart.' Robinson pointed out that 'Classical Pentecostals have again and again been affected by division'.
3. 'Pentecost has something to say about the world itself. The Spirit calls us to be concerned with the problems of race, the poor, the economy, the underprivileged.'

Robinson also noted that Harper had not taken on Boddy's work with working class people, in which the latter was so successful in his parish.

Taking the first two elements together, since Robinson wrote the charismatic movement has affected virtually all denominations, introducing them to Pentecostal experiences and practices. Michael Harper played a significant role in this, extending his work beyond the Church of England to embrace all Christians groups, and is himself now a member of the Antiochian Orthodox Church. Classical Pentecostals themselves have become more open to working with other Christian groups, with Donald Gee and David du Plessis being prominent in early ecumenical conversations. While not fully accepted within Pentecostalism, many have caught the vision of Boddy and the other pioneers that the Pentecostal experience is a gift for the whole church. Walter Hollenweger has identified this belief as a fourth phase of ecumenical development, with conversations between Pentecostals, Roman Catholics and the World Council of Churches.[8] A century on, and despite real problems, Boddy's larger vision of the Pentecostal experience as a renewing force for the existing churches has greater significance than ever. His slogan, 'unity not uniformity', has been unknowingly echoed by countless people since.

Boddy certainly recognised that the Holy Spirit had called him to go beyond his familiar boundaries. The way in which he sought to hold together a Pentecostal spirituality and a range of other important contemporary concerns remains of value and challenge in the church today. I identify four important issues as:

1. Anglican practice and pastoral care.
2. An ecumenical vision.
3. An international vision.
4. Social implications of faith.

The first of these relates to Boddy's parochial vision as someone working in a poor industrial area, and caring about his parishioners. This pastoral vision is still held by many Anglican clergy, but is more difficult to achieve, not least because there are fewer clergy. Boddy did have a succession of curates working with him, but also acted on the need to involve lay people in the work, and the Pentecostal experience gave renewed motivation to his congregation. Time and again he refers to those who have been renewed taking leadership roles in the Sunday schools, choirs, Bible studies and so on. The test of love seen in action was worked out in his parish in this way.

His ecumenical vision has been discussed already; his ecumenism was in the context of an international vision of the church. From his early life he supported mission work, and on his travels wanted to learn from the Christians and churches he encountered, even when he had some disagreements with them. His love for God's people overcame many barriers. At its best, Pentecostalism has always had a global perspective, and it is increasingly viewed as a global phenomenon. At a time when foreign travel was very unusual, Boddy used his opportunities to challenge his fellow clergy and parishioners to look beyond their country and their denomination.

Boddy had always known there was a social dimension to the gospel, learnt from his father's work in Manchester. He did not reject that after his Pentecostal experience, but continued to seek the breaking down of social divisions wherever possible. Whether these divisions were of class, ethnicity or colour he was clear that unity in Christ, made real through the Spirit, was more important. He was known for his work in the temperance movement; this was motivated by the damage he saw in families through the abuse of alcohol. The gospel was not divorced from the reality of daily life for his parishioners.

Lastly, we must turn to the legacy only fleetingly mentioned by Robinson, but which I suspect to be the one that as a pastor he would be most pleased to know about: his continuing influence in the lives of Christians. There are some better known personal links, for despite his failure to develop a team of leaders we have seen how he provided much needed pastoral support and wisdom to nearly all the early British Pentecostal leaders at some stage. It is possible to trace the personal link to the present: one well-known link has been through Smith Wigglesworth, through David du Plessis to Michael Harper, all men who have shown a commitment to the wider Christian community in the way pioneered by Boddy. Another, less well known, link between Boddy and Harper came through the evangelist Canon Bryan Green of Birmingham. He was very supportive of Harper, partly because he had had an aunt who had been a Pentecostal Anglican through the work of Boddy,[9] and partly because he had worked with Jane Boddy in parish missions.[10]

Boddy's style of leadership, that of a benevolent father-figure, was not unusual in the Church of England at the time in working class parishes. It is less common now in the Church of England, but has something in common with the position of pastors in present-day Pentecostal assemblies. Although notionally without formal status beyond that of 'minister of the gospel', Pentecostal pastors function as 'charismatic' leaders, given status through their personal gifts.[11] While there is a strong sociological push in this direction, one also wonders if there was some unconscious modelling on Boddy by emerging leaders.

More pleasing still to Boddy would be the testimonies of ordinary Christians still worshipping in the churches of Sunderland. In the 1980s Peter Lavin was able to find in both Monkwearmouth and Pittington parishioners who remembered Boddy and were able to speak of his personality and work.[12] Remarkably, Boddy was still recalled in oral tradition in 2005, for I have found church members who testify to his pastoral work with members of their family. His work with his choir members (each of whom received a personally signed book when he left Monkwearmouth), his care for the bereaved, and his passionate fight against the evils of alcohol, all are remembered a century later.

For a man with a pastoral heart, symbolised by the shepherd pictured in his memorial window, there can be no higher accolade.

Notes

1 A development from the local Elim fellowship
2 Gott, *Sunderland Refreshing*, 75
3 Hollenweger, *Pentecostalism*, 344
4 *Confidence*, April 1908, 2, and note the use of more than one secretary sharing the workload
5 Kay, *Pentecostals*, 15–16, 65–66
6 The following extracts are from Robinson, *The Charismatic Anglican*, 239–41
7 Harper, *As At the Beginning*, Chapter Four 'A Debt Consumed'
8 There is a useful summary in Anderson, *Pentecostalism*, 249–58
9 Informal conversation between Green and Robinson, 9 January 1976, reported in Robinson, *The Charismatic Anglican*, 239
10 Information supplied by the Community of the Resurrection, Grahamstown
11 Kay, *Pentecostals*, 194–96
12 Lavin, *Boddy*, 2. Anecdotes are scattered through the text

Appendix One

Timeline of Alexander Alfred Boddy (AAB)

1809 Birth of James Alfred Boddy, father of AAB, at Beaconsfield, Bucks[1]

1824 7 August: birth of Jane Vazeille Stocks, mother of AAB, at Huddersfield, Yorkshire[2]

James Alfred Boddy

1834 Michaelmas: matriculates at St John's College, Cambridge

1838 Graduates from Cambridge, third class (in mathematics)
28 January: ordained deacon at Chester, curate at Goodshaw
The Christian Mission published by JAB

1839 24 February: ordained priest at Chester
Appointed Chaplain to the Manchester Poor House

1843 Marries Jane Vazeille Stocks

1844 Becomes Rector of St Thomas', Red Bank, Cheetham, Manchester[3]

1848 Birth of first son, Hugh[4]

1850 9 October: birth of Herbert Antony Vazeille, second son

1851 12 January: baptism of Herbert[5]

Alexander Alfred Boddy

1854 15 November: Alexander Alfred born

1855 11 March: baptised by his father[6]

c.1859 Birth of Mary Pollock in Scotland[7]
1868 January: enters Form II at Manchester Grammar School[8]
Starts helping in Sunday School work[9]

1870 29 October: confirmed by Bishop of Manchester[10]
1871 Articled to R. Worsley and W. Parker, solicitors in Manchester
10 October: father admitted as incumbent of Elwick Hall, Co. Durham[11]
AAB apparently living at Chadkirk, near Stockport[12]
Helps with Mission Room Services; at some point commissioned by the Bishop of Chester as Lay Reader and Preacher[13]

In this period visits Boulogne, and on another occasion Paris.[14]

1873 21 December: brother Herbert ordained deacon, Durham
First curate at Grindon, then Vicar. Domestic Chaplain to Marquis of Londonderry from this point until his death
1874 Canoe trip along NE coast[15]
July: trip to the Alps; on 7th nearly fell to destruction on Mont Blanc[16]
20 December: Herbert ordained priest
1876 Spiritual crisis at Keswick Convention[17]
December: admitted as solicitor by Master of the Rolls
In practice as Assistant Solicitor[18]
1878 Exhibitioner at University College, Durham
1879 J.B. Lightfoot consecrated Bishop of Durham
1880 June: awarded Licentiate in Theology (L.Th.)
19 September: ordained deacon by Bishop Lightfoot
Curate to his father at Elwick Hall, County Durham and also to undertake Embleton in Sedgefield
1881 26 March: his father dies
Possible visit to Sweden[19]
October: curate, St Helen's, Low Fell, Gateshead[20]
18 December: ordained priest
1882 Visits southern Russia and Crimea,[21] via Holland,[22] Italy and Greece[23]
1883 May–June: visits Tunisia and Algeria[24]

1884 Curate, St Peter's, Bishop Auckland[25]
     November: Curate-in-charge, All Saints, Monkwearmouth[26]
     Christmas: sent an assistant curate, Arthur Worsley Smyth[27]
1885 January: *To Kairwan The Holy* published[28]
     Elected Fellow of the Royal Geographical Society[29]
1886 May–June: visits Lapland and northern Russia[30]
     15 August: becomes Vicar, All Saints, Monkwearmouth on the death of the Revd B.C. Kennicott[31]
1888 Formation of the Pentecostal Union by Reader Harris, Q.C.[32]
     James Pollock Curate at Ven Bede, Monkwearmouth[33] (until 1889)
1889 May–June: trip to North America, including Seattle, immediately after the great fire of 6 June 1889; probably his second visit
1890 1 May: B.F. Westcott consecrated Bishop of Durham
     May: trip to Canada, probably his third
     November: parish mission, led by Canon Grant from Kent, with Mary Pollock as a worker[34]
1891 May: possible fourth visit to North America
     Autumn: marries Mary Pollock
     Honeymoon on a Cathedral Tour, including Lincoln, Ely and Lichfield[35]
     James Pollock apparently living with the Boddys while between curacies[36]
1892 Birth of daughter, Mary (May) Vazeille
     With Russian Pilgrims published
     Raises £500 for ironworkers laid off during Miners' Strike
     21 September: 'The Holy Spirit in infinite love came upon me' at an early morning Holy Communion service
1893 23 September: birth of daughter, Jane Vazeille
1894 Mary still ill after her confinement[37]
     Long negotiations about the formation of a new church and possibly parish, St Aidan's, Roker
1895 Birth of son, James Alexander Vazeille
     October: *The Laying on of Hands* published, a handbook for Confirmation candidates[38]
     September/October: Visits Egypt and the Holy Land[39] (certainly returned by 18 November)[40]
1896 May: *By Ocean, Prairie and Peak* published[41]

1897 15 May: *Christ in His Holy Land* published[42]
October/November: cycling visit to Holy Land[43]
26 November: licensed by the Anglican Bishop of Jerusalem, Dr Blyth, as one of his clergy in Egypt[44] for eight months (chaplain in Ramleh, Alexandria)[45]
1898 July/August: returns to Monkwearmouth
1899 23 February: wife Mary healed of asthma, through faith in Christ[46]
1900 25 April: *From The Egyptian Ramleh* published[47]
30 August: *Days in Galilee* published[48]
1901 1 November: H.C.G. Moule enthroned as Bishop of Durham[49]
Member of Pentecostal League of Reader Harris[50]
1903 5 September: his mother, Jane, dies[51] at Grindon Vicarage
15 November: announcement of money for a new church at Roker[52]
1904 November: visits Welsh revival to meet Evan Roberts
1906 April: Asuza Street revival, Los Angeles; the usually recognised beginning of Pentecostalism
22 May: death of his brother Herbert in Orvieto, Italy[53]
30 September: Pentecostal experience for T.B. Barratt[54]
1907 March: visits revival meetings in Oslo with T.B. Barratt and speaks at the meetings. On 5th 'an especial blessing'[55]
August: visits Keswick Convention to distribute leaflets
September–October: visit of T.B. Barratt to Monkwearmouth
11 September: Mary receives the gift of tongues
21 September: daughters Mary and Jane receive the gift of tongues
25–29 October: visit by Smith Wigglesworth
2 December: AAB receives the gift of tongues
1908 1, 2 January: AAB and Mary speak at the Faith Mission, Lochrin Hall, Edinburgh[56]
28–30 March: speaks at Kilsyth, near Glasgow; a Pentecostal assembly formed[57]
April: first edition of *Confidence*
6–11 June: first Sunderland Whitsuntide Convention
July: visits Keswick Conference[58]
September: anniversary services
ten-day visit to Holland[59]
October: a few days in the south of England with Polhill[60]
17–18 October: Mary at first Pentecostal Conference, Edinburgh[61]

8–11 December: attends the international Leaders' Meeting in Hamburg, Germany[62]

1909 9 January: formation of PMU, with AAB as Editorial Secretary[63]

9 February: visit to mid-day prayer meeting in London with Polhill[64]

13 April: present at the opening night of the first Welsh Pentecostal Conference, Cardiff[65]

25–28 May: 'Pentecost with Signs' Conference, London[66]

1–4 June: second Sunderland Whitsuntide Convention

8 June: visits Stanley Frodsham in Bournemouth

9 June: leaves England for fifth visit to USA and Canada, which lasts four weeks[67]

30 June: leaves New York on the *Lusitania*

Early July: brief visits to Liverpool, London, Lytham, Preston, Carlisle on the way home

August: AAB and Mary away from home

St Aidan's Roker formed in this period

c. 26 September – 14 October: visits Germany, Switzerland and France[68]

November: 'A London Declaration on Tongues'[69]

1910 14–16 May: introductory meetings

17–20 May: third International Convention, Sunderland

21–23 June: AAB and Mary in Belfast at YMCA[70]

29 June: in Paddington, London for opening of Home for Pastor Niblock

15 September – 5 October: visits Denmark, Germany and Holland[71]

October: Mary a key speaker at conference at Herne Hil[l72]

1911 10–12 January: London Conference with AAB presiding[73]

27–30 January: conference at Edinburgh with Mary Boddy[74]

6–9 June: fourth International Convention

2–20 November: visit to Germany, including daughter Mary in Selesia[75]

1912 30 January – 2 February: London Conference, convened by Polhill; AAB a key speaker[76]

April: London Pentecostal Meetings, Holborn Hall, organised by Polhill

May: fifth Sunderland Convention; first Consultative International Pentecostal Council held in Sunderland

1 August – 25 October: sixth visit to USA and Canada[77]
4–5 December: second International Pentecostal Consultative Council, Amsterdam[78]
1913 1 January: Pentecostal and Missionary gathering in Stirling, inc. Frank Bartleman, Mrs Polman and Polhill[79]
February–March: Attends Llandrindod Wells meetings, with Stephen and George Jeffreys
10–16 May: sixth Sunderland International Convention
12–15 May: third International Advisory Council at Sunderland[80]
24–30 September: mission at All Saints, with AAB and John Leech, K.C. as speakers[81]
1914 30 May – 5 June: seventh and last Convention at Sunderland; fourth and last International Advisory Council
12 June – August: visit to Canada and USA to speak at four Camp Meetings (seventh visit)[82]
1914–18 European war disrupts the Pentecostal Movement
1915 21–24 May: Whitsuntide Conference, Sunderland for local people[83]
24–28 May: speaks at London Whitsuntide Conference, organised by Polhill
June–July: visits troops in France
1916 publishes *Real Angels at Mons*
12–16 June: speaks at London Whitsuntide Conference, organised by Polhill
1917 28 May – 2 June: speaks at London Whitsuntide Conference, organised by Polhill
23 November: son James shot down by the 'Red Baron'[84]
November: AAB and daughter Jane visit James in France[85]
1918 20–24 May: speaks at London Whitsuntide Conference, organised by Polhill
1919 8 June (Whit Sunday): Bishop Moule speaks at All Saints on 'The Hope of the Approach of the Lord's Return'[86]
8–11 June: speaks at Whitsuntide Conference in Croydon, Surrey
end of August–September: preaching series at St James, Taunton[87]
6 July: Peace Thanksgiving Service in All Saints
5–17 November: visits Belgium, mainly for a Mission in Brussels[88]

1920 10 February: son James marries Marjorie D'arcy[89]
8 May: death of Bishop Handley Moule
24–28 May: speaks at London Whitsuntide Conference, organised by Polhill
August: temporarily in charge of All Saints, Hoole, Chester (to give the vicar a break)
21–22 October: speaks at Conference on the second coming, Sion College, London[90]
30 October: H.H. Henson enthroned as Bishop of Durham

1921 16–20 May: speaks at London Whitsuntide Conference, organised by Polhill

1922 5–9 June 1922: speaks at London Convention, organised by Polhill
September: in charge of Holy Trinity, Kilburn, London[91]
17 December: farewell services at All Saints[92]
Moves to Pittington

1923 January: Jane helps in the new parish; Mary still convalescing[93]
London Whitsuntide Conference takes place without AAB[94]
15 August: marriage of daughter Mary at Pittington Church to W.R.O. Taylor, a clergyman trained at St John's College, Durham[95]

1924 *The Church of St Lawrence the Martyr, Pittington* published
Formation of the Assemblies of God in Britain
August 3, 10, 17, 31: preaches at St Anne's, Soho on 'Christ in His Holy Land' – ten discourses[96]
October: ecumenical week of prayer in Pittington[97]

1925 Birth of granddaughter Evelyn Mary Vazeille
23–30 September: Parish Week of Prayer
October: mission with students from Durham

1926 Last edition of *Confidence*. PMU report reduced to notice of *Redemption Tidings*
20 June: birth of granddaughter Sheila Vazeille
9–19 October: Parish Mission

1927 Birth of grandson, Walter Noel Alexander

1928 25 April: death of Mary, aged 69

1930 10 September: death of AAB, aged 75

Notes

1 Details of JAB mostly from J.A. Venn *Alumni Catabrigienses*
2 1901 Census return
3 *Crockford's Clerical Directory* 1860
4 1901 Census return
5 Baptism certificate, in Ordination Papers, Durham University Library Archives
6 Ordinations Register for 1880, entry 204, Durham University Library Archives
7 1901 Census return
8 MGS school register
9 Ordinations Register for 1880, entry 204, Durham University Library Archives
10 Ordinations Register for 1880, entry 204, Durham University Library Archives
11 Clergy Visitation Return by JAB for 1 January 1880, Durham University Library Archives
12 Deduced from comments in Ordinations Register for 1880, entry 204, Durham University Library Archives
13 Ordinations Register for 1880, entry 204, Durham University Library Archives
14 According to *ABPP*
15 *Confidence*, January 1923, 64
16 *Confidence*, November 1909, 261
17 *Confidence*, 1923
18 Ordinations Register for 1880, entry 204, Durham University Library Archives
19 According to *ABPP*, 10
20 Visitation Returns, St Helen's Gateshead 1882
21 *ABPP*, 10
22 He had been in Amsterdam 26 years before (*Confidence*, September 1908, 7)
23 *TKH*, 255
24 *TKH*, frontispiece, 16 and passim
25 Register of the Clergy 1879–1901, entry 24, Durham University Library Archives
26 *Confidence*, January 1923
27 Visitation Returns, All Saints Monkwearmouth 1886
28 Advertised in *The Times*, 8 January 1885
29 *ABPP*, 19
30 *WRP*, 20, 249 (date of Trinity Sunday), 295 mention of vicarage
31 Visitation Returns, All Saints, Monkwearmouth 1886
32 *ABPP*, 24
33 *Crockford's Clerical Directory* 1907

34 *Confidence*, January 1923, 66
35 *Confidence*, November 1911, 258
36 *Crockford's Clerical Directory* 1892 (or '93?)
37 Letter to Bishop of Durham, 11 May 1894, Durham University Library Archives, file on All Saints, Monkwearmouth
38 Advertised in *The Times*, 4 October 1895
39 *FER* Chapters A-D; *DiG*, 289, plus the evidence that this second visit was in 1897
40 Letter to *The Times*, 20 November 1895
41 Advertised in *The Times*, 11 May 1896
42 Advertised in *The Times*, 15 May 1897
43 *DiG*, 320 gives the Sunday before Advent as 21 November 21
44 *DiG*, 327–28
45 Letter from AAB to Bp Moule, 10 December 1901, University of Durham Archives, file on All Saints, Monkwearmouth
46 *"Pentecost" at Sunderland*, 2
47 Advertised in *The Times*, 25 April 1900, 12
48 Advertised in *The Times*, 30 August 1900, 6
49 Harford and MacDonald, *Bishop Handley Moule* 1922, 190
50 Letter from AAB to Bp Moule, 10 December 1901, University of Durham Archives, file on All Saints, Monkwearmouth
51 From the tombstone at St Peter's, Elwick Hall
52 *The Times*, 16 November 1903, 8
53 J.A. Venn, *Alumni Catabrigienses*
54 *Confidence*, October 1909, 227
55 *Confidence*, March 1909, 58
56 *Confidence*, 1, 1908, 11–12
57 *Confidence*, 1, 1908, 8–11
58 *Confidence*, August 1908, 13–14
59 *Confidence*, September 1908, 6–9 etc
60 *Confidence*, October 1908, 6–9
61 *Confidence*, November 1908, 14
62 *Confidence*, December 1908, 24; van der Laan, *Pneuma* 1988, 10.1, 36
63 *Confidence*, January 1909, 13–14
64 *Confidence*, February 1909, 49
65 *Confidence*, April 1909, 88
66 *Confidence*, May 1909, 114 and advertised in *The Times*, 25 May 1909, 1
67 *Confidence*, July 1909, 143–44
68 *Confidence*, October 1909, 223
69 *Confidence*, December 1909, 286ff
70 *Confidence*, June 1910, 151; July 1910, 155–57
71 *Confidence*, October 1910
72 *Confidence*, October 1910, 227
73 *Confidence*, November 1910, 261
74 *Confidence*, December 1910, 292

75 *Confidence*, November 1911, 258
76 *Confidence*, February 1912, 36
77 *Confidence*, June 1912, 115
78 *Confidence*, May 1912, 277, 284
79 *Confidence*, January 1913, 18
80 *Confidence*, June 1913, 111
81 *Confidence*, October 1913, 204
82 *Confidence*, June 191, 115
83 *Confidence*, May 1915, 84
84 *Under The Guns of the Red Baron*, 160–62
85 *Confidence*, January 1918, 7
86 *Confidence*, July 1919, 39–43, 45–46
87 *Confidence*, October 1919, 55–56
88 *Confidence*, January 1920, 3–5, 10–12
89 *The Times*, 13 February 1920, 1
90 *Confidence*, October 1920, 58
91 *Confidence*, October 1920, 56
92 *Confidence*, October 1922, 50
93 *Confidence*, January 1923, 67
94 *Confidence*, January 1923, 62
95 *Confidence*, April 1923, 83
96 *Confidence*, April–June 1923, 78
97 Advertised in *The Times*, 3 July, 2 August 1924 and subsequent Saturdays.
   Confidence August 1924, 138
98 *Confidence*, November 1924, 150

Appendix Two

Boddy Family Tree

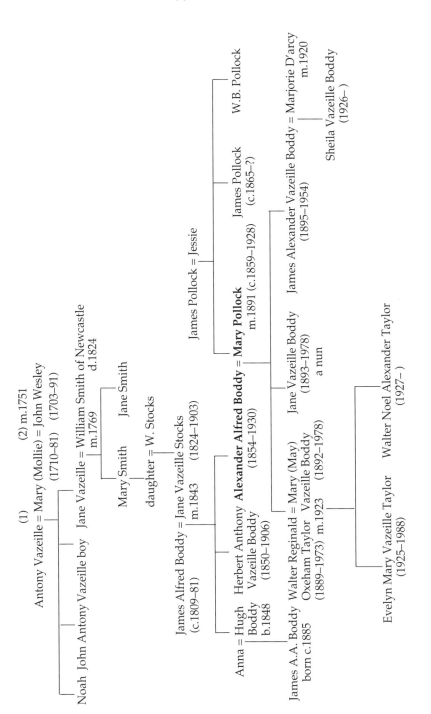

Appendix Three

Assistant Curates at All Saints, Monkwearmouth

Information from *Crockford's Clerical Directory* and Clergy Returns to Diocese, and Norman Joyce, All Saints' Church Monkwearmouth Centenary Booklet

Dates	Name
1880–1884	Robert Simpson
1881–1885	James Ousey
1884–1887	Arthur Worsley Smyth
1886–1891	George Howell Ashworth
1889–1890	Tom L. Brown
1891–1892	James Murdoch Pollock
1893–1896	R.J. Milward
1896–1898	G.A. Grace
1897–1898	F.P. Sandford
1897–1899	T.P. Williams
1898–1903	Frederick Smith
1899–1901	Charles Robert Wheeler
1900–1904	Thomas Harold Walton
1901–1903	Joseph Shores
1903–1907	Gilber Monks
1904–1906	Robert Edward Corlett
1905–1906	T. Davies
1906–1911	John Slater Nye
1911–1915	William Watson
1915–1919	Hamilton Blackwood
1917–1918	J.W. Dobson
1918–1921	Hugh Bourne Dowson
1921–1923	Robert Wilson

Appendix Four

Bishops of Durham

1879 Joseph Barber Lightfoot
1890 Brooke Foss Westcott
1901 Handley Carr Glyn Moule
1920 Herbert Hensley Henson (retired 1939)

Bibliography

Primary Sources

Material by Boddy in date order

ORIG *To Kairwan the Holy: Scenes in Muhammedan Africa* (London: Kegan Paul, Trench & Co., 1885)

With Russian Pilgrims, being an account of a sojourn in the White Sea monastery and a journey by the old trade route from the Arctic Sea to Moscow (London: Wells Gardner, Darton & Co, 1892)

The Laying on of Hands (London: SPCK, 1895)

ORIG *By Ocean, Prairie and Peak: Four journeys to British Columbia and Eastern Canada* (London: SPCK, 1896)

ORIG *Christ in His Holy Land: a life of our Lord, written during and after a special journey in Palestine* (London: SPCK, 1897)

From the Egyptian Ramleh (London: Gay & Bird, 1900)

ORIG *Days in Galilee and Scenes in Judah: together with some account of a solitary cycling journey in Southern Palestine* (London: Gay & Bird, 1900)

Roker Tracts (ed.) (n.p.: Sunderland, n.d.)
1. Born from above (with personal testimony)
2. Forgiveness of Sins

"Pentecost in Sunderland" referred to in LRE Feb 1909 does not appear to be included.

3. Heaven upon Earth
4. Satan's Devices. and the wonder-working Blood
5. The Holy Ghost for us
6. Health in Christ
7. Identification with Christ
8. Spiritualism Denounced
9. Christian Science: A Soul Danger
10. Systematic Prayer
11. The New Creation
12. Divine Necrosis: or the Deadness of the Lord Jesus
13. Faith in his Blood (this is not mentioned in the earliest lists but is included in a list in 1912, *Confidence*, March 1912, 66)

Letter to T.B. Barratt 12/7/1907 confirming invitation and expecting many visitors to Sunderland
Correspondence between Boddy and Jesse Penn-Lewis 1907

Leaflets on 'Tongues' (n.p.: Sunderland, 1907)
1. Speaking in Tongues. Is this of God?
2. Anon. A Pentecost at Home (Tongues as a sign). Testimony by a Busy Mother (ed. AAB)
3. These Signs shall follow
4. A Pentecost with Tongues: a brother's testimony
5. God's signs at Mukti, Miss Abram's story of God's further blessing
6. Tongues in Norway
7. Tongues at Caesarea
8. Tongues in America
9. Tongues in Sunderland: The beginnings of a Pentecost for England
10. Young People at Sunderland: results of Waiting Meetings, Sept. 1907
11. A Prophetic Message, given in Tongues
12. An Evangelist's Testimony: His Pentecost with Tongues. (Letter from Smith Wigglesworth to the Boddys, 5/11/1907)

Letter to T.B. Barratt 29/10/1907 mentioning spiritual warfare and opposition.

Confidence (Sunderland: 1908–26), as taken from CD-ROM, available from Springfield, MO: Flower Pentecostal Heritage Center, 2000

The 'Pentecostal Baptism': Counsel to Leaders and others (Sunderland: 1908) This has two editions; the second has an addition on Foreign Service

Real Angels at Mons (n.p.: Sunderland: 1916)

The Church of St Lawrence the Martyr, Pittington (Hallgarth), Durham (London: SPCK, 1924)

Also:

Letters to Bishops of Durham in the Administrative and Ecclesiastical Archives, Durham Diocesan Records, Durham University Library: 30 Sept. 1887; 11 May 1894; 26 June 1894; 10 Dec. 1901

Contemporary Sources by other authors

"Rev Alex. A. Boddy F.R.G.S.", *Sunderland YMCA Flashes*, Vol.11, No. 8 1895, 86
Barratt, T.B., Diary extracts March-September 1907
Barratt, T.B., *Erindringer* (ed. Solveig Barratt Lange; Oslo: Filadelfiaforlaget, 1941)
Blackburn, A., Memo with extracts from letters from Mary Boddy, 4 June 1905. Held in the Donald Gee Centre, Mattersey Hall.
Boddy, James Alfred, *Euston Hall* (London: Murray, 1834)
Boddy, James Alfred, *The Christian Mission* (London: William Smith; Manchester: Charles Ambery, 1838; reprinted Manchester: Hall & Roworth, 1845)
Boddy, J. Vazeille, *Afterwards* (London: Stockwell, 1918)
Boddy, Jane, "Alexander Alfred Boddy 1854–1930" (Grahamstown, unpublished essay, c. 1970)
✓ Boddy, Jane, unpublished letter to Martin Robinson, 19/9/1975
✓ Boddy, Mary, *"Pentecost" at Sunderland: the Testimony of a Vicar's Wife*, 5–7
Boddy, Mary, letter to a Mr Blackburn of Waskerley, Darlington, concerning 'full Baptism', 28/3/1905)

Engels, Friedrich, *The Condition of the Working Class* (ET, Oxford: Basil Blackwell, 1971²)
Sumner, John Bird, *Charges Addressed to the Clergy of the Diocese of Chester* (London: Hatchard & Son, 1841)
Durham Diocesan Visitation Returns 1874, 1882, 1886, 1891, 1896, 1900, 1904,1908, 1912, 1924, 1928
Ordinations Register for 1880, entry 204, Durham University Library Archives,
University of Durham Calendar 1881
Parliamentary Papers, 1852–3, 89, 'Religious Worship, England and Wales; Reports; Particular Notice of Different Churches; Spiritual Provision and Destitution; and Appendix, containing Summary Tables and Tabular Results.'

Newspaper Reports and Periodicals
Ecclesiastical Gazette, 1839
Sunderland Echo, 30 September 1907
Morning Leader, c. 3 October 1907
Thomson's Weekly, early October 1907
Daily Chronicle, 5 October 1907
Lloyd's Weekly, 'Revival Miracles', early October 1907
Evening Dispatch, Scotland, 11 October 1907
Daily Chronicle, 12 October 1907
North Mail, 'Day of Pentecost: Wearmouth Vicar on Revival Services', n.d. October 1907
North Mail, 'Wearside "Tongues" Mission', 14 October 1907
North Mail, 'Utility of the Gift of Tongues', n.d. 1907
Christian Herald and Signs of Our Times, 'World-Wide Revival', 24 October 1907
Christian Herald and Signs of Our Times, 'Pentecost at Sunderland', 30 January 1908
The Times, 18 May 1910, 4
Daily Mirror, 'General Booth's Brother-in-law at the Pentecostal Convention', 8 June 1911, 6
Newcastle Daily Journal, 1 May 1912, 7
Daily Sketch, 'Baptized in pale blue pyjamas', 16 May 1913 6
Daily Mirror, 'Converts Icy Bath', 16 May 1913, 5 and 1
Daily Mirror, 'Baptisms in sea at Roker', 4 June 1914
The North Star, 24 May 1915, 2

Secondary Literature

Anderson, Allan, 'Signs and Blunders: Pentecostal Mission Issues at "Home and Abroad" in the Twentieth Century' (2000) at {http://www.martynmission.cam.ac.uk/CSigns.htm}

Anderson, Allan, *An Introduction to Pentecostalism: Global Charismatic Christianity* (Cambridge: Cambridge University Press, 2004)

Allen, David, 'The Glossolalic Ostrich: Isolationism and Other-worldliness in the British Assemblies of God', *Journal of the European Pentecostal Association* XIII, (1994), 50–62

Bebbington, David, *Holiness in Nineteenth-Century England: The Didsbury Lectures 1998* (Carlisle: Paternoster Press, 2000)

Bicknell, Richard, 'The Ordinances: The Marginalised Aspects of Pentecostalism' in Warrington (ed.), *Pentecostal Perspectives*, 204–22

Bloch-Hoell, Nils, *The Pentecostal Movement* (London: Allen and Unwin, 1964)

Blumhofer, Edith, 'Transatlantic Currents in North Atlantic Pentecostalism' in Noll, Mark A., David W. Bebbington and George A. Rawlyk, *Evangelism: Comparative Studies of Popular Protestantism in North America, the British Isles, and Beyond, 1700–1990* (Oxford and New York: Oxford University Press, 1994), 351–64

Braley, Evelyn Foley (ed.), *Letters of Herbert Hensley Henson* (London: SPCK, 1950)

Bundy, David, 'Thomas Ball Barratt: From Methodist to Pentecostal', *Journal of the European Pentecostal Association* XIII, 1994, 19–49

Burgess, Stanley M., and Gary B. McGee (eds), *Dictionary of Pentecostal and Charismatic Movements* (Grand Rapids, Michigan: Zondervan Publishing House, 1988)

Cartledge, Mark J. (ed.), *Speaking in Tongues: Multi-Disciplinary Perspectives* (Milton Keynes: Paternoster, 2006)

Cartwright, Desmond, Letter to David Bundy, 27 May 1996, reporting on additions to the DG centre

Cartwright, Desmond, *The Real Smith Wigglesworth: The Man, The Myth, The Message* (Tonbridge: Sovereign World, 2000)

The Centre for the Study of Religion & Education in the Inner City, *The Jewish Community in Manchester* (Manchester: The Sacred Trinity Centre, 1983)

Cox, Harvey, *Fire from Heaven: The Rise of Pentecostal Spirituality and the Reshaping of Religion in the Twenty-first Century* (London: Cassell, 1996)

Cranston, Mike, *Mike's History of the Reader* accessed at {http://www.futurechurchsouthcoast.com/time line3.htm} on 24/1/2005

Eden, George R., and F.C. MacDonald (eds), *Lightfoot of Durham: Memories and Appreciations* (Cambridge: CUP, 1932)

Faupel, William, *The Everlasting Gospel: The Significance of Eschatology in the Development of Pentecostal Thought* (Sheffield: Sheffield Academic Press, 1996)

Franks, Norman, Hal Giblin and Nigel McCrery, *Under the Guns of the Red Baron: the Complete Record of von Richthofen's Victories and Victims Fully Illustrated* (London: Grub Street Publications, 1995)

Gee, Donald, *Wind and Flame* (Nottingham: AOG Publishing House, 1967)

Gee, Donald, *These Men I Knew* (Nottingham: Assemblies of God, 1980)

Gill, Robin, *The Myth of the Empty Church* (London: SPCK, 1993)

Gott, Ken and Lois Gott, *The Sunderland Refreshing: How the Holy Spirit invaded one British Town* (London: Hodder & Stoughton, 1995)

Hamer, Edna, *Elizabeth Prout 1820–1864: A Religious Life for Industrial England* (Bath: Downside Abbey, 1994)

Harford, John Battersby and Frederick Charles MacDonald, *Handley Carr Glyn Moule: Bishop of Durham. A Biography* (London: Hodder and Stoughton, 1922)

Harper, Michael, *As At the Beginning* (London: Hodder & Stoughton, 1965)

Hathaway, Malcolm, R., 'The Elim Pentecostal Church: Origins, Development and Distinctives' in Warrington (ed.), *Pentecostal Perspectives*, 1–39

Hervieu-Leger, Daniele, *Religion as a Chain of Memory* (ET Cambridge: Polity Press, 2000)

Hocken, Peter, 'Cecil H. Polhill – Pentecostal Layman', *Pneuma* 10, 1988, 116–40

Hollenweger, Walter, *The Pentecostals* (E.T. London: SCM, 1972)

Hollenweger, Walter, *Pentecostalism: Origins and Developments Worldwide* (Peabody, MS: Hendrickson, 1997)

Hudson, Neil, 'The Earliest Days of British Pentecostalism', *Journal of the European Pentecostal Association* XXI, 2001, 49–67

Hudson, Neil, 'Strange Words and their Impact on Early Pentecostals: A Historical Perspective' in Cartledge (ed.), *Speaking in Tongues*

Jacobsen, Douglas, *Thinking in the Spirit: Theologies of the Early Pentecostal Movement* (Bloomington and Indianapolis: Indiana University Press, 2003)

Joyce, Norman, *All Saints Church, Monkwearmouth Centenary Booklet* (Gloucester: British Publishing Company, 1949)

Kay, Peter, 'The Pentecostal Missionary Union and the Fourfold Gospel with Baptism in the Holy Spirit and Speaking in Tongues: A New Power for Missions?', *Journal of the European Pentecostal Association* XIX, 1999, 89–104

Kay, William K., 'Alexander Boddy and the Outpouring of the Holy Spirit in Sunderland', *Bulletin of the European Pentecostal Association* V, 1986, 44-56

Kay, William K., *Inside Story* (Mattersey Hall: Lifestream/ Mattersey Hall Publishing, 1990)

Kay, William K., *Pentecostals in Britain* (Carlisle: Paternoster Press, 2000)

Kay, William K. and Anne E. Dyer (eds), *Pentecostal and Charismatic Studies: A Reader* (London: SCM Press, 2004)

Kent, John, *Holding the Fort: Studies in Victorian Revivalism* (London: Epworth Press, 1978)

Laan, Cornelis van der, 'The Proceedings of the Leaders' Meetings (1908–1911) and of the International Pentecostal Council (1912–1914)', *Pneuma* 10 (1988), 36–49

Lavin, Peter, *Alexander Boddy: Pastor and Prophet* (Sunderland: Wearside Historic Churches Group, 1986)

Lewis, Donald M., *Lighten Their Darkness: The Evangelical Mission to Working-Class London, 1828–1860* (Carlisle: Paternoster Press, 2001)

Luscombe, Philip, *Groundwork of Science and Religion* (Peterborough: Epworth, 2000)

Machin, G.I.T., *Politics and the Churches in Great Britain, 1832–1868* (Oxford: Clarendon Press, 1977)

Milburn, Geoffrey, *Religion in Sunderland* (Occasional paper No. 3, Department of Geography and History, Sunderland Polytechnic, 1982)

Milburn, Geoffrey, *Church and Chapel in Sunderland* (Occasional paper No. 4, Department of Geography and History, Sunderland Polytechnic, 1988)

Milburn, Geoffrey, *The Travelling Preacher: John Wesley in the North East 1742–1790* (Wesley Historical Society (NE Branch), 1987; 20032)

Milburn, Geoffrey, *Primitive Methodism* (Peterborough: Epworth, 2002)

Moule, Handley, *Veni Creator: Thoughts on the person and work of the Holy Spirit of promise* (London: Hodder & Stoughton, 1890)

Pope, Robert, 'Wales and the great awakening', *Church Times*, 26 March 2004

Randall, Ian M., 'The Pentecostal League of Prayer: A Transdenominational British Wesleyan-Holiness Movement' accessed at {http://wesley.nnu.edu/wesleyantheology/theojrnl 31-35/33-1-10.htm} on 25/1/2005

Robinson, E.R., 'Myland, David Wesley' in Burgess and McGee, *Dictionary*, 632–3

Robinson, John A.T., 'Joseph Barber Lightfoot', Durham Cathedral Lecture 1981 (Durham: Dean and Chapter, 1981)

Robinson, Martin, *The Charismatic Anglican – Historical and Contemporary. A Comparison of Alexander Boddy and Michael C. Harper* (M. Litt. Thesis, University of Birmingham, 1976)

Scotland, Nigel, *The Life and Work of John Bird Sumner* (Leominster: Gracewing, 1995)

Taylor, Malcolm, *Publish and be blessed: a case study in early Pentecostal publishing history 1906–1926* (PhD Thesis, University of Birmingham, 1994)

Taylor, Malcolm, 'Divine Healing', *Bulletin of the European Pentecostal Association* XIV (1995), 54–84

Turner, Max, *Baptism in the Holy Spirit* (Cambridge: Grove, 2000. Renewal Series 2)

Venn, J.A., *Alumni Cantabrigiensis. A Biographical List of all known Students, Graduates and Holders of Office at the University of Cambridge from the Earliest Times to 1900. Part II from 1752 to 1900 Volume I ABBEY – CHALLIS* (Cambridge: C.U.P., 1940)

Wacker, Grant, *Heaven Below: Early Pentecostals and American Culture* (Cambridge, MA: Harvard University Press, 2001)

Wakefield, Gavin, *The First Pentecostal Anglican: The Life and Legacy of Alexander Boddy* (Cambridge: Grove Renewal Series 6, 2001)

Walker, F. Deaville, *William Carey: Missionary Pioneer and Statesman* (London: SCM, 1926)

Warren, James R., *The Day Seattle Burned* (Seattle: J.R. Warren, 1989)

Warrington, Keith (ed.), *Pentecostal Perspectives* (Milton Keynes: Paternoster Press, 1998)

Westcott, Arthur, *Life and Letters of Brooke Foss Westcott* Vol. II (London: MacMillan, 1903)

Whittaker, Colin, *Seven Pentecostal Pioneers* (Basingstoke: Marshall, Morgan and Scott, 1983)

Wilk, Mariusz, *The Journals of a White Sea Wolf* (London: Harvill, 2003)

Wilkinson, Alan, *The Church of England and the First World War* (London: SCM Press, 19962)

Studies in Pentecostal and Charismatic Issues

Consultant Editors: Max Turner, Andrew Walker
Series Editors: Mark Cartledge, Neil Hudson, Keith Warrington

Andrew Lord

Spirit-Shaped Mission
A holistic Charismatic Missiology

Spirit-Shaped Mission brings together Pentecostal and charismatic theologies of mission for the first time. Part one assesses past theologies, drawing both on scholarly research and the thinking of key church leaders such as John Wimber, who have influenced the Anglican charismatic movement in Britain. Part two addresses different issues that need considering in a holistic theology of mission, including the holistic content, experiential nature, contextual grounding, community focus and spirituality for mission. *Spirit-Shaped Mission* develops a framework for understanding the 'mission of the Spirit' that contributes to Pentecostal, evangelical and ecumenical thinking on the subject.

'This is one of the most innovative and well-written books on the theology of mission that I have ever read.'

Professor Allan Anderson

ISBN: 978-1-84227-264-0

Studies in Pentecostal and Charismatic Issues

Consultant Editors: Max Turner, Andrew Walker
Series Editors: Mark Cartledge, Neil Hudson, Keith Warrington

Max Turner
The Holy Spirit and Spiritual Gifts
Then and Now

What do the writers of the New Testament say about the work of the Holy Spirit. How can we understand spiritual gifts for today? Questions regarding the role of the Holy Spirit and spiritual gifts in the life of the believer and the church today continue to be asked, and remain a source of controversy. In this updated edition of his widely acclaimed book, Professor Max Turner offers a clear scholarly consideration of the Holy Spirit that is rooted in Scripture and relates to aspects of contemporary theology. He carefully explores how three major New Testament writers – Luke, John and Paul – took over and developed Old Testament and inter-testamental notions of the Spirit. Turner then investigates the contemporary theological relevance of these biblical teachings.

'Max Turner's book is essential reading for all who are concerned to know more about the work of the Holy Spirit in the New Testament churches and today.'

Professor I. Howard Marshall

ISBN: 978-0-85364-758-4

Studies in **Pentecostal** and Charismatic Issues

Consultant Editors: Max Turner, Andrew Walker
Series Editors: Mark Cartledge, Neil Hudson, Keith Warrington

Mark Cartledge

Practical Theology
Charismatic and Empirical Perspectives

This is the *only* book on *practical theology* from a *charismatic viewpoint*. It is unique in integrating charismatic and empirical perspectives in practical theology, exemplifying both qualitative and quantitative methods of research. In **Part One** Mark Cartledge offers a proposal for practical theology, reviewing the ways in which theology, and especially practical theology, has related to the social sciences, charismatic spirituality and theories of truth and knowledge. **Part Two** progresses into six empirical studies on charismatic worship, glossolalia and postmodernity, women and prophetic activity, the 'Toronto Blessing', healing and socialization. Each chapter ends with methodological reflection and suggestions for renewed theological praxis, enforcing the value of such methods of study for an understanding of charismatic Christianity.

ISBN: 978-1-84227-200-8

Studies in Pentecostal and Charismatic Issues

Consultant Editors: Max Turner, Andrew Walker
Series Editors: Mark J. Cartledge, Neil Hudson, Keith Warrington

Mark J. Cartledge (Editor)

Speaking in Tongues
Multi-Disciplinary Perspectives

Speaking in tongues (*glossolalia*) is a common spiritual phenomenon in the Pentecostal and Charismatic streams of the Christian church. Such Christians believe that when they speak in tongues they are communicating with God in a language that they have never learned – a spiritual prayer language given to them by the Holy Spirit. This innovative volume seeks to enhance our understanding and appreciation of *glossolalia* by examining it from a range of different angles. Christian scholars from diverse academic disciplines bring to bear the insights of their own specialist areas to shed new light on the practice of speaking in tongues. The disciplines include: **New Testament Studies** – Max Turner; **Theology** – Frank D. Macchia; **History** – Neil Hudson; **Philosophy** – James K.A. Smith; **Linguistics** – David Hilborn; **Sociology** – Margaret M. Poloma; **Psychology** – William K. Kay. A final chapter by Mark J. Cartledge seeks to show how all of these perspectives can work together and enrich a Christian appreciation of the gift of tongues.

ISBN: 978-1-84227-377-7